JUST ABOUT

everything

A RETAIL MANAGER
NEEDS TO KNOW

By the same author

The Modern Nurseryman
    co-authored with Alan Toogood, Faber & Faber, London, 1981
The Garden Centre Manual
    co-authored with Ian Baldwin, Grower Books, London, 1982
The Nursery and Garden Centre Marketing Manual
    Reference Publishing Company, Auckland, 1992, 1994, 2000
John Stanley Says, Volume 1
    Reference Publishing Company, Auckland, 1991
John Stanley Says, Volume 2
    Reference Publishing Company, Auckland, 1995
The Complete Guide to Garden Centre Management
    Ball Publishing, Chicago, 2002

As a contributing author

Confessions of Shameless Internet Promoters
    Success Showcase Publishing, Tempe, 2002
The Modern Public Library Building – Managing Planning
    Libraries Unlimited Press, Westport, USA, 2002

JUST ABOUT *everything*
A RETAIL MANAGER
NEEDS TO KNOW

John Stanley

Kalamunda, Western Australia

Published by lizardpublishing.biz, PO Box 604, Kalamunda, Western Australia 6926

National Library of Australia
Catalogue-in-Publication data:

Stanley, John
Just about everything a retail manger needs to know.

Includes index
ISBN 0-9750118-0-4

    1. Retail trade - Management - Handbooks, manuals, etc.
    2. Personnel management - Handbooks, manuals, etc.
    3. Executive ability - Handbooks, manuals, etc. I. Title.

381.1068

Foreword

The prevailing nature of the international 'global village' economy is stimulating among people a heightened sense of enterprise and entrepreneurship. Self determination is appealing in an era in which long-term security appears to be a thing of the past.

At the beginning of the twenty-first century, there are some 1.2 million businesses operating in Australia, with a workforce of 8.5 million. Significantly, the retail sector is the largest employer in the marketplace, reflecting its importance to the nation and, indeed, to the world.

Government initiatives are fostering and promoting financial independence for all. However, neither legislation nor regulation will ensure success.

Common characteristics of most retail market segments include aggressive competitors, product parity, rampant discounting, short planning lead-times, and wafer-thin margins. Risk tolerance is low and the scope for errors is limited. Minor miscalculations can be terminal.

Retail managers need external assistance, expertise, experience, and creative input. Information sources abound but, sadly, many are general, generic, and lack local retail focus.

This latest book by John Stanley is timely and fills a void which is conspicuous to many practising retail managers. Retailers do not have the time nor the inclination to invest in researching the marketplace for credible consultants and publications. In this book they find both.

The structure of the publication provides for easy and prompt comprehension of a diverse range of topics. Readers will be encouraged by the challenges inherent in the questions which are posed, and reassured by the guidance provided in the nature of the answers given.

It is an original and innovative style which involves the reader in the learning process. The approach will foster personal development.

John Stanley is justifiably an internationally recognised authority on the broader discipline of retailing, with specific skills in merchandising. He brings to focus in this book his widespread first-hand experience in a manner which will accelerate learning. That will impact directly on the bottom line.

The currency of the details provided in the publication imply it should be included in the management and staff development libraries of all retail organisations, large and small. It should be, and doubtless will become, a constant reference source as differing circumstances and challenges arise.

John Stanley is to be applauded for writing the book. The reader will be rewarded by making an investment in securing this invaluable resource.

Barry Urquhart
Managing Director
Marketing Focus, Perth

Contents

FOREWORD v

PREFACE x

TESTIMONIALS xii

Winning over your Customer

How to attract the passing
customer into your store 2

How to promote your business
to children 4

How to promote your business
to Generation X customers 6

How to promote your business
to young adults 7

How to promote your business
to baby boomers 8

How to promote your business
to the older generation 10

How to develop quality services
for special customers 12

How to communicate your beliefs
to customers 14

How to make sure your team
members look professional 16

How to make a positive
impression in ten seconds 18

How to use positive body language
to make the best impression 20

How to train your team to smile 22

How to greet a customer 24

How to communicate effectively
—and make the sale 26

How to sell features and benefits 28

How to remove a customer's
doubt—and make the sale 30

How to turn your customers
into lifetime customers 32

How to improve your customer
service 34

How to develop a customer
loyalty program 36

How to conduct a customer survey 38

How to set up a customer forum 40

How to increase your customer
base 42

How to handle those complaints 44

How to ensure your team
is customer friendly 46

How to profit from your
PA system 48

How to close a sale 50

How to gift wrap 52

How to select and fill
a shopping bag 54

How to farewell the customer 56

Promoting your Products

How to select the right media for
advertising 60

How to use a direct mailer to
promote product sales 62

How to use 'how-to' leaflets
to sell more product 64

How to plan an advertisement 66

How to write advertising copy
that sells 68

How to promote advertised lines 70

How to conduct a general product
promotion 72

How to use demonstrations
to sell product 74

How to get the most out of
your booth at a trade show 76

How to produce signs that
sell products 78

How to use a 'cut case' display 80

How to use a dump bin 81

WINNING OVER
YOUR CUSTOMER

OMOTING
PRODUCT

MANAGING
OUR STORE

MANAGING
UR BUSINESS

vii

How to dummy-up your displays 82

How to display products
to capture customer interest 84

How to display products on pallets 86

How to maximise sales using
the floor of your store 88

How to build a profitable
power product display 90

How to maximise your sales
using hot spots/end caps 92

How to use a wall of value 94

How to become famous
for something 95

How to manage cold spot selling
positions 96

How to manage shelf filling 98

How to create theatre
in your store 100

How to prepare your staff
for the holiday rush 102

How to maximise your holiday
promotion 104

How to sell concepts not products 106

How to introduce a new
product line 108

How to set up a shop window 110

How to create movement
in your displays 112

Managing your Store

How to maximise
your customer flow 116

How to improve your
'first impression' image 118

How to improve your
'last impression' image 120

How to keep your store clean 122

How to walk the floor and
talk to customers 124

How to manage your aisles 125

How to make sure your displays
are safe 126

How to introduce texture into your
displays 127

How to manage product placement
in your store 128

How to use vertical merchandising
to maximise your sales 130

How to use horizontal merchandising
to maximise your sales 132

How to manage relays 134

How to face products correctly 136

How to manage your product
range 138

How to get the most out of
best sellers 140

How to manage slow-moving
products 142

How to manage counter displays 144

How to manage stands
provided by suppliers 146

How to manage perishable
products 148

How to manage shopping trolleys 150

How to write signs that sell 152

How to manage signs in your store 154

How to write a known value sign 156

How to write a non known
value sign 157

How to use signs effectively 158

How to use background music
in your store 160

How to use aroma in your store 162

How to make best use of colour for
effective merchandising displays ... 164

How to make best use of colour
for the store exterior 166

How to make best use of colour
for the store interior 168

Managing your Business

How to develop a retail business
strategy 172

How to benchmark your store 174

JUST ABOUT EVERYTHING A RETAIL MANAGER NEEDS TO KNOW

How to maintain standards
in your store 176

How to work with percentages 178

How to work out mark up
versus gross profit 180

How to set prices that sell products.... 182

How to increase your prices 184

How to set an advertising budget 186

How to maintain a competitive
edge.. 188

How to develop sales promotions 190

How to manage non price sensitive ....
products 192

How to 'open price'
your products 194

How to buy effectively 196

How to manage stockturns 198

How to monitor departmental
performance 200

How to develop an open to buy
policy 202

How to increase your average
sale—and increase your profits 204

How to calculate the margin of
safety for your business 206

How to grapple with absenteeism 207

How to recruit effective
salespeople 208

How to interview potential
salespeople 210

How to get the best value
out of Generation X employees 212

How to develop a mystery
shopper program 214

How to maximise the benefits
of team meetings 216

How to train the team 218

How to develop a good
relationship with the local press 220

How to write a customer
newsletter 222

How to become a sponsor 224

How to keep shrinkage
under control 226

How to reduce shoplifting 228

How to apprehend a shoplifter 230

How to reduce credit card
and cheque fraud 232

How to handle a hold-up 234

How to deal with emergencies 236

How to develop and manage
your store safety standards 238

How to monitor safety
in your store 240

GLOSSARY **242**

REFERENCES **248**

INDEX **250**

About the author

John Stanley

After leaving school, John Stanley became the course manager at Merrist Wood College in the United Kingdom. Since then he has been involved with many different types of retailing. He has worked in and consulted to supermarkets, garden centres, pharmacies, liquor stores, service stations, and hardware stores.

Since 1976, John Stanley has been much in demand as a consultant, with his expertise taking him to clients in over 15 countries. He is also a highly sought after keynote speaker and motivator at conferences and workshops around the world. In addition, John has written several industry-specific books.

He is also a regular contributor to written and audio magazines, and has produced a number of videos on retailing for clients.

In the new millenium, retailing is going to go through some major changes. John's international background, working with multinational and individual one-site companies in Europe, America, Africa, Asia, and Australasia, allows him to pick up on and develop new ideas and trends rapidly. He uses these gifts when working closely with clients in their own environment, advising and encouraging them to profit and grow from his wealth of experience and incredible expertise in the area of retailing.

This book brings together John's skills in one useful format that will show every retailer how to benefit and raise their level of professionalism, and improve their profitability by tapping into John's talents and experiences.

Eight reasons why every retail manager will treasure this book

Every so often something really useful comes along. And, for retail managers, this book is it. By distilling just about everything relating to successful management practice into practical and immediately accessible 'how-tos', the book provides answers to your retail challenges and questions in straightforward language with the minimum of fuss. If you, as a retailer, needed to own just one reference tool, then this book is it! Flick through the pages. If you're still not convinced, then consider these points...

1 This book provides ideas on retailing —quickly.

Retailers are born. I've been told this many times. Successful retailing is a mix of personality and knowledge. It may be difficult to provide you with personality skills via a book, but this volume can certainly provide you with knowledge and management expertise.

Retailers normally obtain their skills via:

Retail courses. These are valuable opportunities to obtain knowledge— yet many retailers find that they are unable to allocate time to the pursuit of knowledge in this way.

Associations. Many retailers belong to trade associations and use these as opportunities to gather information. But, you may not meet all that often and you usually meet with your competitors—which means information may not be spread as freely—or as quickly—as you would like.

Retail books. I have built up a library full of retail books. The information is there somewhere but retrieving it can be quite a challenge, especially

when time is limited.

On-the-job experience. This is a wonderful teacher, but it can be mistake-laden, and you only get it from one perspective—and it does take time... a lifetime in some cases.

Travelling and looking overseas. This is great fun, but expensive—and, again, very time-consuming.

It would be wonderful if all the above could be condensed into one quickly-accessible tool. This publication is just that, a working tool, based on a wealth of retailing experiences from around the world.

2 This book provides proven retail ideas.

This is not a theoretical book. It is based on practical ideas, presented in a practical way. Retailing is about understanding 'grass roots' principles and this book addresses these in an easy-to-understand format that will help you develop your career and your business.

3 This book offers ideas from all aspects of retailing.

If you work in a supermarket,

hardware store, fashion shop, florist or garden centre, you will find ideas in this book that will help you improve your skills. I have had wide experience in various aspects of retailing and have brought these together in this book. Whether you are building a display indoors or outdoors, in a small independent store or in a multinational mass merchandising store, you will find this book addresses your particular needs.

4 This book is so easy to use.

This is a companion to the bestselling *Just about Everything a Manager Needs to Know* by Neil Flanagan and Jarvis Finger. One of the reasons for that book's huge success was its easy-to-read 'how-to' format.

Just about Everything a Retail Manager Needs to Know keeps to the same successful format. This means it is not a book that is meant to be read from cover to cover, but rather a book to be dipped into whenever you need practical help as a retailer.

5 This book will help you as a student of retailing.

In retailing, you never stop learning. We are all students of retailing. What we need are strategies, ideas and 'how-to' tips we can use to keep developing our business and our careers.

One of the aims of this book is to help you, as a continuing student of retailing, to acquire the skills you need easily and in a format to help you absorb the information with the minimum of fuss.

Management Memo

I help myself realise my sales goals by catching myself doing something *right*. [a]

6 This book is an essential tool for the new or experienced retailer.

This book provides ideas, even for the most experienced retailer. None of us can learn all the skills of retailing at one time and be proficient at them all. This book helps you develop your existing strengths and improve your weaknesses. It provides ideas and advice for when you have a problem that needs solving.

7 This book should be shared by your team.

Here is a book that won't sit on your shelf gathing dust. It is a tool your whole team will refer to constantly. Leave a copy in the staff room and let your team find a solution in it to problems as they occur. It can help you improve the retailing skills of your whole team.

8 This can become your total reference library.

In writing this book and its companion *Just about Everything a Manager Needs to Know*, the authors have read hundreds of books and extracted the valuable information from them for you. This means these volumes can literally save hours upon hours of valuable time and money for you. The two volumes provide a powerful tool based on the experience of many world experts, and presented in an extremely accessible and usable form.—J.S.

Here's what people are saying about this book...

In writing this book, the author aimed to provide a *usable* tool for retail managers and students, a publication that would focus on the day-to-day nuts-and-bolts of retailing and be free from the distraction of theories and concepts. The extent to which the author was successful in his quest is reflected in the comments of the following leading retailers from around the world…

Managing a retail supermarket business in today's competitive environment, you must be ready to tackle a broad range of demands. Having the tools to enable you to do this is essential. *Just about Everything a Retail Manager Needs to Know* is such a tool. It will give you the answers you are looking for, without the need for hours of reading. Identify your problem, and you can find your solution in seconds with a step-by-step strategy for implementing that solution. For the hands-on owner/operator, it is the most valuable management tool available.
> Vince Belladonna
> Dewsons Supermarket,
> Wembley, Western Australia

I have known John Stanley for a number of years, first as a speaker, then as a colleague. I recently toured Australia with him on a workshop tour. John is a brilliant speaker, vibrant and entertaining, and his knowledge on retailing is awesome. This book will be a must for every manager. He has written in a style that is easy to read, easy to understand and, most importantly, easy to put into action.

I have rarely seen a retail book which goes into such detail on 'How to'. It is as if he were in the store directing operations.

John Stanley has the ability to walk around and immediately spot a trend,

seize on a new idea, and then enhance these thoughts to increase retail sales. He is truly amazing. Every manager who is serious about their career and their business should buy John's latest book.
> Anne Sugden
> Anne Sugden Enterprises
> Haslingdon, UK

John Stanley has done it again: *Just about Everything a Retail Manager Needs to Know* is the exquisite distillation of his worldwide experience in retailing. We know John and his work as a coach, trainer and adviser—clear, direct and focused on achieving practical results. Here now is the Retail Bible we all have been waiting for. Start your day reading a passage and practice it during the day. The results will be overwhelming and your personal and professional life will benefit from it.
Just do it!
> Johan Van Wambeke
> Manager Benelux
> EK Grosseinkauf, Belgium
> (EK Grosseinkauf is one of the largest non-food co-operations for independent retailers in Europe)

As a team of communications consultants, Image 7 Group is frequently communicating to retailers or their customers. *Just about Everything a Retail Manager Needs to Know* fills the gap between theory and practice. Most retail managers have developed their skills on-the-job by observation or through plain old trial-and-error, *Just about Everything a Retail Manager Needs to Know* is a wealth of knowledge condensed down into easily digestible, bite-sized pieces. It is designed to be a handy guide which is a ready reference when the retail manager strikes an emergency. I believe this book should be on the bookshelf of every shop regardless of size or products sold. There is no doubt... this is the best book of it's kind in the world.

> Brad Entwistle
> Managing Director
> Image 7 Group Pty Ltd,
> Western Australia

At Caltex Australia, we are committed to providing the best possible for our store managers and franchisees, as we strive towards the highest standards of retailing. When I first discovered the Flanagan & Finger's companion publication, *Just about Everything a Manager Needs to Know*, I immediately ordered one for each of our managers. Having just read the latest book in the series, *Just about Everything a Retail Manager Needs to Know* by John Stanley, the first item on my to-do list is to get a copy into the hands of every retailer in our network. It won't just keep us ahead of our competitors; it will keep us ahead of our customers.

> Robert Bentley
> Retail Learning & Development
> Executive
> Caltex Australia
> Perth, Western Australia

I have known John Stanley for many years and have watched his expertise, knowledge and continuous growth in the area of retail selling. I am proud to say he did it the hard way. He learned through practical, hands-on experience. In reading John's book, you will gain wisdom that will help you not only succeed today but for years to come.

> Bobbie Gee
> Author: *Creating a Million Dollar Image for Your Business*
> Bobbie Gee Enterprises
> Laguna Beach, CA USA

John Stanley's latest publication is definitely for people who don't like reading books—which is just as well because most of us in retailing rarely find the time to read all the books that we would like to. That's why the format used in *Just about Everything a Retail Manager Needs to Know* is so useful for managers.

It is clearly indexed and cross-referenced which allows you to hone in on the topic you want to know about quickly and easily. This might be on how to write signs that sell, how to face products correctly, how to set up a shop window or even something as simple as how to use the PA system effectively in your store. There are a whole multitude of topics to choose from and the information given is simple, straight forward and therefore easy to apply. It's a wonderful format, tailor-made for the retail industry. Every manager must have a copy of this book.

> Jurek Leon
> Terrific Trading
> Perth, Western Australia.

Just about Everything a Retail Manager Needs to Know is definitely not a book for the bookshelf. This is a book which will hold its place on any retail manager's desktop. You will have to keep repairing those dog ears because it will get so much use. It offers an easy-to-access format with all the necessary keypoints for managers contained in a clear and concise manner.

Today's manager constantly needs to keep up with the many changes that occur in business and, in most cases, has little time to read large volumes of literature. This is where this book really comes into its own. Its simple format means you can just go for the key topic that you require, gain an understanding, and put that understanding into practice almost immediately. I highly recommend this book as it offers a no-nonsense practical approach to management—ideal for today's retail manager.

> Bill Richardson
> Credit Services Manager
> Australian Liquor Marketers (WA)
> & Johnson Harper
> Perth, Western Australia

Managing the detail of retail, that elusive, misunderstood and often missing factor in many modern stores, becomes all-clear in John Stanley's latest handbook *Just about Everything a Retail Manager Needs to Know*. It's not what we do, but what we forget to do that customers pick up on and it's vital that guidelines are so accessible and within arm's reach. Long overdue!

> Bob Edwards
> Managing Editor
> *Commercial Horticulture* magazine
> Auckland, New Zealand.

In my travels and speaking engagements throughout Canada it will be great to finally have a tool like *Just about Everything a Retail Manager Needs to Know* to recommend to many retailers who are looking for a solid resource.

> Pete Luckett
> Pete Luckett Marketing
> Nova Scotia, Canada

John Stanley is a professional retailer with worldwide experience. The blend of John's experience with the structural approach of the book gives the reader the opportunity to try things that have worked around the world.

Applying his ideas into your day-to-day organisation will give you the best opportunity for success.

> Arthur Trindall
> General Manger Operations
> Foodland Associated Limited
> Western Australia

John Stanley has consulted in many areas such as retail floor layout, merchandising, point of sale material, and staff training. His expert advise has been invaluable in the various stages in our organisation's development.

This book highlights many of the leading best practices gleaned from some of the best retail organisations around the world. It will be a useful reference resource for retailers in all positions of Customer Service, Marketing, and Management.

I encourage you to challenge yourself and your team to improve your business using John's innovative ideas.

> Trevor Cochrane
> Category Manager
> Bunnings Warehouse
> Perth, Western Australia

This book is a wealth of information, covering all topics pertinent to retail, helping you to get it right the first time. It's easy-to-read, precise and comprehensive without being too technical. The author's experience and knowledge of the retail industry is second to none. His enthusiasm and communication skills make him the ideal person to have written this book.

> Andrew Heaphy
> Marketing Manager
> The Plaza Shopping Centre
> Palmerston North, New Zealand

This book is a must for anyone in the 'people' business… I particularly recommend its suggestions for developing customer relations and promoting product. A great investment.

> Noreen Emery
> Principal
> Speech Dynamics
> Perth, Western Australia

During the past decade, we've learnt 'just about everything we needed to know' from John Stanley to develop our business selling plants as a successful retail garden centre… We rate his advice as invaluable in our quest for excellence in retailing. Now it's here in his new book. It will have pride of place on our bookshelf.

> Jackie Hooper
> Zanthorrea Nursery
> Perth, Western Australia

MANAGING
YOUR CUSTOMERS

GING
STORE

GING
ODUCTS

GING
SINESS

DEX

XV

John Stanley's latest tool to help build team motivation, create change and grow your profits.

Just About Retail Team Brainstorming is an audio CD developed to help build your team motivation, create team ownership of ideas and solutions, raise standards, reinforce change and ultimately grow your profits.

Team brainstorming generates ownership of new ideas and creates a driving force for change.

Let the creative juices flow and watch motivation and profits grow!

John Stanley presents 38 hot topics to get retail teams brains rolling with ideas to boost professionalism, team spirit and sales.

This represents 38 weeks of team brainstorming topics for your training sessions. Each topics is between one and two minutes long.

Team brainstorming topics include:

- Can customers read your signs?
- Retail traffic flows
- Best seller policy
- First impressions
- Last impressions
- Should we use name badges?
- Customer loyalty programs
- Dealing with cold spots
- Selling new products
- Are you a maitre de?
- Stock control and stock rotation plus many more.....

Winning over your Customer

*Take time to make friends
before trying to make customers.*

Elmer Wheeler

How to attract the passing customer into your store

Your retail business relies on attracting customers for, without customers entering your store, your opportunities for making a sale are extremely limited. Potential customers, of course, pass by dozens of retailers each day. Your aim is to be one of the few they notice—you have to attract them into your premises. You need to stand out from the rest. It's all about image, about how other people see your business—and first impressions count a great deal in this regard…

1 Assess your building before making changes.

Have you had a good look at your existing building from the outside lately? Is it appealing? Can its facade be improved, made more attractive?

View your external facade from the outside—through the eyes of a customer. It can be a revealing exercise. Consider the entrance, signage, windows, lighting, cobwebs, peeling paint, external fences, driveway, signs (are they drooping, faded, covered with vegetation), pathways, plants, shade, seating, litter, the carpark—there is much to consider.

Decide what should be kept, or cleaned, or changed. Natural materials, such as bricks, limestone and tiles require very little maintenance and for this reason are wisely retained in their original state.

Do certain areas need repainting? Walls in particular may need attention if they are to enhance the street and make your business stand out. Will the addition of an awning or verandah provide shelter for customers and passers-by? Is there a need for seating?

2 Pay attention to your facade's colour.

A building's colour can enhance the viewer's experience or provide an objectionable episode which may result in some customers actually refusing to walk through your door. As a general rule, walls should be painted in a lighter colour and gutters, doors and window frames in a stronger colour. When selecting colours consider these points:

- Single colour buildings are ideal if your signage and shop window displays are dramatic.

- Buildings of contrasting colours will stand out—but make sure the colours enhance the products you sell.

- Heritage colours may be required to beautify an older streetscape.

- As a general rule, use bright colours in small areas only.

View your building as part of the entire streetscape. Your aim should be to enhance the whole block of shops as well as your business.

WINNING OVER
OUR CUSTOMERS

NAGING
R STORE

MOTING
PRODUCTS

NAGING
BUSINESS

NDEX

3

Vol. 1: See 248, 388, 390

3 Consider landscaping the front of your premises.

Ray Kroc, the McDonald's entrepreneur, was adamant that the exterior of his stores be landscaped to the highest standard possible. His view was that customers would judge the cleanliness of the store to a large degree on the level of its landscaping. McDonald's stores rely on a large amount of perennial foundation plants and very few seasonal plants to create the right image. On the other hand, in the United Kingdom, English pubs rely on seasonal plantings to create a more colourful image. These need more care, and do much to make the pubs stand out from other premises.

4 Make your external signs meaningful and readable.

On the outside of your premises, you need to state who you are (and most of us need to say what we do—exceptions being such well known organisations as McDonald's, Shell and Harrods).

Buildings need signs that are clean and simple. Signs usually include words, trademarks, and logos, and they should be displayed in keeping with the tone of the street and overall image of the business.

They must be readable, using a typeface that can be easily seen by pedestrians and people passing in vehicles. Focus on simplicity and boldness—over-decorated signs are often not read. The total size of the sign will be influenced by local council regulations as well as company standards and financial considerations.

Management Memo

One day while on his way back to the office from an important lunch in the best restaurant in town, Ray Kroc, owner of the McDonald's chain in the United States, asked his driver to pass through a few McDonald's car parks. In one he spotted papers caught up in shrubs along the outer fence.

He immediately went to the nearest pay phone, called his office to get the name of the manager, then called the manager to offer to help him pick up the offending rubbish.

Both the owner of the McDonald's chain in his expensive business suit and the young manager met in the car park and got down on their hands and knees to pick up the paper.

As managers we are frequently more interested in the activity inside our business premises than in the building's outside appearance. The appearance of your building and its surrounds is at the front line of your organisation's public image—as Ray Kroc was well aware.[1]

Don't forget to include, prominently, a street number to ensure the Post Office and searching customers can readily identify your premises.

5 Advertise your company—not others.

Remember: you're selling your store—your brand, your business. Do not minimise your organisation's importance, as many businesses do, by promoting the brands of other organisations. Too often a retailer will do an excellent job on the facia—and then spoil it by putting up the signs of their suppliers. Such signs should go outside that supplier's place of business or next to the supplier's products in your store—not on the outside walls of *your* premises.

How to promote your business to children

Children are arguably the most influential group you could target as a retailer. Importantly, they are frequently the key player when it comes to decision-making within the family. For example, many families eat at McDonald's Restaurants simply because the child has been the decision maker. Yet, often, many businesses fail to encourage children as customers; indeed, at times they go out of their way and actively discourage them. But children, as customers of tomorrow and decision makers of today, are a vital focus group…

 ### Develop a policy and keep to it.

Take steps to develop a policy on how your business will deal with children. Your policy will depend on what you sell. Some retailers will look on children as a major target, while others will deliberately, and justifiably, discourage this group of shoppers. Implement the policy, by ensuring all your team members are familiar with it and consistent in implementing your standards.

 ### Introduce baby-friendly facilities.

Many customers, of both sexes, will at times want to come shopping with babies. For this group, you may:

- provide changing facilities in a both-sex toilet.
- allocate parking spots where customers with prams can park, load and unload safely. Many retailers combine their less-abled and pram-parking spots.
- ensure that your company policy requires staff assist customers in getting from the checkout point to their cars with their pram, pushchair or stroller, and purchases. A word of warning: a pram or stroller is an ideal place to store stolen goods, so your policy may need to take account of this.

 ### Provide play equipment.

Children between the ages of four and seven can quickly become bored when shopping with parents, and can become a nuisance in the store. They need entertaining and you may need to consider the provision of a safe and secure play facility, even the employment of a competent, accredited child minder. A fear for many parents in play groups is that someone will snatch their child. To allay such fears, some larger businesses take a polaroid photo of parent and child as they arrive. This gives you and the parent a passport to safety when the parent returns from shopping—and a present you can give them when they leave.

 ### Consider links with local schools.

Eight- to twelve-year-olds have a major influence on where their parents shop. They can also be a very profitable target group of customers.

Many retailers—supermarkets, sports stores, garden centres, hardware stores, and computer shops—have joined with their local school as sponsors of events, and advertise in school newsletters. They have become involved on special occasions such as fetes, sports days, and concerts. They have provided product and become involved in projects based on the items they sell. The aim is two-fold—to bring the product to the attention of the school children, and to make their business known and the first choice in the child's mind. Schools are only too willing to work with the local business community in appropriate ways.

5 Create a children's club.

Many businesses have created loyalty programs for their adult shoppers. In some sectors it is also profitable to create a children's club which focuses on their products:

- a supermarket can organise a Cooking Club
- a garden centre can start a Gardening Club
- an art shop can run a regular Painting Club
- a sports store can organise sports sessions.

Such clubs can be promoted and held on specific days, thereby enabling customers who prefer to shop without children present to do so on another occasion. You get all the kids (and their parent shoppers) to come at a set time, freeing you up at other times to deal with other adults.

6 Establish a children's department.

Consider your overall product categories and whether it is feasible to develop a children's section, where all the products related to this

Management Memo

Oh what a tangled web we weave
When we think that children are naïve. [2]

age group can be displayed.

Remember, you will need to change shelf fitting heights for your younger shoppers and you should define this department by using bright primary colours and childhood themes. The principles of merchandising stay the same but at different heights. By putting this department at the rear of the store, you will encourage parents to shop the whole store.

7 Listen to parents.

You must listen to parents and make appropriate adaptations to the way you retail. Customer suggestion forms should have a space for parents' comments. In the past, these comments have included such useful ideas as:

- "Have a checkout aisle with no sweets in it."
- "Have a child-size shopping cart."
- "Have wide aisles for prams."
- "Do not place products that say 'Keep out of the reach of children' below the 1.2 metre shopping height."

8 Treat children as special individuals.

Always welcome children as individuals; companies that go out of their way to recognise children and treat them as special people are more likely to attract families. You could provide balloons, sweets (if parents approve), or other small treats as acknowledgement that you look on these customers as special.

How to promote your business to Generation X customers

A lot has been written in recent years about Generation X or today's young adults born between 1965 and 1980. Research claims that their desires and interests are different from other sectors of the population and therefore they need to be addressed in a different way. Generation X is another market sector which you may or may not wish to target, depending on what products you sell.

1 Understand Generation X.

These days, young adults are staying at home longer and living with their parents. Researchers tell us that they have a more negative view of the world, are selfish, and will readily question authority. They believe having fun is important, they want freedom, challenges at work, and to be well off. Generation X are generally enthusiastic, creative, and energetic but feel insecure and hunger to be noticed. They do not know how to handle difficult people and situations, and are not trained to give service. But they have considerable spending power.

2 Focus on their interests.

Generation X often lack basic knowledge which older generations take for granted—Australian research has shown the majority of them do not know how to cook a potato!—but it is a mistake to talk down to this group because they are street-smart in a range of other areas, and it could put them off your product and your company for life.

For example, they are considered to be more computer literate than any other sector of the population. They have grown up with computers and are comfortable using email and web pages as a source of information. This, for example, is one key target area for this group.

3 Be aware of fashion trends.

The group is very fashion conscious when it comes to styles, trends, colours, food, and music. As a retailer you need to be aware of the relevant trends by reading magazines and watching television programs that this age group relates to. To attract them, you'll need to embrace their current trends and fads.

4 Communicate with these customers.

The key to building a business relationship with Generation X customers is to be able to relate to them by approaching them in an understanding way and being prepared to listen, and show you are responding to their particular needs and wants.

WINNING OVER
OUR CUSTOMERS | NAGING
IR STORE | OMOTING
R PRODUCTS | NAGING
R BUSINESS | IDEX | **7**

YOUNG ADULT SHOPPERS | See also: 64, 222

How to promote your business to young adults

Those customers whose ages fall within the 25- to 40-year-old range can be classed as young adults. As a general rule their requirements are different to other groups and therefore your products, displays, and promotions need to be tailored to their particular demands…

1 Present products to meet their needs.

The young adult sector is primarily the independent, do-it-yourself market. This market group requires that you have products laid out in a format and presentation that allows them to select all the products they need to do a task effectively when they get home.

2 Provide leaflets and information.

How-to leaflets and basic guides will help this sector. As a general rule they want to learn how to do the job properly themselves—whether this is cooking a meal, building a patio, painting a house, or planting a rose. Which is why supermarkets, hardware stores, paint stores, and garden centres these days usually stock a range of useful brochures for the 'home handyperson'.

3 Ensure your team can pass on knowledge.

Young adults are looking to your team to provide the product knowledge they need to get the job done and to suggest useful tips and hints to make the job easier. For this reason, take appropriate steps to ensure that your staff have the knowledge and information required and are prepared to cheerfully pass on the necessary information and tips to customers.

4 Have your price strategy match their needs.

Young adults look for quality at a price. They are not prepared to spend excessively, but do expect quality and reasonable service. To service their needs you may wish to introduce a 'basic range' within your product categories to meet their requirements, and a more expensive category for the more discerning of your customers.

How to promote your business to baby boomers

The 'post-war baby boom' refers to the increase in births when servicemen returned home from World War 2. The 'baby boomers' are the generation who were born in the late 1940s and 1950s and are now in their 40s and 50s. They have had a considerable impact on society—and retailing—beginning with their 'Flower Power' revolution in the early 1960s. Over recent years the main target market for many retailers has been baby boomers, for they represent the largest single market sector in Western societies.

1 Know today's baby boomer.

To focus on the customer needs of the baby boomer generation, it is essential to understand this market sector. According to Faith Popcorn in *Clicking*, the following features highlight today's baby boomer generation:

Cocooning, or becoming 'home' bodies – In the United States, 33 per cent of people have changed shopping habits for safety reasons. 43 per cent do not shop after dark due to safety reasons. One in three homes has an alarm system.

Clanning, or socialising with like-minded people – They are forming special interest groups.

Wanting Safe Fantasy Adventures – Virtual reality and exotic meals are in vogue.

Pleasure Revenge – Smoking defiantly, diet rebelling, drinking harder.

Small Indulgences – They search for small pleasures… the sale of champagne, perfume, and cut flowers, for example, has increased.

Anchoring – Spiritual awareness is in fashion.

Egonomics – Customised products, 'me' products.

Female Thinking – 'Female think'. Requiring a relationship before the sale.

Mancipation – New age males are more expressive of their emotions.

99 Lives – They are time-poor due to their busy lives. In the United States the Elephant Secretary service reminds them 24 hours a day of important birthdays etc.

Cashing Out – Dropping out or copping out.

Alive – They want to live longer, yet skin cancer has doubled since 1970. The new disease is stress.

Down Ageing – They act and dress as if they are ten years younger than they are.

Vigilante – They distrust major suppliers of goods.

Icon Toppling – If they do not like a company, they will topple it.

Save Our Society – They seek environmentally-friendly products. —so sales of $100 pollution control devices, leaf blowers, and shower-head water savers have soared.

Provide DIM products and services.

The baby boomers now have the reputation for being the DIM (do-it-for-me) sector of society. It is the time-poor and money-rich generation. Baby boomers have been responsible for major growth in the service industries, home meal replacement, and the patio garden. To expand your sales in this market you need to provide finished products or services. Within reason, this customer sector is prepared to pay for these services.

Provide exceptional customer service.

This group of customers is becoming less loyal and more demanding through its insistance on a higher standard of customer service. If their perception is that you are failing in customer service, then baby boomers will shop somewhere else.

Provide time-poor service.

Be aware that baby boomers as a group are short on time and are willing to pay for services that will save them this valuable commodity. With this in mind, consider:

- Home delivery
- Ready presented products
- Gift-wrapping
- Selling on the web
- Providing unique products.

Be fashion conscious.

For many retailers their prime target will be a baby boomer female. Many of these women are fashion

conscious when it comes to style and colour. You need to be a leader, not a follower, when it comes to trends within these areas. And remember, these days fashion shows up in the kitchen, garden, food we eat, living room and ornaments, as well as in what we wear.

Be aware of the wants of baby boomers.

Baby boomers are the ones that are leading the trends towards:

- Safety – They shop where they feel safe.
- Freshness – They purchase products they believe are fresh and healthy.
- Hygiene – They shop at businesses they believe are clean.

Remember, retailing is about perception in the eyes of your customers. You need to promote the areas that are important to them—safety, freshness and hygiene.

How to promote your business to the older generation

Ageing populations are a feature of many western societies. 'Silver Tops' or 'Grey Tigers' are currently an important market sector with specific needs that must be acknowledged and catered for. But, as baby boomers begin to retire over the next two decades, this retired sector of your customer base will increase dramatically. You'll need to be developing strategies now to meet the demands of this expanding group of customers who will require 'silver service' from you...

 ### Promote nostalgia.

Many retailers already refer to this growing group as the nostalgia market and many products, services and even prices of yesteryear are being taken up in the marketplace today to reflect this trend. For example, nostalgia includes aromas and scents, hence the recent growth in herbal related products and cures. To attract this senior customer group, you will need to ensure the nostalgia theme is reflected in your product mix.

 ### Have nostalgia days.

Many supermarkets already encourage this group to shop on specific days, for example when special buses transport residents from retirement villages to shopping centres, entertainment venues, and other retail outlets.

On such occasions it is possible for retailers to target this customer sector in various ways to the benefit of both customer and business. Greying Tigers often get annoyed if their shopping is disturbed by 'screaming kids' and therefore they may appreciate the opportunity afforded to them to shop in 'their' time at their own pace.

You may have Nostalgia Days, Weeks or Months. And if you're brave, you may have a promotion using prices from another era as part of the promotional campaign—even to the complimentary hard-boiled lollies wrapped in newspaper cones!

Remember, when it comes to nostalgia, we remember the good things about the 'good old days'— and they must be our focus.

 ### Cater for the less able.

As we become older we become less agile and our faculties slow down. For this reason, retailers must ensure that their stores cater for the needs of the less able, both in terms of the physical facilities and the services offered:

- Make sure a wheelchair can get to all parts of your store safely.
- Ensure your floors are safe. Check there are no areas where a less able customer could trip or slip.
- Provide seating areas around your store.

- Make sure signs are easy to read. As we get older our eyes deteriorate and we often forget to wear our glasses!
- Have staff as a matter of policy and courtesy help older people carry their purchases to the vehicle.

4 Make your products accessible.

Place favourite products in positions that can be reached comfortably by the older person. Stretching and bending is something this market sector is not prepared (or even able) to do. If product positioning presents a problem, ensure your staff members are on hand to assist when required.

5 Train the team to relate to Silver Tops.

Many younger sales staff find it difficult to relate to older customers. Younger people need to be made aware that the language of today's youth may not be understood by an older client. For example, for older people, 'cool' relates to temperature, and 'fresh' relates to the condition of perishable products. The key is to use the language of your senior customers without being condescending.

6 Make their stress go away.

Canadian fashion retailer Donald Cooper defines customer service as 'anything you do that in some way reduces the stress in your customers' lives'. Make your sales team aware of the stresses faced by the aged population and how they can help minimise the problem. For example, an elderly person with arthritis may

not be able to remove the car's petrol cap at the pump, or open certain containers in your store—providing an opportunity for your team to offer a much appreciated service.

A Western Australian shopping centre, The Park Centre, offers a free shuttle bus service to its senior shoppers.

7 Beware of those talkative oldies.

Many older customers are lonely and go shopping for companionship. This often means they may talk to the sales team excessively, stopping them from serving other customers. Your team members need understanding and patience to show they are listening, but to politely remove themselves from the conversation after a few minutes. Other team members should be observant to what's happening so that they can, under some guise, rescue their colleague without offending the customer.

How to develop quality services for special customers

Many retailers often confuse the terms 'providing customer service' and 'providing customer services'. Customer service is how you treat your customer. Customer services are what you provide them with, other than the products you sell. You need to provide services as part of your customer care policy and the range of services will vary with the type of customer and the style of retailing you are offering...

1 Understand your customers.

Because the list of services you could offer is so large and varied, you need to narrow it down to the services your specific customer segment would expect. Remember, however, you are there to make a profit by selling product. The skill is to provide enough services to impress and attract your regular and special customers, while limiting excessive expense connected with the service you are offering. As a guide, begin by considering the ages and needs of your customer base and link appropriate services to these.

2 Cater for parents with babies.

It's a real challenge having to manage baby *and* the weekly shopping, so you'll win over many mothers by providing special services for them. These may include:

- Baby parking zones. Parents with babies have to manhandle prams and strollers out of cars. Why not provide a car parking area near the door that is reserved for parents with babies?
- Unisex baby changing facilities and breast feeding rooms are now a common provision in many retail situations.
- Do you have supermarket trolleys with facilities built into them to carry babies? Children's buggies can also be made available, free for customers who request them.
- Baby bottle heating facilities.
- A carryout service to the car for parents.

3 Provide for parents with toddlers and small children.

Consider these options:

- In large retail stores, security tags for parents and children can help if children get lost.
- Creche, supervised by qualified personnel for the 2- to 8-year-olds can allow parents to shop without worrying about their children; the result is the parents spend more.
- Children's entertainment programs in larger retail stores can include jugglers, magicians, soft play areas, party rooms, and so on.
- Children's clubs that demonstrate products you sell are becoming more popular and a profit centre in their own right.

4 Consider the disabled.

Among the services for the disabled

customers would be:

- The allocation of parking spaces near the entrance.
- Toilets for the disabled.
- The provision of battery-operated wheelchairs once in the store. This encourages shopping throughout the whole facility.
- Elevators or lifts, if you need them, to accommodate wheelchairs.
- Carryout services to the car park.
- Some stores have personnel trained in sign language to assist customers with hearing difficulties.

5 Assist overseas visitors.

The Japanese word for guest is the same as customer—and therein lies a message. If your business attracts visitors from a specific country then your team needs to be aware of their culture, so that your guests are not offended. Encourage team members to learn an overseas language; this really impresses the overseas customer and puts them at ease. Where appropriate, be able to guarantee delivery to the customer's homeland. The last thing they want is to have to carry delicate items on a long journey.

6 Ensure all your services are open.

Consider this report: "I recently visited a world renowned retail mall, expecting to be overawed by the retailing excellence I was about to see. The centre opened at 9.30 am. I arrived at 9.15am to find the car park locked until 9.30 am for security reasons. I wanted breakfast, but once inside I found restaurants within the complex had signs up saying 'Closed till 10.00 am', and 10.30 am and, in

> ### Management Memo
>
> Boots, a UK company, has been providing its Christmas catalogue in braille for three years, even though only 50000 English people can read braille. In 1990 it started offering an audio cassette version. One in 20 in the 60+ age group is visually impaired and 1 in 4 in the 75+ age group. Is this something you can do for your customers? [5]

one case, midday. It was all so frustrating."

The message here is—do not disappoint your customers. They expect all your services to be operational when the business is open. You may think your excuses are justifiable—but often customers are not prepared to believe you.

7 Gain a reputation for your special services.

The list of services is endless and could include:

- A lay-by service for Christmas or birthdays to provide something special to an individual.
- Allowing customers to take as many items as they like into changing rooms to show you trust them.
- Complimentary refreshments to put them at ease if they have to 'linger longer'.
- Complimentary gift-wrapping and gift cards.
- Accepting foreign cheques, notes, leading credit cards etc.

Brainstorm with your team what services they feel customers would like to experience. We have to accept that customers are taking more and more of our services for granted and are still asking for more—but that's the competitive nature of retailing today!

How to communicate your beliefs to customers

Every retailer must be committed to providing the highest possible levels of fair trading and customer service to consumers. Commitment, however, is one thing; how you demonstrate that commitment and how you tell customers of that commitment is something else. How do you tell your customers what they can expect from you and your store?

1 Understand what customers expect.

It's simple—the customer expects quality goods and quality service. The problem for the retailer comes when the customer's perception of quality is different from yours. It is your job to set the standards and to communicate them to the consumer.

A quality product can be safely defined as:

- A product free of defects, fit for the job it was designed to do, and of a satisfactory quality

- A product accurately described on the box or label in language the consumer can understand

- A product guaranteed against fault within a specific time frame

- If the product is not up to standard, it is clearly marked as such for the customer to easily read.

Quality service can be defined as:

- Service that is delivered to the customer with competent care and skill

- Service delivered within a reasonable time frame

- Service delivered, as agreed to, between the customer and the retailer

- Service provided at a cost the consumer perceives as reasonable.

Remember, however, your job is to exceed customers' expectations. Set a standard that the customer will be happy with, and then train your team to consistently exceed that limit.

2 Communicate your beliefs to your customers.

Stew Leonard, the fresh food retailer in the United States communicates his beliefs on a slab of stone at the entrance to his store. He ensures that everyone—customers and passers-by— knows what he and his team believe in. Some businesses will display posters around the store, while others distribute leaflets or newsletters to shoppers. It does not matter *how* you communicate your message as long as you *do* communicate your beliefs to customers…

3 Be prepared if things go wrong.

We do not live in a perfect world and

there will be times when you will fail your customer. It is important that they tell you—and not your competitor, *and* that you have a positive action plan in place to remedy problems.

Ensure you have a procedure where customers can let you know without getting embarrassed or feeling threatened. Train staff in how to handle complaining customers. Remember, you want those customers to leave, satisfied with your store's handling of the crisis, and with a smile on their face.

Use words which avoid conflict.

Customers frequently get annoyed because the salesperson uses the language of conflict. Train your team to practise 'positive English', as the following examples illustrate:

Instead of 'You did this', try 'Here's what I suspect went wrong…'.

Management Memo

An analysis of the top power words used in the Top 100 Good Headlines reveals the following: [6]

	Number of Appearances
YOU	31
YOUR	14
HOW	12
NEW	10
WHO	8
MONEY	6
NOW	4
PEOPLE	4
WANT	4
WHY	4

Use these in your verbal and silent promotions. They will increase sales.

Instead of 'You shouldn't have done it that way', try 'Here's how I would have done it'.

Instead of 'Why didn't you do it the way you were told?', try 'Help me to understand why what we agreed to do didn't happen'.

How to make sure your team members look professional

Retailing is about perception and your team members are your company's ambassadors. Customers will judge your staff in ten seconds, and since judgements are initially made with the eyes, staff appearance can be a critical factor in your company's success. So, while their communication skills are vital, how your staff are dressed can play an equally important role, particularly in terms of first impressions...

1 Consider the image you're trying to create.

Your uniform provides a very strong message to your potential customers, and the message will vary depending on how customers perceive your business. The uniform can provide the following signals:

Authority: The police officer's uniform and the bank managers suit (yes, it's a uniform) are symbols of authority.
Status: The cabin crew in an aircraft wear uniforms as symbols of status. This says to the customer that the uniformed person has a higher status in a particular situation than the customer.
Colour: Customers associate colours with specific industries and your uniform may need to reflect your industry—barbers (red and white), butchers (blue and white), gardeners (green), cooks (white).

2 Involve your staff in decisions on dress.

Before introducing a team uniform or dress code, first seek ideas from staff. You will find that different genders and ages will have different perspectives as to what should be worn. You need everyone to share ideas. Staff views are important and consensus should be your aim. The team must feel comfortable and proud

to wear the uniform. Your role is to ensure that their views are consistent with the image you require.

3 Aim for consistency.

Success is about consistency in everything you do. This often means you may need written standards on how the team uniform is to be used in your company. Issues for consideration should include:

- Can or cannot the team wear the uniform outside work. e.g. Can they go to the pub in a company uniform?
- Who cleans the uniform, how often, and who pays for it?
- What accessories are to be provided by the team to wear with the uniform, i.e. type of shoes, trousers/skirts, jewellery and other garments?
- What cosmetic style, hairstyle and other personal criteria are important to provide consistency in the team?

4 Develop and publicise a staff dress code.

It is important to have standards that your team can accept. Below is an example, compiled by a retailer with staff input, for you to consider:

Our Dress Code
Because we are members of a professional

retail organisation, we believe we should provide professional selling skills and service. Therefore to help us achieve these objectives, we have the following dress and behavioural code:

All female staff will be provided with two tabards, one of which will be worn at all times when in the retail areas.

All male staff and female outdoor staff will be provided with two shirts, and one waterproof coat. Shirts will be worn at all times when in the retail areas.

It is the responsibility of the employee to ensure these garments are kept clean and in good repair.

Failure to wear this clothing in retail areas will result in the person being sent home with an appropriate loss of pay.

The storeowner will provide replacement garments once the old ones have deteriorated through normal wear and tear.

Jeans may be worn by outside staff, but must be clean when you arrive to work. Torn jeans will not be tolerated. Again , the person will be sent home with an appropriate loss of pay.

For safety reasons, staff will not be allowed to wear open shoes in any areas of the retail area.

Light facial cosmetics are acceptable on female staff, but nail varnish is not permitted.

No facial cosmetics are acceptable on male staff.

Rings, earrings and light necklaces are acceptable on female team members.

Earrings and excessive jewellery will not be accepted on male team members.

Team members will wear name badges at all times in all retail areas.

All clothes worn by the team should be in good repair.

Smoking, eating and drinking will not be allowed in the shop area.

5 Add that touch of credibility.

In retailing, credibility is based on perception, not knowledge. To make your sales team look credible, try including a tool of the trade as part of the uniform. For example,

- garden experts can wear secateurs on their belts.

Management Memo

Appearance does not make the man, but it will pay any man to make the best appearance possible. [7]

- tailors can hang a tape measure around their necks.
- hardware experts can have a tape on their belt.
- clothing retailers can wear the clothes they sell.

6 Consider the use of name badges.

Wearing or not wearing personal name badges depends on what level of customer service you wish to provide. If your aim is to give the impression that your team is friendly towards customers, then a name badge is essential. This allows customers, rather than your staff, to decide at what level of formality they wish to hold a conversation. If you use name badges, consider this advice:

- Have a policy that your team must wear their name badges when on the shop floor.
- Only use the team member's first name on the badge. If you include surnames, you may find some staff receiving unwanted, even obnoxious phone calls.
- Do not put titles on name badges. The title Manager, Supervisor, and so on, does not help your customer service relations. In fact it may result in your customer becoming selective in terms of whom they deal with. Your aim should be to ensure everyone in your team is an equal in the eyes of the customer.
- Have two badges for each person. Keep one badge in the office. If a team member forgets a name badge they can then collect one from the office. Before they collect it, ensure they put coins in a charity box as a fine. (This is a useful motivator and the 'punishment' is less onerous when staff know the fine goes to a good cause.)

How to make a positive impression in ten seconds

Retailing is about making the right impression upfront. Researchers tell us that we have ten seconds at best to make that first impression on the customer. For that reason, everything must be spot-on—your external appearance, inside the store, your staff's appearance and involvement, the products, the check-out... At every stage, first impressions count.

1 See your store through the customer's eyes.

The following checklist focuses on the types of things which a typical customer can react to in the first ten seconds of an encounter. For this reason, they are aspects of your store which require your consideration and attention if you want to leave the customer with a positive impression first up:

Outside your store
- ☐ The store has clean, distinctive entrance directions.
- ☐ The windows are clean.
- ☐ There is no litter in front of the store.
- ☐ The shop windows look inviting.
- ☐ The entrance to the store is swept/mopped.

Inside your front door
- ☐ All the lights work.
- ☐ The primary product display is in position.
- ☐ The product on display is well signed.
- ☐ There is adequate product on display.
- ☐ The floor has been swept/mopped.
- ☐ All safety issues have been addressed.

Toilet facilities
- ☐ There is adequate toilet paper.
- ☐ There are soap and hand towels.
- ☐ The facility is clean.
- ☐ We are promoting the right products in the toilet.

The team
- ☐ They are all in the agreed team attire.
- ☐ They are using positive body language.
- ☐ They are greeting every customer.
- ☐ They are using positive verbal language.

The checkout
- ☐ It is clean.
- ☐ It is uncluttered.
- ☐ There are adequate bags/boxes.
- ☐ All the equipment is working.
- ☐ The checkouts have enough change.

2 Develop a checklist.

To ensure all is well in your store in terms of giving a positive impression at all times, it is wise to compile a formal checklist that focuses on all aspects of the store. This should be a vital tool for retail managers and, if used correctly, is a guarantee that everything that the customer experiences is consistent with your minimum standards—hopefully you can excel this basic standard.

The following is a suggested format for a checklist. You should compile a similar list to reflect the specific nature of your enterprise.

Department	Action Required	By Whom
e.g. **Fashion** All products priced Signage in place Aisles clear Carpet clean Products clean Lights working		

e.g. Indoor Plants
Labelled
Sub-standard stock removed
Irrigation systems working
Area tidy and litter free
Customer info available
Trolleys/Baskets available
Linked sales on show
Benches look stocked
Lighting checked
Shading checked
Heaters unobstructed
Tidy under benches
Preparation area clean/tidy
Storyboards used
Pot plant sleeves available

e.g. Food
Shelves clean
Floor clean
Product clean
Counter clean
Food preparation area clean
Waste bins empty
Signage relevant
Food fresh, well displayed
Linked sales obvious
Impulse purchases obvious

3 Walk the floor with your checklist.

Apart from the quick visual check that should take place every morning before the front door is opened, a much more thorough check should take place at least twice a week. Your formal checklist will prove invaluable in this regard.

4 Monitor what team members are doing.

When customers enter your store, they get the wrong impression if they see idle team members. You therefore need to occasionally check, record, and analyse how the team is performing:

(a) Record your observations regularly throughout the survey day on a customer/team ratio survey sheet. A typical example follows:

Management Memo

Determine who your store customers are and then you can decide what retail niche you're really in. It sounds easy, but for those sitting at the top of the pyramid— and not working at the front lines in day-to-day contact with customers— it can be tricky. [8]

CUSTOMER/TEAM RATIO SURVEY							
Date:	**Observation Times:**	9.30 10.30 11.30 12.30 1.30 2.30 3.30 4.30 5.30					
Name of Team Member	Selling (S)	Ancillary duties (A)	Idle (I)	Break (B)	Total no. of customers in store	**Comments**	
1							
2							
3							
10							

(b) Convert the information gathered into a graph. See a possible outcome provided below. By referring to the completed graph, you will obtain an overall picture of the working status of your staff for that day, in particular who is actively selling and how ineffectively others of your team are involved. You can then reprogram your team timetable to ensure staff are available to serve the customers at vital times of the day.

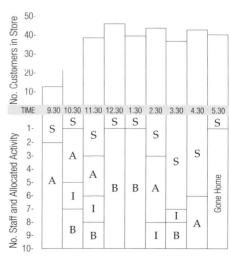

Key: S = Selling; A = Ancillary work;
B = Break; I = Idle

How to use positive body language to make the best impression

Most of us, often without knowing it, communicate a great deal without actually saying anything. Our facial expression, the way we look at someone, our posture, the movement of our hands—all send clear signals about how we're feeling or responding to another person. Body language can send many messages to customers and others with whom we deal daily. It is an important concept for retailers to grasp...

1 Know why body language is important.

Research shows that people interpret body language before they interpret tone of voice and words. In fact, 75 per cent of what we absorb when we meet somebody is based on how they use their body in interacting with us. In retailing we are constantly meeting strangers whom we judge through their body language. That stranger, of course, is also assessing our body language.

In retailing the salesperson likes to be perceived as the dominant person in the encounter —which is why they aim to control the body language game. If the salesperson has positive body language then the outcome of the interaction with the customer has every chance of being successful. However, if the salesperson has negative body language then this can have a negative impact on the selling encounter.

It is difficult to train people in body language, but as retailers we must be aware of, and be prepared to work on, the use of our bodies to best effect in the sales process.

2 Practise positive body language always.

Strangers can often sum up a person in ten seconds—the moment of truth in a sales encounter. Since you have only one chance to make a good first impression, make sure your body language provides a positive start.

Body language is read, often unwittingly, by first observing the face and then the body. Monitor your own body language—keep it positive:

Positive: Make eye contact—we normally read the eyes first.
Negative: Don't look at the person. Look past the customer.

Positive: Smile—and this is really only effective if it comes naturally.
Negative: Frown.

Positive: Keep your hands away from your face.
Negative: Stroke your hair, rub your ear, stroke your beard or scratch your nose, indicating that you are nervous or do not know what you are taking about.

Positive: Use open arm gestures and talk with your hands to show you are open and confident.
Negative: Fold your arms and you reveal you are hostile, bored, or not interested in the customer.

Positive: Stand upright and face the customer squarely.

Negative: Lean against something, and you say you are not really interested in the customer or do not have time for them.

Positive: Touch the customer's hand when giving change back.
Negative: Drop change into a customer's hand or on to the counter, and this shouts negativity.

3 Consider distance from the customer.

How close should you get to a customer when serving on the shop floor? Women generally seek more space than men, but this comfort zone varies with cultures. Australians tend to seek the largest comfort zones, with men prefering two thirds of an arm's length between strangers, while women prefer an arm's length between them and a stranger. But travel to Indonesia or Thailand and you'll find the salesperson will come right up to you and may even touch you—in cultural terms, their personal comfort zones are much smaller.

4 Be aware of cultural differences.

Unfortunately, there are no universal rules for body language. The rules change from country to country, and often within countries. For example, as a sign of respect, Aborigines, Zulus, and Japanese tend not to make eye contact straight away when they meet a stranger. On the other hand, Caucasians see eye contact as an essential precurser to an encounter. And the thumbs up signal is a positive sign in many countries while, in others, it's a rude gesture. So the best advice is to attempt to have your team culturally aware and constantly learning from each other on matters relating to the varying cultural rules of body language.

Management Memo

If you recruit people who are naturally pleasant and positive, acceptable body language will be second nature to them. When interviewing, look for staff who: smile easily and often, have a sense of humour, be themselves, are fun loving, issue compliments easily and often, display common sense, exude self confidence, engage you in conversation—about you in first 15 seconds, are not afraid to admit they do not have all the answers, can laugh at themselves, are touchable and approachable, know the difference between honesty and tact. [9]

5 Know the body language at the checkout.

Culturally, Caucasians tend not to touch strangers very often. Harassment legislation also makes this a difficult area. There's no problem in touching when we shake hands or when we pass money to each other. Indeed, we look on the dropping of change in our hands or the placing of it on the counter for us to pick up as being a negative sign. For this reason, cashiers should always place change in the customer's hand. And smile. Small points like this can make a big difference with customers.

6 Be sincere.

Many retail staff will tell you that they are competent actors—they claim they can 'put on' a positive approach to customers. Actors may indeed be skilled at this, but most of us are untrained in the dramatic arts—and the customer is quick to perceive a counterfeit smile or gesture. The key is to employ positive, pleasant people and to train them in the skills of retailing—and that includes the basics of body language.

How to train your team to smile

Every retail manager will know that they want team members to smile when greeting a customer. But smiling is supposed to be primarily a biological function. Smiling occurs naturally. Yet still many staff members smile reluctantly. The secret for retail managers is really quite simple: if you want your team to smile, you need to create a culture where people *want* to smile... and that may warrant a training program—for management, or team, or both.

1 Consider a change in culture.

Research carried out in the United Kingdom by Nicholson McBride revealed that one in five customers change their shopping habits due to the lack of friendly customer service. And supermarkets came at the bottom of the league table in terms of public perceptions in this area. Customer feedback included:

- 'I often wonder if it is my fault that checkout operators are so rude.'
- 'The staff have no product knowledge.'
- 'They do not really acknowledge you.'
- 'The calibre of people is not the friendliest.'
- 'The quality stores like Waitrose and Marks and Spencer are very good, but the others are like the pits.'

With comments like these, many stores were advised to change their culture or lose their customers. Perhaps it's time for you to address factors of friendliness in your business.

2 Invest in your team.

Many businesses invest in new technology, shopfittings and promotional campaigns, but fail to invest in possibly their greatest asset—their people. All the customer often wants is a positive, courteous response from your staff members, but to achieve that you will need to invest in them and show you care about their job satisfaction and their future. A happy employee is a smiling employee.

3 Conduct an interactive workshop.

A first step in encouraging team members to change is to get them to think positively about their own jobs. Telling the team will often be perceived as preaching and preaching is usually resented.

A useful strategy is to conduct an interactive workshop where team members are encouraged in a free-wheeling environment to think for themselves about their roles—from both their own and the customer's perspectives.

Many companies use an 'outside provider' to lead the workshop since these people are usually more objective than your own leaders and possess the skills and experience to manage such sessions.

4 Seek the facts from customer feedback.

The majority of your team will honestly believe that they are providing appropriate customer service. Many won't be. If you want people to change, you'll have to provide proof that they need to change—which is why you must present a true perspective based on what customers believe. This can be obtained via mystery shopper reports, questionnaires, customer comments, or more sophisticated research. Feed this evidence into the workshop deliberations, without picking out individuals as the focus of customer complaints.

5 Provide formal training.

Once the team has identified the need, introduce a formal training session to correct any problems. The program might embrace:

- A formal presentation of the reasons for change and what specific changes need to be implemented.
- Small group 'think tank' sessions that allow the participants to resolve problems cooperatively with peers.
- Role play sessions that allow team members to practise newly acquired skills and attitudes.
- A question-and-answer environment where all of the trainees feel they can confidently ask questions and will not be ridiculed.

6 Use a competent, fully qualified trainer.

To maximise your investment in training, you should employ an experienced trainer, not simply a presenter. Presenters offer their own views on how to improve. Trainers

Management Memo

Positive business culture comes down to leadership. Around 95% of leaders are traditional and 5% are the 'fabled' service leaders. Consider the qualities of both: [10]

MANAGERS	LEADERS
Traditional	**Fabled**
Focus on power	Focus on empowerment
Top of the hierarchy	Centre of the circle
Autocratic	Participative
Exclusive	Inclusive
Seek deference	Seek consensus
Conscious of rights	Conscious of responsibility
Inwardly focused	Other focused
Bureaucratic	Entrepreneurial

will encourage your staff, with guidance, to share their own views, and seek solutions, and will limit the imposition of their personal opinions. The trainer normally provides a workbook for individual use and for later use as a workplace reference.

7 Measure the results.

If you conduct a workshop session, and then fail to follow it through in the subsequent days and weeks, then your team will be motivated for the short-term only and eventually become disillusioned. You must follow up with mystery shopper audits or surveys to ensure the newly learnt skills are implemented in your store.

8 Remember—*all* the team must smile.

Your business has internal customers (all your own people in their varied roles) and external customers (the public, suppliers, maintenance people and so on). *All* your team need training in friendly customer service to deal with *all* your customers.

How to greet a customer

The culture of retailing varies from society to society. In Italy and Indonesia, for example, the customer is more important than the merchandise and being an effective host is an integral part of store life. In the United Kingdom and Australia, the merchandise is often perceived as being more important than the customer and, as a result, the customer is sometimes ignored while the merchandise is displayed to maximise effect. But whatever the culture, the need for retail staff to greet the customer warmly is seen as desirable...

1 Select staff who enjoy working with people.

When recruiting team members, it's an advantage to select people with personality and who enjoy working with customers. This is not always easy. Too often, managers lack the finer skills of interviewing, while interviewees, having been trained in the nuances of interview, are often able to disguise their true personality. In this regard, a useful interviewing technique is to pass compliments to the interviewee and then to gauge the reaction. A confident, 'people' person will graciously accept the compliment without embarrassment. Such people are likely to be useful additions to your sales team.

2 Insist on a 'meet-and-greet' policy.

In any retail business, it is imperative to have in place throughout the store a minimum 'meet-and-greet' standard. Your staff should, as a matter of course, welcome any customer entering the premises with a friendly greeting and a warm smile.

3 Understand the basics of greeting customers.

Make sure your staff are familiar with the following essentials:

• *Make eye contact with the customer.* People read eyes first. Suggest that your staff make a habit of always noting the colour of every customer's eyes—a sure way of guaranteeing eye contact. And, if in your business you wear sunglasses, do take them off for a few seconds when you meet the customer so that eye contact can be made.

• *Smile.* A true smile can only come naturally. It shows a friendly face and it also is capable of giving your voice a warm, friendly ring to it.

• *Give a sincere welcome.* We can name global franchise organisations with the staff trained to trot out their standard, insincere greetings. Sincerity is important. Allow your team members to use any greeting they feel comfortable with—Hi, G'day, Hello, Good Morning, or whatever—provided it comes across sincerely.

• *If you know the customer's name, use it.* We're all flattered to hear our name being used. If your staff know the name of a regular customer, then they should be encouraged to use it. As well, if they can refer to a recent incident, holiday or other event in the customer's life, they will strengthen the bond with this person. The relationship will move from a customer/salesperson link to a friend/friend bond. Such relationships within your business will increase customer loyalty dramatically.

• *Keep the body language positive.* Remember, our body language can send strong messages—both positive and negative.

• *Focus on the customer not the merchandise.* If, for example, you are building an intricate display, it is advisable to stop for a second, greet a customer, and then carry on with the task. To continue working may send a message that the customer does not matter.

• *Never ignore a customer.* During a busy trading period, how should you greet a customer when dealing with an existing one? Simply glance at the new customer, make eye contact and smile. This alone says: 'Hello and I will be with you in a moment.'

4 Keep the basics on the boil.

Desirable retail habits are often simply 'common sense', but regrettably such essential conduct is not evident all the time. For this reason, it is wise to initiate a procedure for updating all team members every six months in those important, basic retailing skills— including 'meeting and greeting'.

Management Memo

Surveys of customers indicate that they wish to be greeted promptly and properly. In the United States, 80 per cent of customers believe they are greeted properly. Most customers surveyed felt that a greeting within three minutes of entering a store was essential. [11]

5 Check out your business for customer friendliness.

To assess your company's friendliness towards customers, the following checklist should be completed at least annually:

	YES	NO
Have you a service strategy clearly defined in terms of customer benefits?	☐	☐
Do you have a well-defined promise?	☐	☐
Have you a service strategy clearly communicated		
• outside your store?	☐	☐
• inside your store?	☐	☐
Are your systems and procedures always aimed at the customer?	☐	☐
Have you measurable quality standards for all the service areas?	☐	☐
Are they communicated to all members of your team?	☐	☐
Is your recruiting, training and promotions oriented towards customer service?	☐	☐
Each month, do you reward somebody for something really special that s/he does for a customer?	☐	☐
Do you deal with letters of complaint or praise		
• rapidly?	☐	☐
• to the customer's satisfaction?	☐	☐
Is your team involved in the setting-up of service quality standards?	☐	☐
Do these team members participate in chasing errors through quality circles?	☐	☐

How to communicate effectively— and make the sale

US research claims that 70 per cent of people start their working life in retailing—yet only 3 per cent of them really want to be in retailing. In other words, the vast majority of them are reluctant starters when it comes to retailing as a career. Little wonder then that, despite the volumes that have been written on communication, customers come across indifferent communication skills in stores. As well, we fail to train newcomers to communicate effectively. Perhaps the following advice will help…

1 Know when to approach a customer.

Not all customers want to be approached. The experienced salesperson is able to read the signals that indicate a customer wants to be approached. The signs include: the customer is looking lost, looking confused, back tracking to a product, approaching the counter, making eye contact with you, looking impatient, walking towards you. The real skill is in reading the customer and deciding which is the most appropriate way of approaching, and opening up a conversation.

Three approaches might be considered…

2 Try the Greeting approach.

This is the friendly path where you greet people in a positive way. It relies on the use of positive body language as the customer is greeted. The opening might begin with a simple statement such as: 'Hi, How are you today?' The important message is that the greeting must be sincere, otherwise customers could regard you as being 'pushy'.

3 Try the Merchandise approach.

This strategy is used when the customer is seen to be looking at or handling the products. The approach here is to give a brief piece of information on the product as you approach the customer. Examples include: 'Hi, let me tell you that those oranges are delicious', or 'Hi, I've just purchased one of these, and it's working wonderfully', or 'Good morning, did you know those clothes are on special today?'.

4 Try the Service approach.

This is the most common—and most misused—approach. A service approach should be friendly, non-aggressive and offer assistance. Service approaches used come in a number of different guises…

Closed—This style of communication, when used to start a conversation, actually closes down selling. Common closed approaches are: 'Can I help you?' or 'Are you all right there?' Over 70 per cent of customers answer 'No' to the first question and 'Yes' to the second. Since you have given the customer the opportunity to close down the

Vol. 1: See 74, 212, 220, 224, 226

conversation, the result is that the average sale is much lower than it should be.

Open—This should be the most used approach. Open conversation starts with *how, what, when, where, why,* or *who.* It is designed to encourage the customer to 'open up'. Examples include: 'Good morning, how can I help you?' or 'Hi, what can I demonstrate for you?'.

Leading—Here you try to get the customer to agree with you—which is fine if you do both sincerely agree with each other. When leading, end sentences with '…isn't it?', '…didn't it?', '…aren't they?', and '…hasn't it?'. For example, 'Lovely flowers, aren't they?' or 'Now that looks great on you, doesn't it?' If you are not being sincere when using leading statements, the customer will soon become suspicious. This approach can prove futile if you consciously manipulate the conversation.

5 Probe, probe, probe.

Gentler probing encourages the customers to really get into a deep conversation at a personal level about the product they are buying. Probing questions usually make use of the word 'feel'. For example, 'How do you feel about…?'

6 Become emotionally involved in the purchase.

Top salespeople are emotional salespeople and, generally, women are better at this skill than men. An emotional salesperson finds something attractive about the person they are talking to and then compliments them on it. For example, 'I do like your dress' or 'Now that colour really suits you' or 'What a lovely selection of plants you've chosen'. The important thing is to be sincere when using the emotional approach. Emotional salespeople

Management Memo

S ales training is about saying the right thing to customers, but we also need to be aware of the things we must *not* say to customers. For example, it's a sin to say…

'You have to…'
'No, …' at the start of a sentence.
'So-and-so screwed up.'
'I don't know. I'm new to the company' (What you should say is: 'I don't know the answer myself, but I'll find someone who knows'.)
'We can't do that.'
'I'll have to put you on hold.'
'XYZ Co. carry shoddy merchandise and their prices aren't as low as ours.' [12]

quickly become friends with the customer and have a far higher average sale per customer than other members of the sales team.

7 Be aware of the importance of listening.

Your listening skills are probably more important than your verbal skills. A good listener can soon establish the needs and wants of the customer and then recommend the most suitable product. Listeners also give the impression that they are genuinely interested and care about the customer. They then get the chance to do add-on selling as well.

8 Remember the basics.

Finally, as Chris Newton (Results Corporation) summarises:

'To be a successful communicator… Make your customers feel welcome. Enquire about their needs and wants. Talk in their language. Ask questions constantly. Invite them to buy. Leave them on a high.'

How to sell features and benefits

The successful salesperson knows the difference between the features of a product and that product's benefits for the customer. In the end, people are more attracted to a product's benefits than to its features. For this reason, it is important for a salesperson to be able to translate features into relevant benefits if the deal is to be sealed...

1 Understand the changing role of the salesperson.

In any sales encounter, the salesperson will, as the sale progresses, adopt the role of host, consultant, and seller. The following diagram identifies the sequence of these functions:

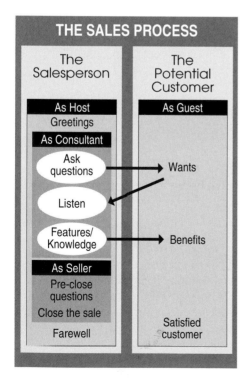

THE SALES PROCESS

The Salesperson	The Potential Customer
As Host	**As Guest**
Greetings	
As Consultant	
Ask questions	→ Wants
Listen	
Features/ Knowledge	→ Benefits
As Seller	
Pre-close questions	
Close the sale	
Farewell	Satisfied customer

2 Understand the importance of 'features'.

Features are what a product is and how it works. Although your sales team need to be familiar with this technical knowledge to have credibility in the eyes of the customer, most customers are not particularly interested in the features of the product. Research tells us that the majority of them make their decision to purchase on the basis of 15 per cent product knowledge and 85 per cent emotion, an important concept for a salesperson to grasp.

So, if you rely on product know-how alone and emphasise features to sell merchandise, you are not relating effectively to the customer. You run the risk of using product jargon, words the customer cannot understand, and are in danger of over-communicating, over-complicating the product—and losing the sale.

3 Understand the importance of 'benefits'.

Benefits are what the product does for the customer and often embody the important emotional areas of the decision making process. Consider the banking service, for example, to differentiate between features and benefits. A bank may argue that its *features* include:

Automatic teller service
Open till 6.00 pm on Fridays
Many branches
Friendly staff
Deposits are secure
Travellers cheque facility
10 per cent interest on savings.

It may argue that the *benefits* of banking include:

Saves you time
Can obtain money any time of day
Gives you peace of mind.

Explore the difference between features and benefits for such products as a household fire alarm, a garden sprinkler system, and a long-life paint—and you'll understand the value in promoting benefits whenever you can.

4 Understand your customer's motives.

I believe people buy a product for one of six reasons (although Pat Weymes' categorisation differs slightly—see the *Management Memo* above). During a sales encounter, a skilled retailer can soon identify the customer's prime buying motive and approaches the sale accordingly. These six buying motives include:

(a) Money gained or saved
(b) Useful or convenient item
(c) Security/Protection
(d) Status
(e) Pride
(f) Pleasure.

Customers become price sensitive when their motive for purchase is identified as being (a), (b) or (c), because they *need* the product. They become less price sensitive when

> ## Management Memo
>
> **B**uying motives can fall into two groups, emotional and rational. [13]
>
> **Emotional reasons for buying are:**
>
> Fear—of competition or being left behind
> Envy—of another's successful achievements
> Vanity—recognition by others that you have made a wise decision
> Love—approved by family and friends
> Entertainment—enjoyment and relaxation
> Sentiment—family tradition
> Pride—being associated with success
> Pleasure—derived from the appearance of the new purchase.
>
> **Rational reasons for buying are:**
>
> Profit—increase efficiency, reduce wastage
> Health—less hazardous, less strain
> Security—well-established firm or brand, or a proven track record
> Utility—easier to use, less effort, time saving
> Caution—fewer service calls, long life

their motive is (d), (e) or (f), because they *want* the product.

5 Train your team in selling the benefits.

As an integral part of your sales training program, you should include the procedure of identifying the features and benefits of your merchandise. During these sessions, your trainees might consider completing the following chart to drive home the importance of going beyond a product's features in the selling process:

Product name and description	Features and functions (what it does and how it works)	Benefits to customer (what it does for the buyer)	Buying motives

How to remove a customer's doubt—and make the sale

Most people do not make instant buying decisions. They need to have their doubts removed by a person they have confidence in—and this is one of the roles of a salesperson. You need to be able to identify a customer's doubts and then, by combatting that uncertainty, you can achieve the sale...

1 Know that customers have doubts.

Doubt is due to one (or more) of four factors looming large in the potential customer's mind. According to John Wren in *Yes, Thanks! I'll Take It!*, these can be summarised as:

- A doubt due to an unanswered question or a misunderstanding in the potential customer's mind.
- A doubt due to lack of clarification or the need for approval by a qualified person.
- A doubt due to not believing the product is going to satisfy the customer's needs.
- A doubt due to conditions that will not allow the customer to purchase when they want to purchase.

2 Welcome customer doubts.

If prospective customers raise doubts, this normally is a clear indication that they are wanting to make a purchase, but they need a salesperson to remove those doubts and to help them make the decision. The presence of doubt is, in reality, a positive opportunity that should be welcomed.

3 Be on the lookout for customer cover-ups.

Most of us conceal our real doubts. How often do you hear people say: 'I'll think about it' or 'I'll talk it over with my partner and get back to you' or 'I was only really looking at this point in time'. Such cover-ups usually hide the real reasons for not going through with the purchase.

According to Jeffrey Gitomer in *Sales Bible*, the real reasons for doubt by customers are normally:

I do not have the money on me.
I have a credit problem.
I cannot decide on my own.
I want to shop around.
I do not understand the product.
I have a friend in the industry.
The price is too high.
I have money, but don't want to spend it.
I need someone else's financial approval.
I have something else in mind.
I'm too rushed to purchase at present.
I don't really need it.
I don't trust your company.
I don't trust you.

4 Discover the real reason for doubt.

Being aware of the above, you are now in a position to discover the real

WINNING OVER
OUR CUSTOMERS

IAGING
IR STORE

OMOTING
R PRODUCTS

IAGING
R BUSINESS

IDEX

31

Vol. 1: See 74, 98, 220, 222

reason for doubt. The customer may not always tell you (especially if they do not trust you) but you do have the opportunity to probe. To discover the real reason, you must be confident and this comes with training, especially in product knowledge, selling skills, negotiations, and listening skills.

5 Be methodical when dealing with doubt.

John Wren advocates four steps when dealing with doubt:

Defuse any objections by listening, showing empathy, and using open questions to discover the real reason for doubt.

Prove facts by using magazines, technical reports, demonstrations, testimonials and any other material that is available to you.

Clarify to make sure the doubt has truly been removed in the customer's mind.

Refocus on the sale, after having removed the doubt.

Situations with customers where doubts have arisen should be discussed in team meetings. These are an opportunity to get other team members' ideas and to look at ways of preventing them in the future.

As a sales tool, develop a portfolio which includes technical literature, customer testimonials, articles in the press, references in books, and any other relevant information. This portfolio can be an excellent sales reference when discussing product selection with a potential customer.

6 Build up staff confidence through role play.

Role-playing those difficult selling situations is an ideal way of

> ### Management Memo
>
> Pick a trading day at random and for the whole day keep a record of how many of your customers say 'no'. That day could become a high point on your sales calendar —particularly if you thereafter use a different selling technique to reduce the number of no's.[14]

providing yourself and your team with the confidence to approach and deal with the doubting customer. It provides an opportunity to make mistakes and to learn from other team members. This is far more effective than bungling a real-life situation with a customer and losing the sale.

Role plays can be undertaken in training sessions or in team meetings. Introduce them as part of your culture so that your staff see the value of such scenarios. If role play is a normal practice, embarrassment will be minimised and staff will not be reluctant to get involved.

7 Always keep to these basic rules...

When talking to a customer with doubts, remember these golden rules:

- Keep calm at all times. Never let your frustration show. If you feel yourself getting agitated, take some deep breaths to help you calm down.

- See doubts as opportunities to make a sale. If you can remove doubts successfully you will often find the customer will become loyal to you and your company.

- Never take any comments personally. The customer is not being critical of you as a person; they have problems with the situation.

- Always be prepared: know your product and have the skills to deal with the customer.

How to turn your customers into lifetime customers

Successful retailing is a long-term affair. It is not simply about making a sale—it is about keeping customers for life. All your team members should know the lifetime value of your customers and how to ensure that they work towards generating life-long customers. Unfortunately, too many retailers start with good intentions, but lack the commitment in building those essential long-term relationships. The following advice will help in that regard...

1 Calculate the lifetime value of your customers.

According to data released by the New Zealand marketing research company Go Direct, the lifetime value of a customer can be as follows:

Supermarket customer	NZ$250,000
Motor vehicle customer	NZ$150,000
Women's wear customer	NZ$ 90,000
Menswear customer	NZ$ 30,000

You can calculate the true value of your lifetime customer by using the following formula:

Lifetime value of customer =
  Average sale of customer x Frequency of
  spending visits annually x Lifetime with your business

In most retail situations, the lifetime value will vary between 5 and 7 years, not, as is often assumed, 20 or 30 years.

2 Keep in touch.

John Goman of American Express believes there are only three ways to build any business:

  Have more customers.
  Have customers shop more often.
  Have customers buy more when they
    come in.

Obvious perhaps, but just as obvious is the point he missed—you also need to work towards building customers for life.

The key to lifetime relationships is KIT—Keeping In Touch. The skills required to develop lifetime links with customers are different from the skills of product selling. So, encourage and train your team to foster lifetime value, to keep in touch with customers, and to build genuine relationships. Not only do they need skills training, but they also need the commitment to make it work.

3 Adhere to the 1-5-15-30 technique of follow up.

John Wren in *Yes, thanks! I'll take it!* promotes the concept of the 1-5-15-30 follow up technique. A decision to use this technique should be based on the type of product purchased, the amount of money spent, and the relationship formed between the salesperson and the customer.

The 1-5-15-30 concept relates to the days after the sale when a salesperson should communicate positively with the customer.

Day 1—a personally handwritten note from the salesperson to the customer is all that is required. This could be along the lines of a short thank-you and a hope that the customer is getting pleasure out of the purchase.

Day 5—a telephone call may be in order. Never start the telephone call with 'Are you happy with…?'. If you do, you may get a negative response. Start with, 'I wanted to telephone you to make sure you were enjoying…'.

Day 15—check again over the telephone.

Day 30—mail an added-value gift related to the purchase.

After 90 days, and every 90 days thereafter, they should receive your newsletter as a loyal customer.

4 Make people remember you as a salesperson.

People do business with people, so your aim must be to build a person-to-person relationship, not a relationship with the business. To do this, you need to make a lasting impression. Depending on your business, consider such strategies as…

- Always hand your business card to the customer, preferably one with your photograph so that the customer is reminded of what you look like.
- Send relevant newsclippings, articles or new information on the product as and when it becomes available.
- If the person is interested in joining a club that relates to the product, then introduce them to a club member.
- Send birthday or anniversary cards. These work more effectively than Christmas cards which get lost in the volume of other cards received.
- At Nordstrom in the United States, individual salespeople keep profiles on their specific customers, enabling them to match new products with identified customer needs/wants.

5 Have written policies that everyone adheres to.

Too many businesses fail because they are not consistent. Consistency comes with having realistic written

---

Management Memo

The 25 attributes of a good business-customer relationship, ranked in order of importance by long-lasting customers:

Being called back when promised

Receiving an explanation of how a problem occurred

Being provided with information on how to contact relevant people

Being contacted promptly when a problem has been resolved

Being able to talk to someone in authority

Being told how long it will take to resolve a problem

Being given valuable alternatives if the problem cannot be solved

Being treated as a person, not as an account number

Being told how to prevent a problem in the future

Being given progress reports if the problem will take some time to resolve

Being able to talk to people without interruptions

Not being put on hold without asking

Being treated with appreciation for their business

Having a person, not a recording, answer the telephone

Being given service people's names and telephone numbers

Getting through to a department on the first call

Being offered suggestions on how to minimise costs

Being able to talk, on the first call, to someone who can resolve a problem

Receiving an apology when an error is made

Being helped without being put on hold

Having the telephone answered on the third ring

Being greeted with a 'hello' or 'good morning'

Being able to reach the service area after 4pm

Being addressed by name

Being able to reach someone after hours. [15]

---

policies that outline achievable strategies and embrace a constant program for training team members.

6 Instigate a reward system.

Team members, as well as customers, need recognition for building relationships and you need to put in place a reward system for your team. Rewards can be low cost, but show that you value the dedicated team member. Consider everything from tickets to the movies, to dinner for two at a local restaurant, to enrolment in a keep fit club.

How to improve your customer service

Numerous surveys have been carried out over the years to determine what kind of things upset customers when they go shopping. After the findings of these surveys are collated and analysed, the customer comments are found to be strikingly similar. If you want to improve your customer service, then obviously these surveys can provide some valuable guidelines for action...

1 Keep your tills open and your queues short.

In a recent Australian survey by Les Barnett Advertising Agency, 44 per cent of shoppers said this was their biggest complaint—not enough tills open at busy times; the result: queues!

The answer seems straight-forward: minimise those queues. Have a policy where another till is opened whenever a queue of four develops. But remember, when you do so, invite the next person in line over to the new till. If you don't, the last to arrive may be the first to be served—and you will still end up with unhappy customers.

2 Keep your staff up on product knowledge.

Over 40 per cent of customers surveyed felt that lack of staff knowledge about products was a major disappointment. It is essential that all team members participate in product familiarisation sessions. Suppliers and manufacturers are often keen to help as it is a win-win situation. Alternatively, rotate the leading of these product knowledge sessions around your team members.

3 Resist charging for wrapping or bagging.

Some 37 per cent of people surveyed complained about having to pay for shopping bags and wrapping services. Bags and wrapping are an opportunity to promote added-value services. Wrapping services at Christmas, St Valentine's Day, Easter, Mother's Day, Father's Day, and Secretaries' Day will be a pleasant bonus for most customers.

4 Limit staff overkill.

Nearly one-third of customers get annoyed by staff who they perceive are pestering them. This highlights the lack of sales training in many retail businesses. Properly trained team members can read customer body language and know when and when not to approach. Hold training sessions on a regular basis to remind team members of these basic skills.

5 Remove disinterested staff.

The complaint that staff show little interest in customers is a reverse of the last point, but again nearly one-third of people surveyed believed this to be a major turn-off. The solution is the same as above— although the key is to recruit keen people with personality. Given the correct skills, enthusiastic team members with personality will enjoy the challenge of selling.

6 Welcome legitimate customer returns.

Being made to feel in the wrong when returning products upset 17 per cent of those surveyed. The majority of customers are genuine when they return products and, as retailers, we should accept their honesty. Again, team training on how to deal with complaints and returns is necessary.

7 Assist customers to load their cars.

Your company should have a policy of when and how to load cars, since 12 per cent of customers complained about this lack of service. One added touch is to provide boot liners emblazoned with your name— customers appreciate that you have taken that extra bit of care.

8 Don't patronise customers.

One in ten customers resented patronising and condescending treatment from team members. The great majority of surveys conclude that staff-customer interrelations lie at the heart of customer complaints about retail outlets. For this reason, regular training sessions on human relations should be an essential part of all your staff development programs.

9 Appraise your staff regularly.

All businesses should carry out staff appraisals at least annually. The following appraisal sheet is a useful first step in turning your staff into winners in terms of customer service:

Assessing Staff Selling Skills APPRAISAL FORM			
4 - Excellent 3 - Good 2 - Average 1 - Poor			
	4	3 2 1
SALES IMPRESSION Appearance and approach e.g. alert, poised, at ease, pleasant	☐	☐ ☐ ☐
SELLING ATTITUDE e.g. Enthusiastic, mature, socially positive, sincere, convincing, humour	☐	☐ ☐ ☐
SPEECH Vocabulary, voice, speed of talk, grammar, pronunciation	☐	☐ ☐ ☐
QUESTIONS Use of open, closed and leading questions	☐	☐ ☐ ☐
LISTENING FOR NEEDS Posture, attention, showing for understanding, identifying needs and/or wants	☐	☐ ☐ ☐
KNOWLEDGE OF SUBJECT Facts, information, personal tips based on experience	☐	☐ ☐ ☐
REASONS FOR BUYING Benefits, advantages to customer	☐	☐ ☐ ☐
OBJECTIONS Recognised, handled tactfully, assurance given, converted into reasons for buying	☐	☐ ☐ ☐
USE OF SALES AIDS Use of product, quality and ingenuity of sale aids	☐	☐ ☐ ☐
ORGANISATION Opening, development, specific answers, close of sale	☐	☐ ☐ ☐
ALTERNATIVE PRODUCTS Use of link (tie-in) items and/or alternative products	☐	☐ ☐ ☐

How to develop a customer loyalty program

A trend in recent years has been the development of loyalty programs in retail businesses. The objective is to 'lock' your customers into your business at the expense of other businesses in the same retail sector. Loyalty programs started in the airline industry and have now spread to other areas of retailing, primarily led by supermarkets in the United Kingdom. Consider these suggestions if you want to retain your customers' loyalty…

 ### Focus on loyalty, not discounts.

When establishing a loyalty program, your objective is to *establish* loyalty, not to *buy* loyalty by simply using a card to offer discounts. Your priority must be to provide regular, dedicated customers with privileges by joining your 'loyalty club'.

 ### Set up a database before you start.

Prior to launching a loyalty program, establish a database of names, addresses and customer interests. First, obtain a database software program for your computer. There are many packages on the market and you should select one which suits your own specific requirements. With the software in place, you can then go about promoting your loyalty program to customers.

The application form for your loyalty program should introduce the benefits of joining your club and request the following information for the database: name, address, telephone number, product range interests. Revise, clean and update your lists every twelve months.

 ### Sell the benefits.

Your aim must be to sell the privileges of being in your loyalty club. This list of benefits will differ across retail sectors, but can include:
- Invitation to special events
- Invitation to guest speakers
- Exclusivity to unique products
- Offer of new products prior to mass release on market
- Upgrade in services
- Exclusive services
- Gifts on birthdays or at Christmas
- Financial incentives to purchase more
- Visits to attractions not open to others
- Network incentives with other retailers used by your customer database.

 ### Be upmarket in presenting the concept.

Your customer base is familiar with credit card use and your loyalty card must be of the same calibre if it is to be appreciated by customers. The words Privilege Card, Gold Card and Club Card are names that help customers accept the card as a privilege.

 ### Devise your loyalty strategy.

Your objective is to win loyalty and repeat business. The airlines do this with their frequent flyer programs where customers are encouraged to accumulate points. The more points they collect, the more prestigious the privileges. In your situation, one successful strategy might be for customers, every time they shop with you, to collect points which can then be converted into privileges over a given time frame. For example:

- Look at your average sale per customer, take that average sale and allow the consumer to collect 10 points if they spend above your average sale.
- The more money they spend, the more points they are given.
- Start your reward program at 80 points (8 x above average sale target). At 80 points any reward should be to the value of the normal average sale.
- Extra rewards could then be obtained at 100, 160, 200, 320, 400, 800, 1500 and 4500 points.

Notify customers at regular intervals so they know where they stand with their points. This is an ideal excuse to communicate with them about a range of other matters.

Should customers pay for joining loyalty clubs? If you put a price on joining the club, you have the opportunity to include a thank-you gift later.

6 Build relations with loyalty members.

Once you have established a loyalty program, you must ensure that your team plays the game. Customers now believe they are special in your business and they expect special treatment. They expect recognition, their names to be used, comments on their last purchase, and joint celebrations of special events in their lives. Here, your staff are key people —and for them to achieve, they must

---

Management Memo

Nordstrom in the United States is recognised around the world for their customer service and for generating customer loyalty. The keys to their success have been identified as follows:

☐ If you treat customers like royalty and let them know that you will take care of them, they come back to you.

☐ Top salespeople do not put things off until the end of the day. They get them out of the way so they can start the next day fresh.

☐ When customers enter a department, salespeople make sure they are acknowledged. They are relaxed and unhurried in order to help the customer feel the same way.

☐ Top salespeople keep the process simple and easy by helping the customer eliminate the things not wanted. They constantly ask for feedback because the more information they have, the better they can serve the customer. Price is never a primary issue.

☐ 'Trust' is the coin of the realm. Salespeople earn the confidence of customers by being well versed in the merchandise they sell. They are not just selling clothes and shoes. They are also selling service.

☐ Top salespeople rely on the tools that Nordstrom provide, including a personal customer book to keep track of pertinent information on every customer.

☐ The telephone is a powerful tool for generating business, improving productivity and saving time.

☐ Follow-through is important. Top salespeople are not looking for the big score. They are committed to nurturing an ongoing business relationship. [1]

---

have access to the database, even know how to use it and update it.

7 Explore 'out house' retailing opportunities.

Loyalty programs allow you to promote and sell your products by mail order to targeted customers. This could be considered as your next retailing opportunity once a loyalty program is firmly in place.

How to conduct a customer survey

Successful retailers know their customers exceptionally well. They know their customers' needs and wants—because they ask them. This is usually done through the use of a mix of techniques, including customer forums, questionnaires, surveys, by walking the floor and talking to customers, and through the use of mystery shopper surveys. One of the simplest techniques is the customer survey. If you want to get a true picture of how consumers feel about your business via a survey, then consider these guidelines...

1 Know why you are conducting the survey.

You are collecting data and you are asking people to commit their time to the task. For this reason, the process must be systematic, targeted, efficient and likely to lead to actionable outcomes. So, before embarking upon the survey, be able to answer these questions:

- What kind of data am I seeking?
- Why do I need this information?
- When do I need the information?
- How will I collect this information?
- Within what time frame will the data be collected?
- How will the information be collated and analysed?
- What will I do with the data I get?
- Will the data really lead to action?

Only if you can provide satisfactory answers to such questions should your survey proceed.

2 Keep the survey form simple.

The key to a successful response rate is to keep survey forms simple and friendly. Limit the information you require to avoid taking up too much of your customers' time. It's better to conduct a series of short surveys than one over-lengthy questionnaire. Limit the questions to one side of one sheet of paper if possible.

Apart from the customer's name, address, and phone number, basic information you may seek could focus upon such issues as:

- what they like about your business
- what they would like to see improved
- what product/s they want that you do not sell.

3 Structure your survey wisely.

Two basic approaches may be adopted in structuring your survey form. The easiest and quickest method for customers is the tick-a-box technique. For example,

Please indicate your satisfaction with our service to you, our customer:

	Very satisfied	Satisfied	Dissatisfied	Very dissatisfied
1. Staff attitude	☐	☐	☐	☐
2. Staff knowledge	☐	☐	☐	☐
3. Staff appearance	☐	☐	☐	☐
4. Value for money	☐	☐	☐	☐

A second approach is the open-ended question format:

1. Why do you like to chop in our store?......
2. What would you like to see improved?.........
3. What products would you like to see added to our range?...............
4. What do you think we do least well?............

Or try a combination of both methods.

You may like to make your survey form stand out. The survey sheet at one Melbourne hotel in Australia depicts a 30cm high ear with the words 'We are listening' across it.

Don't forget to indicate briefly why the survey is being conducted ('We value our customers' opinions and seek your concerns and suggestions to help us improve the quality of our service') and a sincere thank-you for their time.

Provide an incentive.

Some people will fill in survey forms as a matter of course. Some will not be bothered. Others might need an incentive. As a token of your appreciation, you may offer a prize draw to reward one or more of those who complete the questionnaire. If you do this, your customers are more likely to provide you with their name and address, a great help if you are building up a customer database.

Place survey boxes near the exit.

Completed surveys should be placed in boxes near your store's exit. The response will be greater if you provide there a small area with bench and pens where customers can complete their survey forms. Make this location very conspicuous and display a large sign above it in an appropriate spot.

Management Memo

If a company is truly customer-driven, the utmost attention should be given to finding out what customers really think of the business. [18]

6 Show your appreciation.

Winning retailers will tell you that you must respond to all suggestions. If the customer provides a contact point, then you'll be on a winner if you take the trouble to communicate with them, replying in a positive and friendly manner to their positive and negative comments. Your response should ideally be made within 48 hours of their survey form being deposited in the box.

7 Use the survey as a marketing tool.

Writing to a survey respondent provides a great opportunity to begin building a relationship with your customer. Consider sending them a voucher with your letter, as a thank-you gift. The voucher should be valid for about a month and its aim is to encourage the customer to return to your store and increase their average spend.

8 Act on the results effectively.

Use the results of your survey as a stimulus to improving your customer service. The results are only meaningful when they have been interpreted by you or cooperatively by your staff. A survey will only prove its worth when you act on its findings.

How to increase your customer base

The key to building a successful retail business is to build and foster a loyal customer base. Getting new customers is only the first step: you will need to develop relationships with those customers so that these linkages can expand over time into lifetime partnerships. It's possible to do this by converting identified prospects into advocates and using a simple step-by-step formula...

1 Help your customers climb the ladder.

If you think of your business as a 5-rung step-ladder, your aim should be to help as many people as possible to climb to the top of that ladder...

Suspects are those people on the bottom rung of your ladder. They're forever suspicious of you and your store. Money spent on them may be money wasted.

Prospects are on the second-bottom step. You've never invited these people into your store but, if you did, chances are they would willingly enter. An advertising program could be directed to these people.

Customers are people who come to your store, and who are also shared by competition. They are not loyal to your business, probably because you have never asked them to be loyal.

Clients are those on the second top step. They are good customers, loyal to your company, but have never promoted you to their friends and colleagues. Again, you may have not asked them to do so.

Advocates are at the top of the ladder. They use word of mouth to promote you and your business to anyone who wants to listen.

Your aim is to get everyone—beginning on the prospects' step of the ladder—to climb continually to the top to become advocates. Of course, this all takes time, and disgruntled people can quickly drop off the ladder.

2 Begin the search for prospects.

To build a strong customer base, you'll need an advertising budget because you will have to invest on an ongoing basis to identify new customer prospects. You can attract these people through newspaper and magazine advertising, the *Yellow Pages*, radio advertising, word of mouth, sponsoring events, mail-outs and leaflets, and by appealing to them as they pass your premises.

3 Convert prospects into new customers.

A prospect who enters your store is not a customer until you convert them—getting them to buy something from you… and then wanting to come back. To do this, you'll need to apply all your skills of conversion—welcome the prospect to your business, get them interested in making a purchase, sealing the deal to their complete satisfaction, and, if possible, obtaining their name and address so you can follow up the purchase later.

 Convert new customers into good customers.

Your new customer can now be added to your existing customer database. It should be your ongoing objective to convert these customers into good customers (or clients) by involving them in a campaign to increase the frequency of customer visits. Most retailers have details of retail averages in terms of visits for their sector of the market. Your aim is to be higher than this average—for example, if the average customer visits a hardware store six times a year, you want your average to be eight.

Your campaign might include frequent-user programs, an in-house club, a children's club, exclusivity evenings, or other special events.

5 Convert good customers into advocates.

Your goal is to get to know your good customers extremely well, to maximise the potential of the store-customer relationship and, in time, to turn these people into advocates of your business throughout the community. Among the strategies

> ### Management Memo
>
> Advocates can provide testimonials for you to promote your business, but you'll need to adhere to the following rules to make testimonials work:
> - Make them believable.
> - Make them honest.
> - Make them spontaneous.
> - Make it easy for your advocate to give a testimonial.
> - Make sure you respect their privacy if requested.
> - Have the testimonial givers provide them in a form that is usable.[20]

you might consider for accomplishing this would be promotions to them on their birthdays, club functions, Christmas cards and presents, reminders of important events, exclusive invitations to special events—the list is limited only by your imagination.

 Remember the formula…

In the end then, developing a large and loyal customer base and increasing the average sale is a combination of merchandising skills, selling skills and human relations—and a commitment to the following formulae:

Prospect + Conversion = New customer

New customer + Existing customers = Total customer count

Total customers + Frequency of visits = Total customer visits

Total customer visits x Average sale = Return on investment

How to handle those complaints

Every business gets complaints—it's all part of doing business. In fact, in the retail trade, 14 per cent of customers have a complaint and 75 per cent of complaints go to the checkout or counter. Little wonder then that dealing with complaints should constitute an important part of any store training program. The key things to remember are that complaints must not be taken personally and that they should be seen as opportunities to improve your business procedures. To handle complaints effectively, consider this advice...

1 Be aware of the impact complaints can have.

Research into the impact of customer complaints reveals some interesting statistics:

☐ According to recent research 4 per cent of unhappy customers complain —the other 96 per cent of those people with complaints leave your business without you knowing why! We're advised that the average person who has a complaint will then tell 9 to 10 other people, while customers whose complaints have been resolved will tell 5 to 6 people. It is the same old story: bad news travels twice as fast as the good news.

☐ Between 56 and 70 per cent of customers who have a complaint will do business with your store again—if the complaint is resolved. But, 96 per cent will do business with you again if you resolve the complaint within a 24 hour period.

☐ According to *Kwik Kopy Newsletter* (February 1998), US research shows that, in terms of customer complaints, 20 per cent of fault relates to employee attitude and 40 per cent lies with company procedures. The remaining 40 per cent of blame resides with customers having the wrong expectations.

2 Adopt the LEAR technique of handling complaints.

The LEAR technique of dealing with complaining customers is very simple—and very effective...

L isten
E mpathise
A sk Questions
R esolve Problem.

3 Listen and show you're listening.

Listening to customers complaining is one thing—but the important thing is for the customer to believe you are listening to them. To show you are actively listening, there are six steps you should follow:

(a) Make eye contact.

(b) Nod in agreement.

(c) Give verbal encouragement.

(d) Display positive body language.

(e) Ask relevant questions.

(f) Give a summary and feedback.

By showing you are listening, you have taken an important step in defusing the issue and in resolving the problem.

4 Empathise with the customer.

Empathy is putting yourself in your customers' shoes and seeing the situation from their perspective. The key is to ask how you would feel in their position. Again, it's important to actually show the customer that you are empathising—by actively listening, rewarding and acknowledging. Showing empathy does not mean you agree, but you must be genuine and use positive body language. Use empathy statements such as:

'I can understand your disappointment.'
'You were right to let me know.'
'You did the right thing in returning the item.'
'I know how you feel.'

5 Seek clarification through questioning.

Ask open questions as you attempt to diagnose the problem and never attempt to justify your situation. The customer is not interested in your problems and justification may just make them angry.

When dealing with complaints:

DO   Listen.
        Isolate the problem and restate it.
        Make the complaint a positive opportunity for your company.
        Know your subject.

DON'T   Interrupt.
        Argue.
        Evade the issue.
        Lose your temper.
        Reintroduce an objection that has been dealt with.

Management Memo

A complaint is a 'gift' to your business and should be treated as such. Too many businesses take a negative view of complaints, when in fact they are a positive opportunity to build your business. Consider this eight-step formula for dealing with complaints:

1. Always say thank you
2. Explain why you appreciate complaints
3. Apologise for mistakes made
4. Promise to do something about it immediately
5. Ask for the necessary information to solve the problem
6. Correct the mistake promptly
7. Check the customer is satisfied
8. Prevent the mistake happening in the future.[21]

6 Resolve the problem.

Resolve the problem to the customer's satisfaction as quickly as possible. Consider the lifetime value of the customer, not the cost of resolving this particular issue. Once the problem has been resolved, make sure the rest of the team knows what has taken place. This feedback to staff will help your team deal with similar situations in future, perhaps provide you with additional ideas for the next time, and help you to take appropriate action to ensure this complaint never resurfaces.

How to ensure your team is customer friendly

The retail trade is often in the firing line over low levels of customer service. A recent public opinion poll found that Australians were 'concerned and bothered' about AIDS and nuclear war— followed by the rudeness of shop assistants! A *Time* magazine survey discovered that 85 per cent of customers felt service could be improved, and in their book *The Customer*, Bob Ansett and John McManamy condemned our service policy. The message is clear: we must become more customer friendly...

1 Develop a customer service policy.

If you do not have a written service policy, you should write one, for this must be the first step in achieving a friendly customer service culture throughout your organisation. Indeed, the implementation of any staff training program must be based on a company service policy—or how will participants know what standards are required by the employer?

Your policy should at least cover the following areas:

- *Service Strategy.* Where does your organisation fit into the marketplace? What level of excellence do you require?

- *Customer Communications.* How do you communicate your service strategy to your customers?

- *Clear Standards.* Write down your quality standards, courtesy standards and speed of delivery.

- *Deliveries.* Design a customer friendly system.

- *Employee Communication.* Outline a strategy for telling all employees what your standards are and a procedure for reprimanding them when they drop below those set standards.

- *Employee training.* Detail what steps you will be taking to ensure your staff receive appropriate training in the skills of customer service.

- *Chasing errors.* Do you have a procedure in place to tackle complaints? Your aim should be to reach zero defects in your policy and customer service.

2 Train the team to be customer friendly.

Take steps to ensure that all team members who face or talk to customers are trained in the skills of selling. With your company's service policy as the yardstick, your trainers and staff know where the organisation stands with regard to customer service standards.

Some companies provide training through in-house facilities and staff, while others use outside agencies. Training should include the entire team. We often forget that the most important person in the team is the checkout operator as they see every customer—and even the storeroom staff deal with internal customers.

For starters, any training program should include:

- using body language in retailing
- using open, closed and leading questions
- being a good host, consultant and seller
- the skills of benefits selling
- using pre-close and close questions.

3 Following up your training.

Unfortunately, many companies put people in training courses and assume that, thereafter, the problem of customer service has been solved. Formal training is only the start. Training must be followed up. The new skills must be reinforced in the workplace and, once people have been trained, they need appraising to see how, and to be told that, they are improving.

4 Compile a selling skills appraisal form.

A typical staff appraisal form appears on page 35. This should be used to measure the selling skills of your staff on a regular basis—at least once a year. Ideally, the form should be completed by two people—the person being appraised who makes a personal judgement on their current performance, and by that person's

> ## Management Memo
>
> Providing the right customer service varies between male and female shoppers. According to research carried out in Singapore:
> - Male shoppers earn more than females.
> - Males shop less, but spend more when they do.
> - Females rely on word of mouth; males rely on the newspaper.
> - Females are more impulsive; males are more planned.
> - Males are more influenced by the service provider; females are influenced by colleagues and friends.
> - Males consider packaging, services, and merchandise; females consider sales promotions, brands, and price.
> - Females shop longer hours. [22]

supervisor. Both parties then meet to compare ratings. Clearly, if the employee believes their selling attitude is 'excellent', and the supervisor allocates a 'poor' rating, then this is a topic for exploration and a decision as to what action should be taken to improve the employee's skills in this area.

5 Institute a customer friendly staff award.

Reinforce the importance of customer friendly service by introducing a staff award, to be presented monthly to the team member who best demonstrates the standards and qualities espoused in your company's customer service policy.

How to profit from your PA system

The public address (PA) system is a great way to promote your business—and it costs you next to nothing! Many firms fail to use their public address system effectively because they see it only as a means of communicating with staff or announcing specials. If you can use your PA creatively, it will become a promotional medium that will enable you to increase sales and customer goodwill by simply using equipment already installed and without the extra expense of advertising. Make your PA work for you by following this advice…

1 Adopt a professional approach.

Being professional means being well prepared. Ensure that you and your staff know how to get the best results from your PA by understanding the medium you are using.

Whether you have a 'fixed' or 'roving' microphone, it is vital to remember that you are selling with voice—so the choice of a presenter requires more than simply selecting someone who 'just happened to be handy' or had the confidence to pick up a microphone. Arrange regular practice sessions for your staff or, better still, for a voice coach to give them some professional training. Nothing is more off-putting to customers than the 'nasal whine' or 'shotgun speech' often associated with PA announcements in retail stores.

2 Encourage staff participation.

Because most people have a fear of public speaking, it is no easy task to find staff who are willing to use the PA. The answer is to make training a more attractive proposition. Offer incentives and rewards such as:

- a trophy for the 'PA Person of the Week'
- a 'Customers' Favourite Commentator' award
- bonus points for participating – with store discounts as a prize.

To develop the increased confidence that comes from an ability to speak in public, the following tips will prove useful…

3 Plan what you want to say.

Being well prepared means knowing what you propose to say, as well as how you intend to say it. Work from an outline rather than a script so that you don't give the impression that you are simply 'reading aloud' over the PA. The aim is to sound spontaneous:

- Speak from notes–not from a fully scripted presentation.
- Keep the wording clear and simple.
- Jot down key points and special items.
- Arrange the points in logical order.
- Decide on your main message–

and say it twice: once at the beginning and again at the end.

• Practise 'ad libbing' from your outline.

The result will be a more personalised and professional use of the PA.

4 See your voice as a selling tool.

Making a connection with your customers means making it easy for them to listen. People tend to 'tune out' if your voice is too loud, too soft, too fast, or too slow – or just plain boring.

To 'sell well' on the PA, your voice requires:

Clarity. People need to hear and understand what it is you are saying. Speaking too fast or not distinctly enough is a major PA problem. Saying the alphabet slowly and clearly with lots of mouth movement is an excellent way to warm-up.

Colour. People need to stay interested in what you are saying. A monotone makes them 'switch off' and start thinking about something else. If you stay interested in what you are saying, it will be reflected in your voice and make it more expressive.

Confidence. People need to be convinced of what you are saying. Research shows that enthusiasm and confidence are contagious. Let those feelings show in your tone and your customers are much more likely to respond.

5 Be innovative.

Make the PA a means of getting-to-know your customers, and vice-versa. You can, for instance:

• Introduce yourself and your staff over the PA. If you have a large store, introduce a different department each week.

Management Memo

Noreen Emery of Perth-based Speech Dynamics, the professional voice coaches for the retail industry, suggests that retailers should resist the temptation to bring in someone from outside to sell on their PA.

The whole idea is to strengthen customer and staff relationships. A familiar voice or face will help to personalise your store and provide the sense of belonging that maintains your customer base. [23]

• Run a competition aimed at matching staff photographs with staff names.

• Give meal ideas, kitchen tips, or handyperson hints over the PA, then direct people to the appropriate department.

• Set up a weekly promotional theme, e.g. 'Sweet Week', 'Low Calorie Week', 'Family Favourites Week', etc.

• Work with your local community in promoting forthcoming events over the PA and tie these in with the benefits of buying at your store.

• Hold 'Valued Customer' days in which you target specific groups with discounts or give-aways.

Be creative, use your imagination and you will discover many new opportunities for building profits and promoting business over your PA.

This topic was provided by Noreen Emery, Speech Dynamics, Perth, Western Australia.

How to close a sale

The point at which you ask the buyer for an order is the close. Much of the effort in planned selling is wasted if you fail to close the sale effectively, so it is evident that attention to the close is vital to your success...

1 Tackle closure with confidence.

No matter what technique is used to close a sale successfully, it is important that the process be undertaken positively, realistically, logically, confidently, and with appropriate timing. Remember:

- Always assume that you are going to get the order.
- Use positive phrases. Never use statements such as 'Would you like to have this?', or 'Will this be enough?'
- Be persistent. Never give up at the first 'no' but be aware of the point when the order is totally lost and further persistence will cause offence.
- Link your closing comments logically to the overall sales presentation.
- Let your whole tone reflect your confidence in the proposition and give the impression that you expect to sell the product.
- Keep your body language positive.
- Maintain eye contact with the customer.

2 Select the appropriate close to seal the deal.

Closure can usually be accomplished using one or a number of techniques. The type used will vary according to the situation and it should be the close (or closes) most appropriate for that situation. Very often more than one close will be used.

Consider, and apply as required, the following:

Summary Close—Sum up your sales story, particularly if you have been interrupted by customers, telephone etc. And then get down to quantities.

Physical Close—Some types of promotion make a very positive 'physical' close possible. You may, for example, be selling a bonus offer to the buyer and there is no more effective way of closing than actually giving them part of the bonus on the spot. 'That's your bonus— just on this small order here'.

Buyer's Remark—The buyer will often make some remark which will give you a lead into the close. For example, 'You were saying just now, Mr Buyer, how popular this line has been recently'.

Minor Point—Very often the buyer has almost decided to purchase yet requires a minimum amount of persuasion to get final agreement on an order. A very effective method of closing in such circumstances is to check some point of detail with the buyer, such as, 'Will you be wanting a copy of the order?' or 'Let me see… will you be wanting it delivered to 21 or 23 High Street?'

Apparent Concession Close—Sometimes a part of an order may be too large, or contain unacceptable sizes or colours. This may or may not be deliberately planned. An acceptable way to close is to seemingly give way on one part of the order—for example, 'Obviously the 5 litre size is too much for you, Mr Buyer, so can we provide you with the 2.5 litre and 1 litre sizes?'

Verbal Proof—This type of close is used when you quote the examples of other customers. For example, 'I have a customer on the other side of town and they felt this particular offer was ideal for their situation—which is very similar to yours'.

Fear Close—This close puts the point that the customer will be missing something if the order is not placed now. You can stress that the deal is too good to miss or that, if the customer does not take the product then, the opportunity will be lost (appeal to the relevant buying motive).

Isolation Close—Very often you will attempt to close yet find that the customer says 'no' to the order. You

---

Management Memo

The important thing to remember about sealing a deal is—never give up, as the following statistics reveal…

44% of sales people give up after one 'No'.

22% of sales people give up after two 'No's'.

14% of sales people give up after three 'No's'.

12% of sales people give up after four 'No's'.

In other words, 92% of sales people give up!

Perhaps what they didn't know was that 60% of all customers say 'No' four times—before saying 'Yes'! [24]

---

should attempt to find the reason for not buying. This is an objection, so by addressing the objection in isolation, you can use it as an opportunity to close.

Alternative Close—When using this type of close you get the customer's acceptance by asking which of two alternative orders is prefered. The buyer may then miss the fact that a third alternative—of not buying at all—is also an option.

Assumptive Close—Assume you are going to get the order and simply proceed to write it down, although care must be taken with this close to ensure the timing is right. This is a very effective close when well executed.

Usually one of the preceding types of closes dominates but, more often than not, a combination of two types is successful in practice.

How to gift wrap

Gift wrapping is an essential part of retailing today and your team should be trained in this art. A store that is gift wrapping professionally will be perceived as offering more value for the customer and will be able to charge more for its products because of this extra service.

1 Establish a gift wrapping centre.

Position the gift wrapping station away from your main counter. If customers are in a hurry and are being held up because a staff member is gift wrapping for another person, you will have one happy customer and a number of unhappy ones.

At your gift wrapping station make sure you always have readily available:

> scissors, sticky tape, seasonal tape (birthday, Christmas etc.), seasonal gift wrapping paper, glitter pens, glitter stars, glitter glue set, string, ribbon, sticky back bows or rosettes, Blu tac, gift tags, and a pen.

You should always have a checklist near your gift wrapping station to ensure you have adequate quantities of the items you need.

2 Master the art of wrapping boxes.

Most of us are relatively skilled at wrapping plain boxes. Most of the time the paper needs to be only slightly larger than the item being wrapped.

Step 1: Place box in centre of paper.

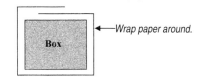

Step 2: Secure one end

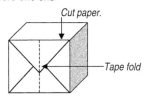

Step 3: Repeat the process at the other end.

Step 4: Add rosettes, ribbons, glitter and so on, as requested by your customer.

3 Learn how to wrap awkward shapes.

Awkward shapes usually present the gift wrapper with a problem and call for a measure of creativity from your staff member.

Of course, the key is, whenever possible, to find a box in which to wrap the gift. On other occasions, creativity and experience are helpful assets.

Consider the art of wrapping a bottle...

Step 1: Roll the bottle up in wrapping paper:

Step 2: Tape the side as shown:

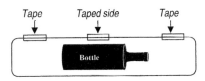

Step 3: Create a cracker by using ribbon:

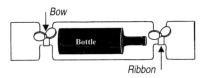

Step 4: Add a rosette to give the impact:

An objective of retailing is to add value and, in doing so, you will often find yourself gift wrapping two bottles rather than one…

Consider the art of wrapping two bottles…

Step 1: Roll up the bottles in wrapping paper and tape. Fold the ends under each bottle and seal with tape:

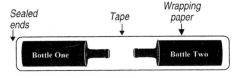

Management Memo

Make sure your team *practise* gift wrapping prior to them wrapping in the store. It's important that they look proficient and expert when dealing with your customers. [125]

Step 2: Twist the bottles in opposite directions and fold the bottles down:

Step 3: Tie the bottles together using ribbon or a different coloured paper:

Consider the art of wrapping sweets or similar items in a cone…

Step 1: Mark the half way point on paper:

Step 2: Roll the paper into a cone using the half way mark as the point and then tape it:

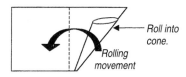

Step 3: You now have a cone you can fill with relevant product. Once you have filled it, twist the top closed and tie with ribbon. You will then need to tidy up the top with a pair of scissors.

Ref: Asda Supermarkets, UK

How to select and fill a shopping bag

Selecting the best 'carry home' system for your customers is becoming a major issue in retailing. We need to be aware of the cost involved, customers' needs, environmental concerns, as well as the best means of looking after the product safely. But whatever system is used, if the shopping bag has been packed poorly, the resulting negative reaction could damage your business reputation. Considerable thought should go into the selection and filling of shopping bags, and your staff need to be trained to handle this task correctly...

1 Be aware: bagging is an expensive exercise.

Spend a little time thinking about the importance of shopping bags to your company's bottom line:

- The Wakefern Food Corporation in the United States studied 5,000 bag transactions in 1997 to evaluate the best way of managing bag-filling in supermarkets. Grocery bags cost 0.6 to 1.3 per cent of the average sale, the cost varying depending on the type of bag, size and handling system.

- The costs of bags directly relates to the training of your team. For example, if an assistant puts 12 items in a bag, rather than the average of 6.3, then a typical store could save $29,500 a year.

- Some stores have a re-use policy on bags. A typical store gets 10 per cent of its bags back, especially if they offer a 2 cent refund policy. When you consider a bag may cost 4.4 cents, this is a sensible strategy.

- Some companies do 'double bagging', i.e. put one bag inside another to give strength. This is a costly exercise and the use of a stronger bag may prove to be more economical.

- According to the US *Competitive Edge Report* (January 1997):
  - 80 per cent of consumers re-use their grocery bags at home as rubbish liners.

- 58 per cent of consumers prefer paper bags, whilst 36 per cent prefer plastic bags.

- Consumers like bags to have handles, be strong, stand up in the car, be re-useable and be the size that they can easily handle.

- In Europe, especially in supermarkets, retailers are now issuing environmentally friendly bags that are provided for life.

- Again, in Europe, customers can purchase large plastic boxes which are loaded in the supermarket and placed directly into their cars.

All of which means that you should spend time considering the most appropriate bagging strategies for your store.

2 Be environmentally aware; customers are.

Consumers are becoming more environmentally aware and expect you as the retailer to share their concerns about the environment. On Prince Edward Island in Canada, for example, retailers are no longer allowed to sell drinks in plastic containers; they have to be glass. Review how you can become more environmentally aware and consider:

- degradable bags rather than non-degradable bags.
- Tesco's Supermarket in the United Kingdom supply customers with a 'bag for life' which the customer brings back on return visits.
- Car boot liners may be more appropriate than individual bags.
- Safeway Supermarkets in the United Kingdom supply customers with plastic trays rather than plastic bags. These trays are kept by the customer and are used to take food from the store to the car and from the car to the pantry.

⌓ Become socially aware.

Society is becoming more educated and more demanding. This is especially true when it comes to excess packaging of products. Always be one step ahead of your customers. Select a system that is socially acceptable for your customer base. This varies around the world. For example, in Indonesia a person who is easy to barter with has products packed in a white bag, a reasonable barter has goods presented to them in a black and white bag, while a tough barter results in products being presented to the customer in a black bag. This assists other retailers to know in advance what a consumer's buying skills are.

⌓ Ensure your staff consider the filling task.

Prior to packing any bag, have your team members get into the habit of thinking about what they are going to do, before they do it. In this way, they can select the most economical carrier for the job in hand. Several options may be considered:

- a paper bag
- a plastic bag
- an environmentally friendly 'bag for life'
- a plastic box, purchased by the customer for loading and placing directly into cars
- a cardboard box.

⌓ Develop a bag-filling technique.

Bag filling is an art, and in mastering the task, the following techniques should be adopted:

- Open the bag and build a foundation.
- Use large solid products to build a foundation to the bag.
- Always split weights. Your aim should be to make each bag the equivalent weight. Equal weight bags are easier for the customer to handle.
- Fill the bag correctly by building the wall of the bag first and then fill the centre.
- Second wrap wet items.
- Keep frozen products together.
- Put 'squashy' products on the top.
- Never put odour products and poisons with food products.
- Place breakables in the central funnel of the bag.
- Keep soap, cheese and other smelling products away from butter, eggs and meat.
- Place the receipt in the bag.

How to farewell the customer

First and last impressions are so important in retailing. When a customer enters your store, you should be an effective host. When the customer leaves the store, the same advice is true if you want that person to return...

1 Remember your objective...

Your primary aim in farewelling customers is to get them to return to your business but, more specifically, your aim should be to get them to return to *you*.

Often you may be the last person the customer will see in the store. Alternatively, you may be passing them on to a checkout operator. Whichever applies in your retail situation, you should ensure that your store has a policy in place where a staff member is responsible for farewelling each customer.

2 Be genuine.

Your parting words must be seen to be part of a genuine farewell. Many customers become cynical when your team is programmed to recite, parrot-fashion, to every parting customer, 'Have a nice day'.

Unless your staff *genuinely* want to build a relationship with customers, they will sound insincere and they could be doing more damage than if they had remained silent.

3 Adopt a four-point plan.

To ensure your store farewells are sincere, have your staff adopt the following four-point plan:

• *Always thank the customer.*
Every person should be thanked for doing business with you. This should take the form of a heart-felt 'thank-you for shopping with us'.

• *Be positive in your body language.*
Customers enjoy being served by self-assured, happy people. Body language does much to reflect this. Smile, at least. If your body language shows you couldn't care less, or want to rush them through the checkout, then this will be noted by the customers as they leave the store.

• *Make a parting aside to the customer.*
Always include a personal comment to customers as they leave to help foster a one-to-one relationship. Such comments could relate to:
• what they have just purchased
• what they are wearing
• what they plan to do over the coming weekend
• the weather
• their hobby
• their pets, family etc.

• *Invite them back.*

Invite them back to the business, by using words like, 'I look forward to seeing you on your next visit' or 'I'll see you next time'. This is far more personal than 'we', and will stay in their memory longer.

Promote forthcoming events and specials.

If you can start a parting conversation with the customer, it also provides you with the opportunity to remind them of upcoming specials and events— without giving the impression that you are selling.

Use the customer's name.

If you can obtain a customer's name, use it. People like their names being asked for—and used. If a name is offered, you should use it in the closing conversation. Of course, names can also be obtained from cheques and credit cards. If you can pronounce the name with confidence, use it; on the other hand, if it's a difficult pronunciation, don't. You may embarrass yourself and the customer.

Be aware of customer needs.

Be astute when closing a sales encounter because, by observing the needs of the customer, you can extend your service and their gratitude to the store. For example, in an ideal world, it would be excellent if every customer was

> **Management Memo**
>
> **Who are our customers?**
>
> *Customers...*
> are the most important people ever to enter our store.
>
> *Customers...*
> are not dependent on us; we are dependent on them.
>
> *Customers...*
> are not interruptions to our work; they are the purpose of it. We are not doing them a favour by serving them; they are doing us a favour by giving us the opportunity of doing so.
>
> *Customers...*
> are not outsiders to our business; they are part of it.
>
> *Customers...*
> are not cold statistics; they are flesh-and-blood human beings, with feelings and emotions like our own, and with biases and prejudices.
>
> *Customers...*
> are people who bring us their wants and needs. It is our job to satisfy those needs, to both their advantage and ours. [27]

offered a car loading or delivery service, but this is not always cost effective or practical. However, it may be possible, even desirable, if you tried to offer this extra service to:

• disabled customers
• pregnant shoppers
• parents with prams or strollers
• elderly shoppers
• general customers in inclement weather.

Treat everyone as an individual and as a special person, and you will build up an abundance of lifetime shoppers.

Promoting your Products

*Don't sell me clothes. Sell me neat
appearance, style, attractiveness.
Don't sell me books. Sell me pleasant
hours and the profits of knowledge.
Don't sell me tyres. Sell me freedom
from worry and low-cost-per-mile.*

*Don't sell me things.
Sell me ideals... feelings...
self-respect... home life... happiness.*

Sears Roebuck & Co.

How to select the right media for advertising

When business is good, it pays to advertise. When business is bad, you've got to advertise. Advertising is the mouthpiece of business. It is essential. Retailers are offered a multitude of avenues to promote their products and the biggest challenge is deciding how to best invest your advertising dollar to get the maximum return. Advertising your business and products does not have to be haphazard. You can plan, measure and monitor your advertising activities...

1 Consider your audience.

If you do not know your target audience, and you blanket advertise, you will be wasting your advertising budget. Everyone's target market will be different, which is why you need to consider, firstly, such general variables as:

- the geographic location of your store and your audience—passers-by, workers, or residents
- the age group you wish to attract
- the gender you are targeting
- the primary socio-economic group you are hoping to draw upon
- the occupations of your audience.

2 Target your specific audience.

Having reflected upon your general advertising framework, you should then become more focused on the individual customer. Marketers often use the term SPADE to focus retailers on their real target audience:

S tarter   The person who initiates the enquiry
P urchaser The person who pays for the goods
A dviser   The person who influences the decision
D ecider   The real authority on what to buy
E nd user   The consumer of the product.

This may be one person or five different people. At each stage they are looking for different benefits. Your final advertising thrust should reflect this customer analysis by promoting to the selected target audience the benefits of your product.

3 Select the appropriate advertising media.

Once you have decided on your real target audiences, you can then decide on the appropriate advertising media you should use to get their attention. Among the media available to you are:

National newspapers—Expensive, but ideal for nationwide retail chains.

Regional newspapers—Have immediate impact but remember, yesterday's newspaper is old news.

Local newspapers—Have excellent household penetration and can be very cost effective.

Trade magazines—Well read and very targeted.

Local directories—Very effective, but you

WINNING
OUR CUS
MANAGING
YOUR STOR
PROMOTING
YOUR PRODUCTS
NAGING
R BUSINESS
DEX
61
Vol. 1: See 392

must plan well in advance.

Radio—Local radio and community radio are becoming more and more popular. This is a useful medium to consider.

Posters—Often linked to major advertising campaigns.

Street benches—Useful in high traffic areas. The message should be rotated every few months.

Public transport advertising—Moving messages on buses, trains and taxis must be simple, bold and short. Get them right and they work.

Television—Regional television is very cost effective. Only large retailers can afford metropolitan television. Ask your local television station; their advice is valuable.

Sponsorship—Always sponsor local events attended by your target audience. It gives credibility to you as a neighbourhood retailer and one of the 'local good guys'.

Parking meters—These work in the United Kingdom: over 35,000 meters are used by 5.5 million motorists a week.

Point of sale display—Remember, internal advertising is always more cost effective than external advertising. You know you will hit your target.

And the list goes on.

 ## Do your homework.

Before deciding on which medium best suits your business, do your research. Contact as many advertising outlets that suit your target audience as possible. Ask for details on costs and evidence as to how effective they are at reaching your target. Always keep notes of discussions so you can refer back to them at a later date.

 ## Keep to the advertising standards.

Most countries have advertising standards and an authority that

monitors such standards.

Regulations on advertising vary from country to country, but the following guidelines should always be adhered to:

- Advertisements should be legal, decent and truthful.

- Advertisements should be prepared with a sense of responsibility to the consumer and society.

- Advertisements should conform to the principles of fair competition.

6 Monitor the penetration cost of advertising.

It's important to look beyond the cost of the advertisement. Look at its penetration rate. It's not an easy assignment but—how many of your target audience did it reach? Begin with your team. Advise them of what advertisements you have taken out and have them monitor if a new customer has come in as a result of your advertising campaign. In this way, you can determine how much it costs to get a new customer. In many cases, a new customer has to return to your store three times before you make a profit from them. Your staff need to know this and commit themselves also to your advertising initiative.

How use a direct mailer to promote product sales

Customer newsletters are communication tools; direct mailers are selling tools. Both are separate retailing vehicles, serving different roles. A good newsletter has the potential to stay in a household for weeks. On the other hand, in the majority of cases, a direct mailer has a short life—often being despatched to the bin within 7.5 seconds of the customer taking it out of the mail box. For this reason, direct mailers must get directly to the point with a clear, immediate message to the potential customer...

 Sell, sell, sell upfront.

With a direct mailer, your aim upfront is to sell. You need to sell your name, the products you want to promote, and the benefits of these products to your customers. Due to the limited amount of time the consumer gives you to get your message across, it is common to feature price fairly heavily and dramatically. Colour is often used to create impact and the primary colours of red, blue and yellow are often splashed across the front page.

 Use coupons to encourage a sale.

You need an instant reaction from direct mailers. Through its appeal, you want customers to visit your store or to return a purchase order via a coupon in the mailout.

One useful motivator is to include a coupon with the mailer, offering the customer a special deal if it is used in association with the store purchase. If used effectively, the reader will in time get into the habit of looking for coupons in your mailers.

 Focus on gaining the customer's attention.

Direct mailers should be no larger than your store newsletter. Since customers do not have the time or the inclination to read, your message must come across quickly, visually, clearly, and dramatically.

Plan a targeted distribution for greater success.

Mass mailers are often dropped in letter boxes in bulk. Focused direct mail, however, allows you to target more specifically so that you can achieve a higher success rate. Ideally, your aim is to get a specific person to open this specific mailer. Of course, your chances will increase substantially if you use a coloured envelope, a real stamp, and you handwrite the envelope. Usually, the extra effort is well rewarded.

Consider a follow-up strategy.

Depending on your type of retail organisation, you may wish to have a policy of following up the mailout with a telephone call. If you are mass mailing, this would be inappropriate and not cost effective. However, if you are directing the mailout to a specific customer group, then a follow-up telephone call would be desirable and increase the effectiveness of your direct mail initiative.

6 Make the mailer work for you.

According to Results Corp in Queensland, Australia, you will get greater value from your direct mailers if you reflect and act upon these research findings:

- The emotional appeal of products generates 45 per cent more enquiries than a technical appeal.

- Pre-paid postage coupons produce 47 per cent more enquiries than non pre-paid cards.

- Illustrations showing products in use are 30 per cent more effective

> ●●●●●●●●●●●●●●●●●●●●●●●
>
> ## Management Memo
>
> In Australia, the typical promotional budget is split as follows: [29]
>
> | | |
> |---|---|
> | Advertising | 35 % |
> | Personal Selling | 30 % |
> | Promotional Marketing | 15 % |
> | Direct Mailing | 10 % |
> | Other | 10 % |

than products alone.

- Photographs beat line drawings by 50 per cent.

- Simple advertisements are 30 per cent more effective than complicated ones.

- Photographs with the product close up and the person in the background are ten times more effective than those in reverse.

- Coupons are 12 per cent more effective on the outside column than the inside column of your mailout.

How to use 'how-to' leaflets to sell more product

Customers are a diverse lot—from various age groups, social backgrounds, and a wide range of experience. There are those who are time-poor and relatively affluent—the 'do-it-for-me' group of customers, and those in the 'do-it-yourself' category. Help guides or how-to leaflets are aimed at the novice user and the do-it-yourself market. In providing this helpful literature you educate the customer in the hope that they become advocates of your business—and spend more money in your store…

1 Keep the leaflets simple.

Always design how-to leaflets with your target market in mind. These people often do not have technical knowledge, which is why they need the leaflet. So, keep it simple, keep it attractive, and avoid technical jargon related to your industry.

Although pictures are easier to understand than words, text will also be necessary to get your message across. Use short sentences and bullet points or short numbered statements rather than lengthy paragraphs of text. For example, a garden centre leaflet on the topic *Which containers should I buy for my patio?*…

When choosing your container…

☐ *Consider the area of patio and the architecture of the site.* If it is a natural look you are after, select stone or terracotta pots. If it is a modern environment, select plastic or fibreglass containers.

☐ *Consider the size of plants you want.* Select pots that are large enough for those plants.

☐ …and so on.

2 Talk the language of your customer.

Use words like *you* and *yours* when writing for the customer. Do not use language such as *I* and *we* when related to you as the retailer, for it sounds like you are dictating to your customer rather than holding a conversation with them.

3 Ask the questions customers would ask.

Your leaflets should highlight the common questions customers would ask. For example:

Where do I start?
Which _____ should I select?
Which _____ do I buy to get success?
How do I put it together?
How do I look after _____?

4 Provide extra information in separate boxes.

The basic text is what the customer needs to know to be successful. Decide what additional helpful bits of information the customer should also know, and then highlight these items in separate boxes. These should-also-knows could include:

- Time saving tips
- Fun ideas
- Did you know...?

5 Include a shopping list in the flyer.

Remember your objective: to increase the average sale per customer. The leaflet gives you the opportunity to cross merchandise, add-on sell, and provide a complete package—including products purchasable from your store—to do the job successfully. These additional products could be purchased now, in the future, or in stages. Therefore, your leaflet could include such lists as:

- Tools you will need to do the job.
- A shopping list to be successful.
- Items you will need to maintain value.

6 Pay attention to legibility.

Ensure that people can easily read your leaflet. The most easily read typefaces are serif-based, i.e. letters with small feet (or serifs) such as this typeface, while sanserif typefaces (those without serifs), such as the heading above, are best used for headings and signage. Research by the Newspaper Advertising Bureau of Australia supports this.

	Comprehension Level		
	Good	Fair	Poor
Layout with Serif Body Type	67%	19%	14%
Layout with Sanserif Body Type	12%	23%	65%

The words were the same; the only difference was the typeface.

7 Bring colour into your leaflet.

Colour will help the customer

identify your leaflet, as well as clarify certain illustrative points. Try using a different colour for each leaflet. Make the cover of each leaflet very simple, yet very distinctive. And of course, ensure your logo and/or store identification is clearly recognisable to the customer.

8 Position your leaflets in the store.

Don't place your leaflets on the counter where they will soon become untidy. Leaflets need stands, and these are best positioned near the counter where your team can use the leaflets as an 'added-value' tool. An alternative is to place the leaflets next to specific products. So, you'd place a cheese recipe leaflet next to the cheeses; and a garden container leaflet next to the containers.

9 Train your staff in their use.

Make sure all your team have read the leaflets, for the story they tell to the customer must correspond with that outlined in the leaflet. If not, you'll end up confusing your customer with the result that store credibility will be lost. As well, ensure your staff are briefed on the most effective way of using the material as a value-added benefit.

How to plan an advertisement

Your customer population is confronted by thousands of advertisements every day of their lives. Your aim is to make yours the one that is noticed—and that's not an easy task. However, by following some simple guidelines you can take some important steps to give your advertisement a chance in the highly competitive retail world. Your aim must be to reveal the message you hope to get across to your target audience in a simple, logical, and effective way.

 Plan an effective layout.

A good layout embraces four essential factors:
- Sequence
- Focus
- Simplicity
- Eye appeal.

Begin with these key components in mind and, on completion of the advertisement, check that your layout reflects this essential formula…

 Get your sequence correct.

To make sense in life, it is important to get things in logical order, in sequence. In advertising, sequence is also important, and the acronym AIDCA can help us in this regard. When preparing your advertisement, try to make your advertising content capable of creating AIDCA in your readers when they follow this sequence—

Attention—your advertisement grabs readers' attention immediately.
Interest—if you don't get the readers interested, you've lost them.
Desire—your advertisement must be capable of arousing the readers' eagerness to possess the product.
Conviction—the reader makes a decision to purchase.
Action—the reader actually takes steps to purchase.

 Focus your readers' attention.

Ask yourself—what is the most important part of my message? It is this that you want your audience to concentrate upon, and there are a number of techniques you can use to accomplish this. For example:
Highlight the message.
Change the typeface.
Use colour.
Use a pointed finger.
Use arrows.

 Keep it simple.

The KISS principle (Keeping It Simple, Sells) applies to many aspects of the retail business, and simple eye-catching advertisements are always your best approach. The only catch is that, a simple advertisement isn't always as easy to achieve as you would hope. Indeed, you may need to compile your advertisement a number of times to

accomplish that desired simplicity.
Remember also that space sells, and
a cluttered advertisement is often
overlooked by the reader.

5 Give your advertisement eye appeal.

To attract and hold the attention of
your target audience, your
advertisement will need five
components:

> An eye-catching headline and sub-headlines
> Copy or text
> Illustrations
> White space
> Your name, address and logo.

Since our minds work in pictures, not
words, pictures will help get your
message across. We also prefer to
read in lower case, not capitals, and
we prefer the serif typeface, as used
in newspapers. A printer can advise
you on the best typefaces to use.
Finally, make sure the advertisement
is in keeping with the image you are
trying to develop for your business.

6 Adhere to these proven rules...

Most newspapers and magazines
have studios that concentrate on
creating advertisements. If you lack
confidence in this area, use their
available expertise. At the same time
it is worth knowing a few simple
rules so that you can draw up your
own advertisements if required...

■ Decide on your approach—on a 'hard'
sell or 'soft' sell. Hard sell is price-
dominated, soft sell is benefits-
dominated. The decision will depend on
your image, target audience, time of year,
and product.

■ Compile a checklist of what you'd like
to say in your advertisement. In addition

to product details, this may include a
map, telephone, fax, email, and web page
details, car park facilities, years
established...

■ Westerners read from left to right and
absorb information quickly in a Z
pattern:

The major products you wish to promote
must be in the path of the Z. The less
important products are set off to the side.

■ Place your name and address at the
bottom of the advertisement—your
objective is not to sell your name. The
headline should be selling a product,
service or idea.

■ Remember: a picture speaks a
thousand words. Use illustrations and
pictures to catch your reader's eye:

Use copyright-free clip art that is
available in computer software packages
or clip art books. Newspapers often
subscribe to artwork services, and
manufacturers and suppliers often have
illustrations that you can use.

How to write advertising copy that sells

Writing advertising and promotional copy is a skill. If it weren't, we'd be reading every advertisement we see. Good copy answers six important questions that a potential customer is going to ask: Who are you? What are you trying to sell me? Why should I buy it? Why should I come to your store? Where are you located? When are you open for trade? You have to get this information across in such a way that the potential consumer will *want* to read your advertisement—then buy. The following advice will help you do that...

 Identify your USP.

Every successful business has a USP—a Unique Selling Proposition. You must identify your USP and be able to explain it to your target audience in a way that captures their attention and, hopefully, has them beating a path to your door.

 List your selling points and benefits.

Selling points are inherent factors about your business and your products. Can you identify yours? They'll need to be mentioned in your copy. Selling points could include:

- Biggest range in the city
- Large car park
- Massive sale this weekend
- Thousands of items under the one roof
- Been in business 75 years.

The benefits are what the consumer is looking for when purchasing products from you. For example:

- Immediate home delivery
- Reliability and trust
- Save money.

Consumers always buy benefits over selling points and you must highlight these in your copy.

 Be creative, competitive and located.

Writing style is critical. You need to create a desire in customers to buy products at your store. You may need to write competitively—if your audience already has the desire to purchase, your job is to channel that desire into *your* particular location over any competitors'. And you may need to tell your hard-won consumers where you are—let them know how to find your store.

 Make your copy sell.

Keep the AIDCA formula in mind when preparing your copy:

Attention must be gained with such words and phrases as: You, Did you realise, You see, More interesting still, Now, New, Your...

Interest must be generated. Put a smile on their face. Tell them facts they do not know.

Desire must be created. Put yourself in the customers' shoes, raise their doubts and then answer them.

Convince them that the purchase is in

their best interests.

Action must be stimulated. Your job is to ask them for their business. Tell them what you want them to do. For example:

- Pick the telephone up and speak to…
- Fill in the coupon and mail to…
- Visit the shop and ask for…
- Fax your response to…
- Order now from our website at…

Many retailers will write excellent copy and then neglect to include a procedure for getting an order. You must remember: your aim is to sell something!

5 Write a headline people want to read.

The most important part of the copy is the headline. It must attract and hold the readers' attention. Headlines that work usually promise benefits to the reader, and therefore encourage them to read on. Your USP may be the focus of your headline.

For a headline to really grab the readers' attention, it should:

- Mention the reader and their interests.
- Use current news if it is relevant to your message.
- Provoke curiosity.
- Promise the benefits upfront.
- If it is a product you are promoting, say what it does or how easy it is to use. Remember, price is not a benefit when consumers are making initial decisions.

Management Memo

When you have written advertising copy, read it through and count how many times you have written *I*, *I'm* and *we*, and how many times you have written *you* and *your*. You should have used the *you* and *your* at least three times more than *I*, *I'm* and *we*. Your aim is to communicate with another person about them and their interests, not tell them about yourself. [32]

6 Use a PS to drive the message home.

Most people will read headlines, scan the text and focus on the end. Research has shown that postscripts enjoy a readership as much as seven times higher than 'body' copy. So, to boost the power of your message, to reinforce your major point, consider using a P.S. to sell product, stress benefits, or call the reader to action.

7 Remember these basic guidelines to better copywriting…

Successful copywriters adhere to certain basic rules, included among them being the following…

- Use simple and clear English.
- Do not use long words or jargon.
- Use local language.
- Be credible and avoid half-truths.
- Always use facts and figures.
- Do not promote technology early on in your copy.
- Tell it the way it is.
- Do not use too many adjectives.
- Do not try to be too clever.
- When you have written it, get someone else to read it and check it. It must sell—and be error-free.

How to promote advertised lines

It takes planning and organisation to promote advertised specials. To be effective and to maximise your financial investment in the promotion, your external campaign must link in with the internal store promotion to drive home the message to consumers as strongly as possible. Consider the following points in preparing for your next sales promotion...

1 Plan well ahead of the event.

The purpose of promoting advertised lines is simple—to sell more items of that line than if you were *not* advertising. This means your store buyer must anticipate the extra demand and buy sufficient stock accordingly. And this must be planned well ahead. There is nothing more embarrassing for a retailer than to have an advertisement working in the marketplace, only to find that product is unavailable when the customer comes into the store.

2 Determine where to place the products.

The aim of using advertised lines is to attract consumers to your store, not to your competitors' premises. Do you want them to purchase only advertised items once they have arrived at your store? Or is the intention to attract the customer to shop more widely in your store? Such questions will determine placement of the advertised products in the shop.

There are three locations to consider when deciding where to place the advertised lines:

- Place all advertised lines at the front door, so it is obvious you are promoting in-store the items you are promoting externally.
- Place advertised lines together at the back of the store or towards the exit to encourage shoppers to walk the whole shop.
- Scatter the advertised lines throughout the store to encourage the customers to shop beyond the advertised products. The result should be an increase in the average sale per customer.

3 Ticket the advertised lines dramatically.

Clear ticketing of advertised lines is essential. Tickets should be placed early on the day of the external advertising and be removed at the close of the last day of the promotion.

Tickets must look 'fresh'. Ripped, old and faded tickets distract from what you are trying to achieve—a special for NOW!

The ticket should indicate that this is an advertised line, using appropriate wording:

'As Advertised', 'This week's special!', 'Catalogue Special', 'Special! Now!', 'Was $7.95 Now $4.95!', 'This week's price is…'.

4 Increase the facing of advertised lines.

Advertised lines must look as if you have pre-purchased in bulk to provide your customer with this special deal. Therefore, the facing of the product on the shelf should be increased to make it look like a volume special. You may also need to move the product from a lower or higher shelf so that it is now positioned in the sightline of the average-height consumer.

5 Use the right ticket system.

Promotional tickets are available in several formats. For example:

Stick-A-Tickets are shelftalkers which have sticky tape on the top edge. This pre-taping of sheets of tickets saves valuable time and money when ticketing the displays. Simply tear off a Stick-A-Ticket and apply it to any surface. They leave no residue when removed and are available in a range of bright, colorful designs, which immediately grab the attention of customers in any store. They can also create impulse buying of specials, new products, reductions, or simply sell more of those slow lines.

Non-Reusable Price Tickets are priced tickets printed on high quality card

Management Memo

Inexpensive 'Take One' 200mm x 100mm printed leaflets can be printed at little cost. Yet with thought, they can be a powerful selling tool! Use for recipes, new products, special offers etc. [33]

and may be used in conjunction with standard marking pens or the commercial brand POS-PEN ticket writing system. Sizes suit ticket frame systems.

Reuseable Price Tickets feature bright designs on laminated stock to make them reusable and in a size to suit ticket frame systems. They can accommodate either dry erase pens, or permanent markers with ink removers.

6 Keep your staff informed.

All your sales team should be aware of what advertised lines are going to be promoted, when the promotion is scheduled to start and finish, and where the products will be located in the store. Customers quickly get frustrated if they have made a special trip to your store only to find that your team members are unaware or unsure of the products or even of the event taking place.

And, of course, the advertising department must keep the merchandising department in the picture at all times—and vice versa.

How to conduct a general product promotion

A lot of money and effort is spent by manufacturers and retailers to promote products in stores with the aim of creating interest in that product, product category, or store—and, of course, increasing sales revenue. But for such promotions to be successful, considerable thought and planning should precede the promotional activity, as the following guidelines suggest...

1 Know what a promotion involves.

A promotion has three key elements:

- *Extra value to tempt the consumer*, which may be a financial temptation (e.g. $2.00 off, or two for the price of one, or cashback offer) or an offer on their next purchase.
- *Media promotion* to inform the general public that the promotion exists.
- *Internal store display material* that directs the consumer to the product once they are in the store.

2 Understand why customers purchase promotional lines.

Prior to promoting, you need to reflect upon the NEADS of your existing customers:

N What product are they buying NOW?

E What do they ENJOY about the products they are buying now?

A Why would they ALTER their buying habits to purchase the promotional line?

D Who is the real DECISION MAKER when it comes to purchasing the product?

S Analyse all their needs and wants— and make the promotion their SOLUTION.

3 Provide extra value.

To tempt the customer, you must offer additional value. To achieve this, you need to match their buying motive with the promotional product. According to US retail consultant Ed Mayer, there are many reasons why people buy and you need to match as many of these as possible with your product:

- ☐ To make money
- ☐ To save money
- ☐ To save time
- ☐ To avoid effort
- ☐ To gain confidence
- ☐ To achieve greater cleanliness
- ☐ To attain fuller health
- ☐ To escape physical pain
- ☐ To gain praise
- ☐ To be popular
- ☐ To attract the opposite sex
- ☐ To conserve possessions
- ☐ To increase enjoyment
- ☐ To gratify curiosity
- ☐ To protect family
- ☐ To be in style
- ☐ To have or hold beautiful possessions
- ☐ To satisfy appetite
- ☐ To emulate others
- ☐ To avoid trouble
- ☐ To avoid criticism
- ☐ To be individual
- ☐ To protect reputation
- ☐ To take advantage of opportunities
- ☐ To make work easier.

4 Display products to their best advantage.

Customers must be directed to promotional products once they are in the store and therefore the position of these products is critical. For high customer exposure, place products:

- near entrances and exits
- at the top and bottom of escalators in multilevel stores
- at the ends of runs of shelves or fixtures
- in front of checkouts.

5 Place internal display signs near the product.

Promotional signage should be placed next to the product, be relevant to the product, and remain there only for the life of the product. It is not uncommon for retailers to remove a promotional line and leave the promotional signage. The result of this is a confused customer who cannot associate product and sign.

6 Promote products to targeted customers.

Customers can be divided into five groups with different shopping habits and needs, and requiring different incentives to buy products.

Loyals always buy specific product and always from you. Your aim is to reinforce existing habits, not change them. This can be achieved by having promotions that increase the use of the product or by cross selling. For example, if they always use a specific growing medium when potting plants, you may recommend a specific fertiliser to go with that product.

Competitive loyals are loyal to your store, but not loyal to a specific product in a category. This may be due to habit, snobbery, or value. Promotions based on value work very well with this group.

Switchers switch stores and brands to provide variety in their lives. If you can create interesting promotions these people could well become loyal to your business.

Price buyers always buy on price and shop

around to get the best price. Promotions aimed at this group have to be based on price—but only if the consumer is a heavy user of the product; otherwise you could lose valuable gross profit.

Non users are rarely purchasers, due to price constraints, lack of understanding of value, or lack of need. You will need to make a decision if it's worth the effort targeting this sector of your market.

7 Select a promotion to match the customer.

If you are now aware of your customer groupings, you are now in a position to select the appropriate promotional tool to attract the various sectors. In *Sales Promotion Essentials*, Don Schultz and partners advocate use of the following:

Current loyals. Coupons, special packs, sweepstakes, premiums, and trade deals
Competitive loyals. Sampling, contests
Switchers. Coupons, special packs, contests, premiums
Price Buyers. Coupons, refunds, trade deals.

8 Know when to promote in a product's life.

When promoting products always consider the product life cycle. The cycle varies depending on whether it is a fad or a basic line. Promotions are best undertaken during the market growth phase of a particular product or product line. The ideal promotional phase is when you are seeing rapid growth in the sale of the product.

How to use demonstrations to sell product

Customers like to feel, taste, smell, touch, and generally get involved with products. The more interactive you can make their shopping experience, the more inclined they are to buy. One cost effective method of introducing interactive retailing is through the use of demonstrations. These presentations usually relate to such activities as food sampling, tastings, cooking, gardening, and home décor, and must include a 'doing' element...

 Plan your demonstrations.

If you want to send a message to your customers that you are an interactive store with a vigorous approach to retailing, then demonstrations are an effective strategy to embrace—but your demonstrations must be worthwhile and regularly scheduled. For example, if you start organising demonstrations for Saturday mornings, you must keep doing them every Saturday, or run the risk of disappointing, even losing, your customers.

For this reason, demonstrations should not be undertaken lightly. They must be planned well ahead to make sure you attract the people and the products for demonstrations, and to ensure you have sufficient product in stock to sell during the event.

 Train your demonstrators.

Select demonstrators who are presentable, and have personality, communication skills and a flair for this type of work. They must be trained in all aspects of the product

they are talking about. This means, for example, that, if it is a food demonstration, then the instructor needs to be knowledgeable not only about the product itself, but conscious also of food hygiene regulations and wear the recommended gloves and headwear.

3 Position your demonstration to make sales.

In the food industry, research tells us that 70 per cent of customers will sample food provided by a demonstrator. The technique is highly effective. And, if you position the demonstration strategically, 30 per cent of those who have tasted will purchase.

Clearly the demonstration can be a major selling tool. It should be positioned in a wide aisle where people can stop and watch and talk without the feeling they are being hassled by other shoppers who are trying to pass them.

Demonstrations are best located at least one-third of the way into the customers' shopping experience. This gives them sufficient time to become comfortable and relaxed in your store.

 Position the product to make sales.

Many demonstrators place the product right next to them—and, unwisely, nowhere else. Although some customers will purchase immediately while at the demonstration, others, particularly men, usually prefer to think it over for a few minutes without pressure or harassment from the demonstrator.

So, have product at the demonstration for the immediate impulse buyer, but also have a display 3 to 5 metres past the demonstrator for those customers who want to reflect on the purchase. Make sure this display is signed with a message like 'As being demonstrated today by Mary'.

 Sell the promise.

Apart from selling product, your aim with demonstrations should be to cultivate your customers so that they will come back to your store for further demonstrations on subsequent occasions. Have a noticeboard in your store highlighting the topic for next week's demonstration. If you can sell the promise, you may find that 'word of mouth' advertising and reputation will become major marketing tools for you.

 Look professional.

Demonstration tables are available from most retail promotional supply

companies. These look a lot more professional than the homemade variety.

If you are using outside demonstrators, make sure they are wearing either the supplier's company uniform or your company's uniform. As far as your customers are concerned, they are part of your team and should look like it. Remember to debrief outside demonstrators at the end of the session. You may get some valuable tips on how to improve your store.

Keep a record.

Keep a record of all demonstrations. Note when they were carried out, by whom, and the consumer reaction. Record the increase in sales of the product you were promoting, for if your sales figures showed no improvement, you may have used the wrong product and/or the wrong demonstrator.

Share your results with the supplier of the product as this will help both of you to build on the success of such demonstrations in the future.

> **Management Memo**
>
> I strongly recommend that you put team members in a workshop prior to giving demonstrations to the public. This will strengthen the appropriate skills and help them to critically analyse their own abilities in this area. Get them to give a demonstration to the team before you let them loose on your customers. Public speaking is one of the biggest human fears. They are far better to overcome their initial fears in front of friendly faces than in front of strangers. [35]

How to get the most out of your booth at a trade show

Many retail operators look towards trade shows, local shows, and craft and charity events within their catchment area as a means of exposing their products and their message to a broader customer base. But no matter what the product or the message, the results will always be better after careful planning, a little creative thinking, and adherance to the following advice...

 Select a prime location.

One of the keys to a successful trade exhibit or demonstration is your location within the overall site. As early as possible, reserve a position, preferably one of the following:

- near the entrance/exit to the trade hall
- an end display at the junction of major aisles
- a location enroute to the toilet or coffee bar. (Being right next to the coffee bar is not ideal—you'll have plenty of traffic, but the people will have other things on their minds.)
- a booth next to major national suppliers— they will generate traffic for you.

 Plan to make an impact.

Be daring. Do something different. You have to catch the attention of passing customers, and this can be done in a number of ways. Successful ideas have included:

- Use bright colours or noise.
- Consider give-aways, whether they be sweets, a non-alcoholic drink, balloons, or a complimentary product.

- Place new products to catch the eye.
- Dress staff in bright colours.
- Introduce movement of some kind.
- Devise a competition with appropriate prizes.
- Create mystery.
- Make your display sufficiently innovative so that it stands out from those around you.

 Build a workable booth.

Planning is essential in designing a booth that is more than just a box. Consider the following points:

- Don't take things for granted at the exhibit site: check beforehand such basics as power points, ceiling height, access, lighting, and so on.
- Give yourself plenty of time to build the display. You may be able to dismantle it in an hour, but it may take a day to construct. Build the display in your store prior to exhibiting; it will save you critical time if you strike an unforseen

problem on the day.

- Design a booth where potential customers feel they can get involved, rather than just walk past. If they get involved, they are more likely to spend.

- Make sure your display has a clear visual centre of attention. And is your message clear to an outsider?

- Accuracy is absolutely essential when it comes to spelling and grammar on posters, banners, and literature.

- The biggest frustration can be getting to and from your location site, particularly at larger shows where you will normally be allocated a parking site, unloading facilities, and times. Be aware of these limitations and allow accordingly for the inconvenience.

- Make sure you have more than ample literature. There is nothing more embarrassing than running out of your sales material half way through the first day. Trade venues make a lot of money photocopying catalogues for desperate exhibitors.

4 Either sell—or build up a list of contacts.

It is foolhardy to staff your booth with untrained or unsuitable personnel. It is hard work being a sales representative or demonstrator on a sales booth, but the result for an enthusiastic and well prepared person can be most rewarding.

Make sure your display or demonstration booth has ample supplies of Show Inquiry Forms where your staff can record vital information about customers and

Management Memo

Exhibiting requires preparation not only because it is a complex marketing activity but also because of its intensity and concentration and of its propensity to expose shortcomings. On the other hand, the value of effective preparation and the resulting economic use of resources employed is enhanced by the value of the resulting smoothness of the exhibition operation and the general good impression created. [36]

inquirers. The forms should seek such information as:
- Contact's name, address, telephone, fax
- Contact's position in the company
- Products they are interested in
- What they find appealing about the product
- Who makes the buying decision in their company or household
- Date or details on agreed follow up
- When they would like to buy.

5 Know why follow-up is so important.

Gathering information about potential customers is important but irrelevant if those leads are not followed up. According to the Australian Trade Show Bureau, surveys of those attending trade shows have revealed that:

- 60-70 per cent of attendees expect to make a purchase of an exhibition product within two months of the trade show.
- 60 per cent of all attendees do make a purchase within twelve months of the show.
- But 83 per cent of trade show contacts are never followed up by a representative from the company within the next 12 months.

When it comes to making sales, the message is clear for those staffing your booth—follow up the contacts made at the show.

How to produce signs that sell products

For retailers, signage is a key focus area that can increase customer awareness of your business and highlight the products that you sell. Signs can be used outside or inside your business as valuable promotional tools. To use signs effectively, consider the following guidelines...

1 Understand the essentials of outdoor signage.

To be effective, outdoor signage must take account of the following elements:

- the speed at which viewers are passing (on foot or in vehicles)
- the height and width of letters used
- the style of printing
- colour combinations
- the amount of words used
- the message you are trying to get across.

External signs need to be planned from the site entrance through to the exit. They should project the corporate image.

2 Provide entrance signs that can be seen.

The crucial demand for entrance signs is that they can be readily seen and allow ample time for potential customers to decide to turn into your parking area. Ideally, therefore, entrance road signs need to be sited in advance of your site entrance.

The distance from the entrance should be based on the speed of passing traffic. The following table should act as a guide:

Speed Limit	Sign distance from turning
50 kph	500m
65 kph	675m
80 kph	750m

Once the sign site has been agreed upon, the appropriate size of the lettering needs to be determined—large, clear, and obvious to prevent any customer confusion.

The UK Ministry of Transport's recommendations for road-side signs provide useful guidance:

Distance to be read (m)	Letter height (cm)	Number of words at 50 kph
15	4.5	4
30	9	8
60	18	15
90	28	22
120	35	30
150	45	43

Letters also need to be at least a fifth as wide as they are high.

3 Know why customers need in-store signs.

Customers require in-store signs to identify advertised lines, explain hidden benefits, indicate value and price, and highlight new trends and products. Signs can also explain the difference between lookalike products, remind customers to purchase, clarify your policies, and help customers find products. As a retailer, you need signs to encourage 'trade ups' to better margin products. They allow you to convince customers that they need the product and to encourage them to purchase in order to increase average basket spend.

4 Attend to in-house signage.

In-house signage includes all the signs within the site, whether they be inside or outside. Permanent outdoor signs should be on Foamex or similar material, while outdoor promotional signs can be on Foamex or Corflute (Correx). Corflute (corrugated plastic sheet) is adequate for seasonal outdoor promotional signs for retailers with outdoor stock. Departmental signs should be written in lower case as they are more easily read. They should be customer friendly. For point of purchase signs, today's computers, printers, colour photocopiers, and laminating machines allow product signs to be made professionally by your staff on location.

5 Use words that sell.

Certain words have positive suggestive meanings on signage and should be used whenever possible. Words that sell include:

At last, Attention, Back by popular demand, Check out these, Exclusive, Finally, For the first time, For those who insist on the best, Good news, Huge savings, Hurry, In a class by itself, It's here, New, New low price, Only… gives you, Quality doesn't have to cost you, Reasons why you should, Save big, State

of the art, Switch to, Take a look at these features, Take the…challenge, The… advantage, The smart choice, Urgent.

6 Use the right sign at the right time.

Signage should be used at key times in a product's life cycle. The following diagram illustrates the life cycle of a typical product and shows the key times when you should use signs to promote the product to achieve maximum sales.

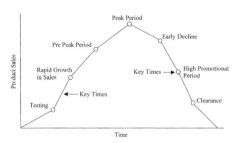

The product will remain the same, but the message will be different at various stages in its life cycle:

Point in life cycle	Sample words to use
Testing	NEW!
Rapid sales growth	IT'S HERE!
Pre peak period	ATTENTION
Peak period	Take a look at these key features
Early decline	Check out these
High promotion period	Attention
Clearance	Huge savings

How to use a 'cut case' display

Many products, such as cans, bottles and packet items are delivered to your store in cardboard boxes. These boxes can be used to display the products very cost-effectively, giving the impression also of greater value to the displayed product.

1 Consider the horizontal cut method.

The following steps will give you a display that is easily handled in the store. Beginning with the unopened box of product...

First, use a sharp knife and cut the box around the top and bottom horizontally, leaving a border of 6 cm from the top and bottom of the box:

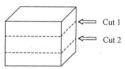

Second, remove the top lid of the box and turn it over and place it alongside the remainder of the box:

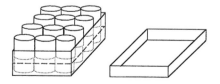

Finally, move the central sleeve from around the centre of the box to the top layer of product. Squeeze the sleeve and transfer the top layer of product to the top lid. You now have two display boxes from the same box.

2 Consider the diagonal cut method.

Again using a sharp knife...
First, cut from the top of the back of the box to the bottom of the front of the box using diagonal cuts and then join the cuts along the top and bottom of the boxes:

Then, remove the cut top and you are left with a display carton, which can go straight on display or a shelf.

3 Play it safe.

You need a very sharp knife to cut through cardboard—a 'Stanley'-type knife is recommended. Don't cut deeply into the box—if you do, you will damage the products inside. Remember, safety first. Protect yourself when cutting. Always cut away from your body and your other hand. Don't leave open knives around for other people to hurt themselves. Finally, displays can end up quite tall, and for this reason it is important that you build them securely so that they do not put customers or staff at risk.

How to use a dump bin

According to studies by the Russell R. Muller Retail Hardware Research Foundation in the United States, sales increase by 43 per cent when retail stores place products in dump bins. Dump bins are generally used to give the impression that the product is reduced in price and the customer needs to be quick to get a bargain, before the item sells out completely. The bins are normally 600mm-wide baskets or scatter tables. To take full advantage of this sales strategy, consider the following points...

1 Position the dump bin in the right location.

The dump bin must be positioned on a major racetrack in the store. Only use dump bins where the customer still has 1.5 metre clearance between the bin and the general merchandise shelf. If the space is any narrower you will discourage browse shopping and some customers will get annoyed due to the cluttered appearance of the store.

2 Focus on one product line.

The product display should focus on one specific category and, preferably, on one product type only—for example, one size and brand of dog food, or one style of sweaters.

Products must be scattered in the dump bin. It is not a place for tidy displays. Product should look like it has been dumped, giving the impression that it is a special once-only price and deal.

3 Sign them clearly.

Dump bins must have a sign which promotes the fact that this is a priced special and must be cleared quickly.

Dump bins require clear and dramatic signage.

4 Limit the bin's life.

The life of a dump bin with a specific product must be short lived. In a supermarket change the product in the bin weekly; in a hardware store the maximum life of a dump bin product should not exceed one month.

5 Keep the bin filled and fresh.

Dump bins must be kept full of stock. Bins below half full do not work effectively. They work exceptionally well as they give the impression of a 'fresh' bargain. Also ensure the bins are safe and that the team has product knowledge of items on display.

How to dummy-up your displays

Dummy displays are used to create a false impression, to hoodwink the customer into thinking that large quantities of product fill the shelves whereas, in reality, the display has simply been made to look that way. Dummying-up is a particularly useful skill in country stores where retailers cannot afford to hold large amounts of stock, yet need to provide an illusion to let the consumer believe that they are holding a large amount of product.

1 Dummy-up your relays.

It is quite common to have a shelf that is deeper than the number of products available in that line. If you do not dummy-up, you will find that, as the product gets pushed further back on the shelf through depletion, it becomes hidden by the shelf above. Cardboard boxes are ideal for the job of making the shelf narrower—and therefore to appear fuller:

If you do not dummy, the product is lost to the customer's eye.

Dummy-up with an empty box and the products will move to the front of the shelf where they are visible.

← Empty box

There are a number of other techniques you can use to dummy-up displays to create the impression of volume and to provide more impact to that display...

2 Use empty boxes in power displays.

If you are building a power display, but do not have enough product to give the impact you desire, try using empty boxes in the central void:

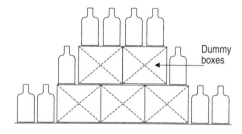

Dummy boxes

3 Use pyramid displays with a false centre.

Alternatively, you can use stands that are shaped like a pyramid with a hollow centre. This will give you the same effect as using dummy boxes.

WINNING
OUR CUS

MANAGING
YOUR STOR

PROMOTING
YOUR PRODUCTS

NAGING
BUSINESS

DEX

83

4 Dummy-up the complete base of your display.

If you need to bring your display to the consumer's sight line, use cardboard boxes to create a base upon which to build your exhibit:

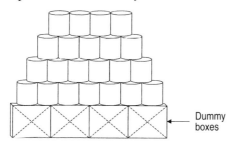

Dummy boxes

strings, artificial seafood, bread, meat and cheeses. But be warned: some customers will pick them up by mistake.

5 Fill high spots with dummy product.

Use empty boxes or empty containers of the product to fill high shelves, out of the reach of customers, if you want to create an attractive and full display wall of product. Suppliers will often be prepared to give you empty products for this type of display.

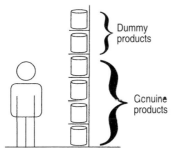

Dummy products

Genuine products

6 Consider using artificial products.

Many suppliers now provide realistic looking replicas which can add a splash of colour to your displays—particularly food displays. These accessories include artificial fruit, vegetables, vegetable and fruit

7 Dummy-up deep shelves or display tables.

Fruit and vegetable retailers are often forced to dummy-up deep benches and tables to give the impression that they have more product than they actually do. They use crates to provide the desired effect:

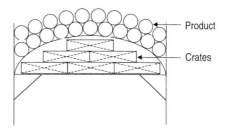

Product

Crates

8 Don't forget the magic.

When using boxes and similar items to dummy-up your displays, cover these with coloured paper, hessian or some other material. Customers want to see the magic of retailing, not the mechanics. And they do not want to see how you build your displays—so work on them at night or behind a curtain and allow the final exhibit to be a surprise.

How to display products to capture customer interest

The aim of merchandising is to increase the sale of a product by displaying the product in a way that stimulates customers to want to buy. The approach adopted will vary, depending on the type of product, your image, customers' expectations, available space, position in the store, and the purpose of your merchandising strategy. However, whichever merchandising style you adopt, the key is to keep it simple and to follow these guidelines...

1 Catch your customer's eye through repetition.

Displaying an item or sign in a repetitive way attracts the customer's eye. To create this impact through repetition you must keep heights, shapes, colours, direction and sizes identical. Additional interest in such a display can be achieved by using a distinctive prop or an eye catching poster.

2 Step your products to provide variation.

Steps develop an interesting display. The key is to keep the height of the step the same and ensure that all the products face the same way. The essence is uniformity.

The objective of a stepped display is to lead the consumer's eye in a specific direction and, in this way, create movement.

Customer
line of vision

Many merchandisers will use a wider step at the base of the display and then use narrower steps as the display achieves height. An appropriate sign atop the structure drives home the sales message.

3 Use a pyramid to sell more product.

The triangle or pyramid always seems to sell more products.

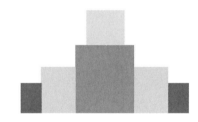

Pyramids are easy to construct and, with experience, a merchandiser can create a wonderful impact with a group of pyramids.

Pyramids can be built from a wide range of products. If the product does not enable you to develop the pyramid shape, you can use a poster at the peak to create the required outline.

WINNING
OUR CUS

MANAGING
YOUR STOR

PROMOTING
YOUR PRODUCTS

NAGING
BUSINESS

DEX

85

4 Consider zig-zag displays.

Terry Curry of Predictions in Melbourne believes that, once you become skilled at building pyramids, you can then progress to zig-zag pyramids. This structure zig-zags its way to the top of the structure and presents a very pleasing and eye-catching exhibit.

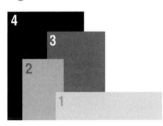

In a zig-zag arrangement, no level is the same height as the last one and therefore you can use a number of zig-zag arrangements to develop a larger display.

5 Try radiating your displays.

Alan Wheeler from the London Institute of Design suggests that another effective exhibit is the radiation or spokes-of-a-wheel display. The hub of the wheel is often raised to give a focus towards the centre of the structure. In this display you have the opportunity to develop ideas based on different colours, shapes and sizes.

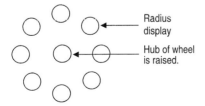

Radius display

Hub of wheel is raised.

Management Memo

Research carried out in the United States shows a 43 per cent consumer recall from static displays and a 94 per cent consumer recall from rotating displays, plus 80 per cent of consumers could remember the product. [39]

6 Be on the lookout for ideas from elsewhere.

Always keep your eyes open and look at displays in other retail environments. Adapt any good displays you find in retail industries other than your own. Your aim should be to stand out from the crowd of competitors in your industry—and any ideas you can creatively acquire from elsewhere will certainly help you do that.

7 Provide a tool box for the display team.

A box of tools and equipment specifically for use in setting up displays will save considerable time and frustration. The tool box should contain such items as:

staple gun, staples and staple remover
pins of different sizes
hammer and screwdriver
pliers or pincers
a selection of nails
screws and screw hooks
cotton (black and white)
nylon thread
adhesives
double-sided masking tape
pencil
measuring tape
scissors
a duster.

How to display products on pallets

Pallets are used for bulk displays to give the perception that the consumer is getting a special price because the retailer has purchased the product in bulk. Pallets can be used in outdoor and indoor locations, but a handling system, usually a hand or mechanical pallet jack, will save a great deal of cost in terms of employee time and labour. Pallets traditionally were made of wood, but plastic versions are now available.

1 Stress safety with pallet displays.

Pallets traditionally are placed on the shop floor, bulk-stocked with products which are usually fairly heavy. This means that product should be stacked to a minimum height of one metre and a maximum of two metres so that the products are at the correct shopping height for the consumer. Of course, the weight and nature of the product will mean that some items must be displayed at lower heights. Products must be stacked safely, due to the height of the pile and their weight. For the majority of products a brick-lay pattern is the most secure.

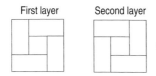

First layer   Second layer

2 Face bagged products in front of pallets.

Large bagged products are commonly displayed on pallets. Sales can be increased by placing a bag or two in front of the pallet facing the direction of the consumer. This clearly displays the product and provides greater impact, especially since most bags on the pallet are usually stacked to appear end-on to the consumer.

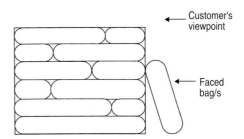

Customer's viewpoint

Faced bag/s

3 Provide point of purchase information.

Generally, retailers do not use point of purchase material as effectively as they should. For maximum effect, signs with relevant sales and product information should be placed on special stands—not simply (and often untidily) taped on to products facing the customer.

Where you have a gap in the centre of the product display on the pallet, it is far more impressive to use a stand, placed on the pallet, with the sign above the product:

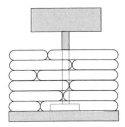

● ●

Management Memo

I f employing team members to move pallets around your store using mechanised equipment, it is essential that they be trained and have passed the appropriate examinations to prove they are competent in this role.[40]

4 Try up-market palleting for improved sales.

An alternative display that is very effective indoors, particularly with the more high value products, is to use a side stand with a display table attached to highlight an individual product:

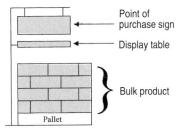

Point of purchase sign

Display table

Bulk product

Pallet

Some pallet products come in a cardboard box that fits on the pallet. These boxes can be cut and hinged back to provide very effective promotional backboards to the display. When these backboards are available they should be used:

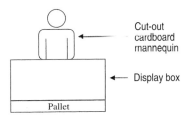

Cut-out cardboard mannequin

Display box

Pallet

5 Delegate pallet-display responsibilities.

A team member should be made responsible for the day-to-day management of the pallets. Bags often get ripped, possibly causing a safety problem, and reducing the overall impact of the display as well. Taping of torn bags may not be the answer. It is often more effective to remove damaged bags from the display completely. It is the staff member's responsibility to monitor pallet displays as well as assist buying customers with their purchases.

6 Place pallet displays strategically in the store.

If heavy items are being displayed on pallets, it is far more convenient to the customer to position the pallets towards the end of their shopping experience. The need to load large bags in shopping trolleys at the start is not only annoying; it will also discourage the customer from purchasing more items, the result of which could be a lower average sale per customer than you would like.

How to maximise sales using the floor of your store

To promote their brands and products, retailers have traditionally concentrated on using the walls and shelves of their stores and on hanging items from the ceiling. They tend to forget that every customer walks on the floor and that the floor can influence customer buying and provide an opportunity to promote the business...

1 Have a floor hygiene program.

According to research, cleanliness is one of the important considerations when a customer selects a retailer. They may take a clean floor for granted—but they find untidy and grubby floors unacceptable. The cleanliness program you implement for the floor is therefore critical. Floors should be mopped, swept, or vacuumed on a daily basis, an activity that must take place when the store is closed. Apart from the safety aspect, your customer does not want to see you cleaning the floor. They just want a clean floor.

2 Ensure you have a safe floor.

Floors must be slip-free. Apart from the untidiness of it all, a slippery floor is a safety hazard you can ill afford in the legal sense. During the working day, you may have accidental spillages. If this is a potential problem in your store, you need a floor cleaning procedure in place. With some products, a mop and bucket may be sufficient. With certain chemical spills, a bucket of sawdust may be required to soak up the material prior to mopping. And make sure those employees on the mops are trained to remove dirt from the floor and not simply spread it.

3 Consider using floor advertising.

Floor graphics are a unique way of selling using floor space. These can range from sticky printed labels on the floor to high quality base material that will last a considerable period of time. Floor graphics can complement national promotional campaigns, especially when we are told that 60-80 per cent of a customer's time is spent glancing at the floor.

Floor graphics can be used to increase sales for new product launches, for branding your store, to promote special events, and to provide directional signage for specific product promotions.

Floor graphics can come supplied on plastic, 3M, Flexon or similar materials, and can be used on waxed, vinyl, ceramic tiles, sealed wood, terrazzo, sealed concrete or marble surfaces.

Remember that the floor is the most under-used promotional area in your store and therefore the right promotional message can literally stop customers in their tracks.

Make use of cross selling opportunities.

Floor graphics are ideal where you would like to do cross selling, but for technical reasons this is not possible. For example, one product may need refrigeration and its associated product may not—try a cream spill graphic and accompanying message below the strawberry stand. Floor graphics are a unique way of linking such products.

Go high tech.

The latest trend is in the use of in-store laser promotions, which are transmitted through static or moving images on the floor. The technique is already being used in nightclubs, expos and demonstrations, and innovative companies have begun introducing the technique into retailing.

Investigate floor selling.

Point of purchase sales and impulse selling has always had a positive effect on sales. More than 70 per cent of purchasing decisions are made off the cuff inside the store and, for this reason alone, any effective in-store promotional strategy—such as floor selling—should be considered. For further details, contact Floor Advertising and Management, Insight Floor Marketing Australia. email: insight@nw.com.au.

Management Memo

The successful retailer combines outside advertising with customer-targeted in-store advertising.

Problem: Your customer is inundated with advertising noise everyday. Often, the only thing they remember is your store name or the fact you have a 'sale'. Retailers can get trapped by unproductive advertising where they and their competition compete to see who can give up the most margin. The primary (and sometimes only) goal of advertising is to get customers into your store. Once you have spent thousands of dollars to get customers into your store, then what?

Solution: The most effective, measurable, and least expensive place to advertise to your customers is in your store. When customers are in your store, they are receptive to your message and they are ready to make a purchase. Think of advertising as a process that begins outside the store and continues while the customer is in the store.

Here are three key points to an effective overall advertising program:

• Combine your outside advertising program with effective in-store advertising. Outside advertising is a means of getting customers into your store. Sign everything that is advertised with *high performance signs*. By combining outside advertising with strong in-store advertising, retailers squeeze the most out of every advertising dollar.

• This is a must— *Sign beyond your advertising.* After spending thousands of hard-earned dollars to get customers into your store, do not allow your store to become a cherry picker's paradise. Compliment your outside advertising with strong feature/benefits signs on more than just the advertised items. Give customers this message: I have other merchandise that you want and need.

• *Utilise creative in-store advertising* consistently and regularly. For example, in addition to using high performance signs, create inexpensive in-store flyers. They are a simple, yet strong reinforcement of your advertising messages. And, since they are inexpensive, you can use them regularly—whether there is a sale going on or not. [41]

How to build a profitable power product display

A key to successful retailing is to be consistent in your relay merchandising and entrepreneurial in your displays. The power display is the most important display in your store, not only because it uses the most profitable square metre of retail floor space available to you, but also because it should set the upfront image for the whole store. Power spots need to be planned and managed, and a few pointers will maximise the return of your investment...

1 Position the power display in your prime location.

The aim of a power display is to maximise sales and set an image. For this reason, position your display where you know 100 per cent of customers will see 100 per cent of product.

Your prime position is usually where customers enter the store. Do not locate the display right at the entrance, however. Since your customers need to adjust to the environment before looking at products, give them about four metres walking and adjustment space prior to building the display. In small stores you may have to build the display slightly closer to the door.

2 Plan your display.

The life of your power display is based on how often a regular customer enters your store. If customers, on average, come in once a week, then change the display once a week; if it's once a month, plan the display to rotate on a monthly basis. And if your store is located at a busy

bus stop used by people going to work each day, you may find that changing the product on the power display three times a week is justifiable in terms of increased sales. All of which means that you must plan at least three months ahead in terms of what product will go on your power display. Design a planning chart for that purpose...

Product	Action	Who is responsible?	Deadline	Assistance required

3 Focus on one product only.

As the term suggests, this is a 'power' display which infers that you should concentrate your sales efforts and your customers' attention on one product. Only in this way will you achieve the essential impact you seek.

4 Build a pyramid to maximise impact.

Pyramids sell more than any other shape, so it's only common sense to keep to this shape. Start building the display on a rectangular base of either product or a 'dummy' base and, to maximise sales, make sure the customer's eye hits the middle of the display.

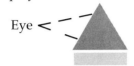

Eye

5 Make sure your display is well signed.

Your display is incomplete without a sign which should be dramatic and obvious, stating clearly what the product is and its price. Other information may also be relevant. Refer to 'How to write signs' (p. 152).

6 Give the impression you have a lot of product.

The retail saying 'Stack it high and watch it fly' was no doubt coined with power displays in mind. In essence, you must make your display look impressive and full—all the time. If you don't have a lot of product, use dummy boxes at the base or in the centre of the display to make it look larger. Never let the display go below half full. Its life cycle should be—full to half-full to full to half-full...

7 Keep an eye on your display.

The manager's role is to plan power displays and to ensure that the display is:
• built impressively and reflects your store's image in the eyes of the customer
• topical and fashionable
• safe in the bustle of passing

> ## Management Memo
>
> The Russell R. Mueller Retail Hardware Research Foundation carried out research in the United States to judge how profitable power displays were for businesses that built them critically. The research showed that sales of that product increased by 540 per cent!
>
> This figure was achieved by taking a product from a relay merchandise position and placing it in a power position. The price stayed the same, only the position changed.[42]

customers and staff
• checked every day to ensure it reflects the image of the company
• dismantled immediately the promotion is over, and replaced with the next promotion.

HOW I SEE OUR POWER DISPLAY

	Needs lots of work	Needs some more work	Looks good	We've got it right
Power display is clearly visible.	☐	☐	☐	☐
Power display is changed at regular intervals.	☐	☐	☐	☐
Eye level merchandising is correct.	☐	☐	☐	☐
'Power' planning calendar is up to date.	☐	☐	☐	☐
Signs are correctly written.	☐	☐	☐	☐
Power display has the correct product on display.	☐	☐	☐	☐
Display is safe and shoppable.	☐	☐	☐	☐

Team members have a role to play as well. They should ensure that:
• the display is kept full to half-full at all times
• a point of sale sign is always clearly visible to the customer
• displays are kept clean and tidy.

How to maximise your sales using hot spots/end caps

Every store has its hot spots—positions that the majority of your customers' eyes unavoidably focus on. Traditionally they are at end caps—those prominent locations at the ends of relays. The more hot spots you can create, the more sales opportunities you can achieve. Hot spots should be positioned in every product category in your store and your team should always be aware of products on display in these positions. To maximise the potential of your hot spots, be aware of the following points...

1 Know where to best position your hot spots.

Your team should know where to position hot spots in your store. A hot spot is a prominent or visible location where customers' eyes are naturally drawn. These focal points are usually at the end of merchandise relays or at specific points which the customer cannot avoid when walking around the store.

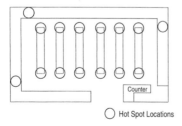

○ Hot Spot Locations

HOT SPOT CALENDAR		
Month	Products for Hot Spots	Allied product to be promoted alongside Hot Spot
January		
February		
March		
April		
May		
June		
July		
August		
September		
October		
November		
December		

2 Plan your hot spot displays.

Always use topical products in hot spots. To achieve this you will need to plan these locations well ahead to ensure you have the right product in the right place at the right time. Your planning needs to consider seasonal and fashion changes, and your hot spot should also reflect the image you wish to create in your store.

3 Build your hot spot displays wisely.

Four points are important in this regard:

- Hot spots need to present products to the customer at their sight line. This means you may sometimes need to dummy the base with boxes to raise the display to the correct position.

- Never plan for a hot spot display if you do not have enough product to make the display look full and to provide impact.
- Hot spot displays must always have a sign to work effectively or you will not maximise your return per square metre.
- Whenever possible, try and create a pyramidal shape to the display. Research shows pyramids sell better than any other shape.

4 Maximise the value of hot spot products.

Consider the following advice:

- Products being specially promoted by your store should be positioned on hot spots or end caps.
- Hot spot displays need to be managed so that product levels go from full to half full to full. To maximise return, displays should never go below half full.
- The products on the end cap should reflect the range of product that is being merchandised in the relay-merchandising plan behind the end cap. For example, if you're building an end cap or hot spot in a shirt department, the end cap should reflect the shirts you are promoting within the category.
- The display must be shoppable in the eyes of the customer, for the products on display should sell at least three times faster from this display than from a relay merchandise position.

5 Adopt a team strategy.

Take steps to develop your team to capitalise on the advantages that hot

spots can offer…

- Team members must know what products are on display at hot spots, and must know why these products are on display.
- They should know the features, benefits and price of the product, so they can readily promote the items from these positions.
- Team members should be accountable for checking end caps daily and facing up products as required. End caps and hot spots must be kept clean and dusted at all times.
- Customers often select products from the relay merchandise—then see the hot spot. They then 'dump' product on the end cap as they select, instead, the promoted line. Your team should be aware of this behaviour and ensure that the displays are kept clear of such clutter.
- Team members should develop the skill to promote 'add-on' lines that relate to the product being promoted at the hot spot. For example, if formal shirts are being promoted, the team should use this as an opportunity to promote coordinated ties.

How to use a wall of value

The 'wall of value' concept is used in a number of mass merchandise stores in the United States, and to a lesser degree elsewhere. The stores mail out a flyer to customers promoting a wide range of products sold on price. Once the customer arrives at the store they find the 'wall of value' at the rear of the store with the promoted products lined up next to each other.

1 Ensure only wall products are promoted in the flyer.

To make the concept acceptable to the buying public, it is important that the flyers promote only those products on the wall of value, and the wall must contain only those products advertised on the leaflet.

2 Locate more profitable products on the way to the wall.

Make sure customers, on the way to the wall of value, pass similar products which have a higher gross profit. This is the real key to success, for the aim is not to sell from the wall, but to offer a more profitable substitute for the store on the way to the wall. These products need to be clearly visible to the customer on end displays and must have good 'on product' signage. Some businesses do this extremely well and it works admirably.

Do not locate wall of value at the front of the store. Experience shows that this results in customers not shopping the complete store, with a consequent decline in overall sales per square metre.

3 Make the wall of value work.

Keep in mind the following points:

- The 'wall' is a true description. Products literally cover the wall and a typical display for one product may be as wide as three metres and stacked up to the ceiling. The display will then have a price sign on it at the eye level of a typical customer.
- If customers prefer the wall products to the ones on the way to the wall, then you still have the opportunity to increase your sales as they leave the store.
- It is important the wall is kept full of products to give the impression it is providing value.
- In the supermarket sector, the wall is normally changed weekly with new products being displayed. In other sectors of retail, the wall is changed at the same time frame as the average customer enters your store (i.e. if they come in on average once a month, then you need to change the display once a month).

4 Experiment with variations of the wall.

One supermarket uses the most central aisle in the store as an aisle of value. Traditionally this was the least visited aisle and it has now become the most visited area of the store.

How to become famous for something

For many consumers, retailing can be a boring experience with so many stores selling the same things in the same way. At the same time, new stores are opening and reducing the opportunities for many retailers to increase their market share. The secret is to become the customer's favoured store—but first you have to be noticed...

1 Know what success really involves.

According to Donald Cooper, the Canadian fashion retailer and consultant, the key to success is that you have to become, in sequence:
• noticed
• remembered
• preferred
• trusted.

This means that you must work on a strategy aimed at having you stand out from the crowd.

2 Dare to be different.

Perth-based consultant Barry Urquhart emphasises that in the future you'll have to dare to be different. You'll have to think and act 'outside the box' so your store is noticed by the consumer—in a positive way, of course. This means creating adventurous services, displays, staff costumes, and total experiences for your potential customers.

3 Seek fame— and fortune will follow.

To be a destination, you have to provide your customers with a destination product range. Research your market and find out where other retailers are *not* providing the full width and depth of product range and associated services. Then set about developing this product range and gain a reputation locally as the expert and the most comprehensive supplier of this product.

It could be you have the best selection of diamond rings, Italian shirts, milk shakes, or camellias. The key is that you have to become famous for something.

4 Do not be shy about your strengths.

Too often retailers establish the range that they are famous for, but fail to let the customer know. Assumption is one of the leading failures in business. Never assume your customers know what you do.

5 Brainstorm ideas with your team.

Being different and famous takes team commitment. Believe in the concept. Involve all team members.

How to manage cold spot selling positions

Every store has 'cold' spots—those areas in the store that customers normally overlook or do not want to visit. These are usable areas of your store and should not be surrendered as 'dead space'. Often it can be a real struggle to turn them into 'live space'. How can you encourage your customers to visit these quiet, backwater areas?

1 Identify your cold spot areas.

Every store has its cold spot, an area where few sales are made. The first priority is to identify these areas, and here are several strategies you might adopt:

- Follow customers around, and plot their route. In this way you will have a clear pattern of customer flow and the areas not shopped.

- Look for dead-ends and badly lit areas in your store. Customers tend to avoid such areas.

- From your records, identify product areas that are achieving lower sales per square metre than you have anticipated.

- Find stock areas where product is getting dusty due to slow stockturns.

- Identify areas where displays are cluttered and difficult to shop.

- Monitor the notoriously poor selling positions—right behind the windows, and the areas immediately to the left and right of the entrance.

- Locate areas where product is hidden behind other shopfittings or the counter.

- Identify areas within your retailing environment, referred to by the team as 'the back'—chances are it is a cold spot.

2 Bring some life into cold spots.

To increase your overall sales per square metre, your objective will be to increase customer usage of the cold spots you have identified. Perhaps you simply need to inject some life into these areas. Perhaps a little reorganisation is all that's required. There are a number of actions you might consider:

- Do you have the right product in this area? For example, impulse lines in the rarely visited parts of the store will not sell. On the other hand, if you move a purpose line into this spot, you will force the customer to 'shop it out' in this area. Supermarkets often place such essentials as toilet paper in a 'cold' spot (aisle) to force customers to shop there.

WINNING
OUR CUS
MANAGING
YOUR STOR
**PROMOTING
YOUR PRODUCTS**
NAGING
BUSINESS
DEX
97

- Try converting your cold spot into a browse area. In a hardware store, for example, it could be an ideal location for a power tool department, or a seedling or bedding plant department in a garden centre.

- Consider using a cold spot as a customer service facility, for example:

  Changing rooms
  Information booths
  Toilets
  Enquiry counters
  Seating
  Refreshment facilities
  Demonstration areas
  Parking for trolleys or baskets.

- Re-examine your customer flow. It may be a cold spot because the store layout is wrong. Re-merchandising may bring traditional cold spots to life.

- Consider using cold spots for key cutting, shoe fitting, fitting rooms, lay-by, or parcel pick up.

- Inject some movement into the area. Consider a water fountain or a moving display of some kind.

- Introduce noise, such as the sound of a water feature or products that make a noise—no problem for a pet retailer.

- Experiment with colour. Blues and whites are cold. Reds and yellows are hot. Use 'hot' colours in a 'cold' area.

- Consider the use of smells. Negative odours, such as fertilisers, will create a cold spot while positive aromas, such as

> **Management Memo**
>
> G ood displays can become dead displays due to lack of attention to detail. Items often left unfinished include pins not removed from garments, dirt and dust not removed from surfaces, glass not cleaned, soiled signs, signs with no borders, tools left in the display, and lighting not checked. [44]

coffee or hot bread, will draw people to them.

- Perhaps try a combination of a few of the above ideas in one of your cold spots.

3 Be prepared to change.

Always be prepared to experiment in terms of altering your customer flow. Only in this way will you be able to maximise the number of hot spots and minimise the cold spots. Retailing is a changing environment. If you do not experiment, you will never know what successes you might have achieved.

4 Involve your team.

Always involve the team in managing and monitoring the cold spots. If everyone on your staff is aware of the problem, and proactive, those cold spots will soon warm up.

5 Always monitor cold spots.

Once you have identified a cold spot and made appropriate changes, ensure that you monitor and manage the area so that you can be confident the improvements have worked.

How to manage shelf filling

Shelf filling is an ongoing task that has to be carried out in the majority of stores. Supermarkets often employ night filling teams to tackle this job, while smaller stores may be required to carry out the task during the trading day. Shelf filling is often looked on as one of the routine, unskilled tasks in the store. It is, however, a skill that needs to be reflected upon and developed to ensure that it is carried out cost effectively and methodically, in keeping with the company's image. Begin by considering the following advice...

 ### Plan your shelf filling.

If you don't think about and plan your approach to shelf filling, you will make poor use of the time allocated to the task and invariably end up with a flawed display—good product mixed with damaged products, loose packaging, torn labels, and dirty shelves. Therefore, prior to any shelf filling activity, always ensure that the team involved is fully conversant with appropriate procedures and aware of the standards you expect of them.

 ### Ensure stock is available to meet demand.

It is simply inefficient in terms of cost and time if your shelves lie empty as a result of poor planning. For this reason always ensure that sufficient stock is placed on the shelf to meet consumer demand for a given period of time. The minimum period of time for sufficient items to be on the shelf should be at least one trading day, but you may need to ensure that you have enough stock on the shelf to keep you in business for at least a trading week.

 ### Clean the shelves before filling them.

Consumers select stores for a variety of reasons—and cleanliness is one of them. It is therefore not only important for your overall store environment to be clean and tidy, each shelf must be clean and tidy as well. So, an important task for managers is to ensure that the shelf filling team gets into the habit of cleaning the shelves *prior* to putting stock on them. And remember, cleaning a shelf means cleaning the shelf edge strip as well.

 ### Keep the workplace safe.

When filling shelves, staff will normally bring boxes out of the warehouse or down from above the shelf. It is important that your team keep aisles safe at all times, particularly if the shelf stacking is being carried out during trading hours. This can be achieved by making sure that boxes are placed on one side only of the aisle and that customers have safe access down the aisle. Safety and tidiness are the two considerations here.

WINNING
OUR CUS

MANAGING
YOUR STOR

**PROMOTING
YOUR PRODUCTS**

NAGING
BUSINESS

DEX

99

5 Abide by the FIFO rule.

First in, first out (FIFO)—that's the golden rule when it comes to shelf filling. When filling shelves you must take the old stock out, put the new stock at the back, and then face up using the old stock. Your aim must always be to rotate stock. If you don't apply the FIFO principle, you could end up with old stock that becomes unsaleable. Of course, FIFO is critically important with food and perishable products.

Accountants tell us that it costs you 1 per cent per month of the buying price for a product to sit on the shelf. In other words, if a product has been on the shelf for 12 months, the costs go up 12 per cent to bring the same return as in month one.

6 Face products correctly.

Products should be put on the shelf the correct way up with the promotional side of the label facing out towards the customer. Make sure price and date codes are clear, accurate, and visible to the customer. At the same time fix loose or torn labels. Any damaged products should be removed from the shelf and recorded in a shrinkage book.

7 Face up items not replenished.

You won't be refilling every product on the shelf, but you should face up items that are not being replenished. Take the remaining items on the shelf and move them forward to give the impression that the shelf is full.

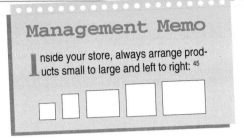

Management Memo

Inside your store, always arrange products small to large and left to right: [45]

8 Consider indenting.

A leading UK supermarket has a company policy of indenting the shelf every three metres. Indenting is where you face up, but leave one gap on the shelf to give the impression that one item has already been sold.

Indenting is most effective on a slow moving product line. It can work incredibly well. Customers tend to gravitate to the indented product line, assuming someone has already purchased from this section of shelf.

9 Clean up afterwards.

Boxes on the floor are a safety hazard to team members and customers. As soon as you've finished, you must remove all empty boxes, rubbish, cleaning materials, and anything else that has been left on the sales floor.

10 Check what message you're saying to the customer.

When the job is finished make sure all shelftalkers are next to the correct products. A frequent mistake in many stores is to fill the shelf—and then forget to realign the shelftalkers. This can cause customer confusion and may result in lost sales.

How to create theatre in your store

Retailing is about inspiring people to buy. Whatever sector of the retail industry you belong to, you need to create some excitement to entice customers back to your store rather than to your competitors. International retail and marketing consultant Barry Urquhart believes the key is not being better than your competition; the key is being different to your competition. Theatre displays give you the opportunity to dare to be different. They are about inspiration and magic...

1 Plan well in advance of the event.

Theatre displays need to be planned at least three months ahead—although some would argue it should be six months or more. In the United Kingdom, Christmas theatre displays are planned 12 months in advance.

Displays work better if the whole team participates in the planning stage and are then encouraged to get involved in developing the promotion itself. At the initial planning meeting, decide on the theme, what props will be used, and on the budget.

Remember, the key is that you need to be different to attract the customer. If you do something different, people will talk about you to others which means, to encourage 'word of mouth' communication, you might even need to be a little outrageous in what you do.

2 Build theatre around events.

Theatre displays should revolve around international, national, regional and local events as well as promotional themes specific to your

industry sector and company. The following major events may provide an excuse (if you need one) to build a theatre display:

January: New Years Day, Chinese New Year (varies)
February: St Valentine's Day, Idhul Fitri
March: St Patrick's Day
April: April Fool's Day, Easter, Secretaries' Day (varies around the world)
May: Mother's Day (some countries hold in other months), May Day
June: End of Financial Year (not all countries)
July: Independence Day (US), Bastille Day (Fr)
September: Father's Day (not all countries have Father's Day in September)
October: Harvest Time, Halloween
November: Guy Fawkes (UK)
December: Christmas

Compile your own promotions calender and have it in full view of your team:

PROMOTIONS CALENDAR		
Period	Main Promotions	Secondary Promotions
JANUARY	1. 2.	1. 2.
FEBRUARY	1. 2.	1. 2.
MARCH	1. 2.	1. 2.
APRIL	1. 2.	1. 2.
DECEMBER	1. 2.	1. 2.

VINNING
OUR CUS

MANAGING
YOUR STOR

**PROMOTING
YOUR PRODUCTS**

NAGING
BUSINESS

DEX

101

3 Sell the magic not the mess.

Customers want to believe in the magic of your theatre activities—they don't want to see theatre displays being built. You have two options. You either build displays when the store is closed or you place a large black drape around the work area and reveal all when the central display is completed. Some stores display signs saying: 'All will be revealed in… one hour', thereby creating expectation in the customer's mind and allowing your team to build the display while the store continues to trade.

4 Train the team and make them actors.

Theatre is about acting. If you really want to create for your customers a memorable visit to your store, get the team to dress the part. If it's Christmas, wear Christmas hats; if it's St Valentine's Day, wear a big red heart. Make sure that team members have features and benefits knowledge about the theme-linked products on display and are able to advise customers on how to use the products.

5 Record the event for future reference.

Theatre displays normally occur on a yearly basis. When the display is completed, take photographs to place in a scrapbook for referral next year. If you don't, you'll have trouble remembering the details in twelve months time. Make notes in the scrapbook of what worked, what you need to improve upon next time, and how successful the promotion was in dollar terms.

Management Memo

Make your sidewalk [pavement/outside footpath] head and shoulders above other retailers on the block. The theatre starts on the sidewalk. If someone surveyed your store from across the street, you want your entire package to stand out. This includes the shop window, signs and overall storefront. You need to ask:

- Can I change the colour of the sidewalk?
- Can I put a large mat at the entrance?
- Can I plant flowers or place pots to give the store an attractive image?
- Do I have benches facing the shop window?
- Do I clean the sidewalk twice a day? A dirty sidewalk is a turn off.
- If it snows in my part of the world do I clear away the snow on a regular basis?
- If it is sunny, how can I provide shade? [46]

6 Measure the success of the project.

If you don't measure it, you can't manage it. Record how much you invested in creating the display and the increase in sales you achieved. Use this as a target to beat next year.

7 Dismantle the theatre display promptly.

As soon as the event has finished you must dismantle the display. Nobody wants to see Christmas still around on January 1st or St Valentine's Day still being promoted on February 15th!

8 Meet with staff after the event.

Hold a team meeting to review the success of the promotion. Get ideas, and note them down, on how you can improve the promotion next time. If you provide costs and sales success information to the whole team, they will share ownership of the initiative, and you will motivate them to make the promotion do even better on subsequent occasions.

How to prepare your staff for the holiday rush

Christmas is one of the most important trading periods of the retail year in the Western world. The impact it has on sales will vary with each retail sector but, whichever sector you belong to, it is critical that you maximise the sales potential of this peak festive season. One of the keys to success is a staff trained and ready to handle the extra demands of this exciting time for retailers...

 Motivate the team.

Christmas should be an exciting time for your team even though it is one of their busiest work periods. To maximise your success over Christmas, you should involve the team in the planning stages. Have a Christmas planning meeting well before the holiday sales period to discuss your plans, your staff involvement, and to canvass their ideas.

Be objective in terms of precise goals—targeted total sales, average sale per customer, number of items per transaction, and conversion rate. Compare the anticipated targets with last year's results and discuss how this year's targets will be achieved, recorded, and measured.

2 Implement a holiday countdown campaign.

Have a Christmas countdown campaign where each day everyone can compare results against targets. Daily progress could be entered on a whiteboard summary chart in the staffroom as part of the motivational strategy.

3 Reduce stress in the team.

Many people find the lead-up to Christmas a stressful period. Your objective is to reduce this stress. Consider these strategies offered by Jurek Leon of Terrific Trading in his Christmas ideas newsletter:

- Employ someone to keep the lunch room looking fresh and tidy during the Christmas rush.
- Place a VCR in the staff room and rent some humorous videos for viewing in free time.
- Hire a masseur to give mini complimentary massages to staff (and even as a Christmas service to customers).
- Conduct a joke-a-day competition with staff.
- Schedule time off for staff to do their own Christmas shopping.
- Make an effort during this busy period to 'catch team members doing something right' and to reward them publicly.

4 Focus on staff employment needs.

Your team will get exhausted during this period and you may need to

WINNING
OUR CUS

MANAGING
YOUR STOR

PROMOTING
YOUR PRODUCTS

NAGING
BUSINESS

DEX

103

change rosters and hire temporary staff. Sign up temporary team members well before December. Contact local colleges and retail training providers who may have trainees requiring retail experience over the Christmas period. Hire special staff to answer your phones and free up your sales team to sell.

Deal with poor performance as it occurs. If you leave it until after Christmas, your high performers may well become disillusioned with those staff members who aren't pulling their weight during this rush period.

5 Train the team.

Every staff member needs to be on the ball for Christmas and a short training program will prove beneficial:

- Provide adequate training based on the ten most commonly asked questions over the Christmas period:
  - Does it come equipped with batteries?
  - Can I return it if it is not suitable?
  - Will it work overseas?
  - Have you a follow-up service?
  - What happens if it's the wrong size?
  - Is it guaranteed?
  - What instructions are provided?
  - Can the recipient change it for another colour after Christmas if they don't like the colour?
  - Do you have other sizes, if it must be changed later?
  - Do you gift wrap?
- Train the team on how to remain cool and calm in times of stress. At

> ### Management Memo
>
> If you have a large Jewish clientele, you should consider Chanukah decorations, a candelabra, signs saying Happy Chanukah... For a Muslim customer base, Idhul Fitri is the major annual celebration.[47]

this time of year, they must act like Santa's helpers—even when there is a line of frustrated shoppers demanding VIP treatment. Even simple advice, like doing deep breathing exercises on the job, will help them at this time.

- Conduct an induction program for new casuals so that they quickly become a part of the team.
- Clever sales assistants should be able to be quick off the mark with gift suggestions for the hard-to-please relative or the friend who has everything. Have you provided your team with lists of such suggestions?

6 Keep your staff on their toes.

Christmas is a time when the team should be order makers, not order takers, i.e. approach the customer and not wait for the customer to approach them. This means your staff must be well drilled in the basics of Christmas selling:

- Welcome the customer with a Christmas greeting.
- Use open questions.
- Sell during busy periods.
- Add-on sell.
- Ask for the sale.

How to maximise your holiday promotion

Christmas is that one time each year when a business can attract shoppers who would otherwise walk past the store. For most people, Christmas shopping is a chore, and any retailer who can successfully promote their business will attract more customers at this festive time—and, importantly, generate more sales.

1 Plan special Christmas promotions.

Christmas is a competitive time in the retail industry. Retailers need to do something different in terms of customer service, even entertainment, to attract the customer. Your promotion can be varied and exciting, and include, for example:

- Take up a local charity cause over the Christmas period and be visibly seen to promote it.
- Network promotions with such local retailers as the Health Shop and a Gym.
- Have a Christmas party for senior citizens and young toddlers—not at the same time, of course.
- Organise special customer events during the lead-up to Christmas.
- Have a value-added promotions period, featuring lucky dips, balloons with gifts in them, and the like.
- Install a Christmas suggestion box where customers can offer their ideas.
- Send Christmas cards to your regular customers and put a handwritten note of thank-you in the card.

2 Create atmosphere.

Focus on all the senses to make an impact on the Christmas customer:

Taste—offer them refreshments and samples of Christmas goodies.
Fragrance—use Christmas spices.
Noise—have carols being sung in the store. Ideally, get your team together during the day to sing to your customers. Or employ wandering minstrels during peak periods.
Touch—provide seasonal products and items that your customer can touch, such as Christmas trees, ornaments and large cuddly toys.

3 Build Christmas displays.

For many of us, one of the magical moments of Christmas was, as children, going to town to look at the window displays and Christmas lights during this festive period. Depending on your circumstance as a retailer, Christmas displays can be real winners in terms of customer support. Your display can be animated, fun, zany, interesting, unusual, newsworthy, educational, or magical—but, whatever you do, 'dare to be different'.

4 Make Christmas special for customers.

Jurek Leon, of Terrific Trading, provides a host of ideas to help retailers get the most out of the Christmas trading period. Among his tips on improving customer service during this time are:

I'll make you glad to talk with me:
- Make everyone feel special.
- Remember, every customer is different. Treat each as an individual.
- If you see someone without a smile, give them one of yours.
- Occupy the children.
- Occupy husbands/boyfriends.

Welcome your customers:
- At peak times have a specially designated person welcome your customers. Make sure they are clearly identifiable by your customers, perhaps with a sash over their shoulder.

Cater for the elderly:
- Provide chairs at strategic places for your elderly customers.
- Provide cold drinking water and other refreshments.

The male shopper:
- Male customers are less comfortable and confident about trends, sizes, colours, fragrances. Think about how you can assist them to feel more assured.

Photos:
- Introduce a photographer to photograph families and friends in front of a festive backdrop.

Gift-wrapping:
- Provide gift-wrapping as an inclusive service. You can pre-wrap a gift for customers who want to buy in a hurry or you could do on-the-spot wrapping where the customers can choose their own paper and ribbon and can then enjoy seeing it wrapped professionally.
- Make sure you have trained wrappers.
- The service cheers up customers and it's great for males since it provides a complete package.
- Train your wrappers to smile and talk as they wrap.
- Select volume merchandise and pre-wrap 30-40 per cent. This can be as

simple as a ribbon around the goods.
- Take steps to ensure long wrapping queues are avoided at the busy times.

Make it easy:
- Do not have customers waiting to be served.
- Provide different service options—gift vouchers, phone orders. Many professional people often do not have time to shop, so provide a service where they can phone up, receive a gift list, then phone back and place an order which can be delivered to their home or office.
- Have an area dedicated just for children (no adults allowed) with someone to help them select gifts for brother, sister, parents and grandparents. Goods should be priced accordingly.
- Have a Christmas catalogue from which children can buy presents for their family. There could be a $2.00 page, $5.00 page, $10.00 page and a $20.00 page.

Keep people informed:
- Today's customers are hungry for information. Provide Christmas-oriented 'tip sheets' for customers.

Management Memo

The first step to a profitable Christmas is to determine what attracts customers to your business and to promote that aspect heavily. Your promotion should centre on different or unusual products, perhaps a specialised hamper service or free gift wrapping.

The second step is to determine what promotional strategy will attract people to your shop. Some retailers base their promotional strategy around the image of Christmas. A common example is the 'Christmas Ham', which is no different to the ham offered throughout the rest of the year—but the word 'Christmas' attracts customers.

The way you promote your message will also influence the number of customers you attract. Perhaps you can advertise in the media, decorate your store, have a point of sale display, or use face-to-face selling.[48]

How to sell concepts not products

It is possible for a retailer to make more money than normal selling the same product. To achieve this, you need to take the existing product and change its perceived value in some way. This means thinking outside the box and presenting the product in a different way. It's called adding value, and it's all about selling a concept rather than the product...

1 Make *your* product stand out from the rest.

Today's consumer is exposed to a wide range of products. Your product not only has to compete with similar products, but you have to compete with other retailers selling that same product.

To gain the attention of today's sophisticated customer, the quality of your product, as perceived by the customer, has to stand out. You need to differentiate your product from a competitor's product.

You can alter your product in a variety of ways so that it is different from that of competing retailers—by grouping products differently, combining with other products, or using different packaging, and so on. You must make the product appear to be worth more in the eye of the customer, hence the term 'adding value'.

2 Try using colour.

Adding value can take a variety of guises, and the use of colour plays an important role. Colour is a fashion concept, and customers perceive some colours to have greater value and significance than others. In hard economic times, for example, 'classic colours' such as navy blue and indigo are preferred by customers because people tend to become conservative when the economy slows down.

In Australia in the 1970s Mission Brown was the fashionable colour for houses, replaced later by Brunswick Green, and even later by pastels and the Tuscan influence. The result is that today, most people, after purchasing a house painted with Mission Brown, quickly repaint it using a more modern colour. According to colour specialists, the last decade or so of the twentieth century saw an emphasis on the environment– so 'earth' colours and greens became fashionable.

To maximise sales through adding value, retailers need to keep a close watch on colour trends and study what is happening in the marketplace. When using colour to add value, remember the evolution of colour trends: Colour tends to start with expensive, high end products, but colour saturation occurs when medium priced items are promoted using that colour.

3 Build events around your products.

If you tie your product to events in some way, you can get more money for your product. For example, promote roses for St Valentine's Day, strawberries for Wimbledon, and chrysanthemums for Mother's Day.

4 Investigate the use of low investment strategies.

To increase the worth of your product, you need to use low investment value-adds to obtain a high investment return. Some low investment opportunities could include:

- gift-wrap the product
- tie bows and ribbons on the product
- group products together in a different way
- add balloons, gift cards etc.
- use more upmarket colours in the presentation
- change the language used to sell the product.

5 Learn from the experience of others.

The trade magazines often relate value-add success stories which provide excellent case studies for you, as a retail manager, to reflect upon. To illustrate the impact of changing concepts, consider for example a company that has retailed chocolates for nearly a century. The company had built up a reputation for quality chocolate sold by weight, but in recent years had found its market share in decline. The challenge was to reposition the

Management Memo

In value-added terms, think globally whenever you can since the world is getting smaller and people are travelling more often. This means you should have at your fingertips, for example, a series of delivery charges. These could include:

- Express delivery—we'll deliver it today.
- Normal delivery—we'll have it to you within five days.
- International delivery—we'll deliver it anywhere.

And don't forget to cost in gift cards, wrapping etc. as part of the package. [49]

company in the marketplace, while still building on its reputation for a quality, niche product.

The first priority was to move the emphasis away from the traditional product and to sell the perceived benefits to the consumer. This was achieved by introducing a seasonal collection of chocolates. Then the chocolates were categorised in a different way— the Continental Range, the Premier Range, The Specialities, the Fine English Range, and so on.

They also introduced 'The Year of Chocolate' concept. Customers were encouraged to join a chocolate club and each month were sent a different range of chocolates with a message on a gift card. On birthdays, customers received an extra treat— Champagne Truffles, and extra gift packs were provided for St Valentine's Day, Mother's Day, Easter, and Christmas.

Yet, during all this time, the product essentially stayed the same. But the concept changed and the price increased. The result—sales increased!

How to introduce a new product line

New products are the life-blood of retailing. They are seen as a means of enhancing our lives and, for this reason, are of considerable interest to shoppers. Which is one reason why retailers and suppliers spend many days at trade shows around the world searching out new product lines. The key to any product's success, however, rests with the retailers and how effectively they are able to introduce these new items to the customer on the shop floor...

 Train your team in the benefits and features.

The introduction of a new product into your store demands that your team be provided with information about the item. Some manufacturers and suppliers forward fact sheets for sales team members; the majority do not. If necessary write your own fact sheet on the product and distribute it at a team meeting prior to the store launch. The sheet should include the date of the launch, the location of the product in the store, retail price, and features and benefits of the product. Allow time for a short question and answer period. The relevant category supervisor should lead this short training session.

 Position the product strategically in the store.

The product must be seen by all your customers if it is to make an impact. It should be positioned in the store either in a major impulse buying area, or taken out of the category and displayed as a stand-alone item in the major racetrack or near the entrance.

 Attend to signage.

This is a new product. It must have a sign that tells customers so and that promotes the product dramatically. In big letters you should use such words as:

'New!'
'Newly selected for you!'
'New in Store'
'Your new...'
'Latest Fashion'.

The word NEW! is a major customer motivator and should be used whenever possible.

 Provide information to enhance the sale.

Consumers love information, especially the type of information they can share with their friends. If you can source fascinating data to enhance the product and its acceptance, you should pass this on to your team and customers. Depending on the product, a gift shop, for example, could feature such interesting information as: where the product was discovered, the part of world where it is made,

WINNING
YOUR CUS

MANAGING
YOUR STOR

**PROMOTING
YOUR PRODUCTS**

NAGING
BUSINESS

DEX

109

the origins of the people who make it, what it was traditionally used for.

5 Use demonstrations to generate interest.

This is a new product that your consumers have never seen before. It is therefore important that they are shown how to use it, or what it looks like, how it is put together, or what it tastes like, how it feels, or what it is like to wear. It is your job to bring this product to life.

6 Promote. Promote. Promote.

Give any new product maximum exposure. Take any opportunity you can to promote the new item. Here are some useful ideas that have worked in the past:

- Send a complimentary sample to your favourite radio or television newsreader or chat show presenter.

- Have a demonstration outside your store, a strategy that works exceptionally well in shopping malls.

- Forward an article and a photograph to your local newspaper.

- Send a complimentary sample to a local celebrity or expert in the product field, such as the gardener, hardware specialist, or cook, who writes a guest column in the local newspaper.

- Ensure a team member takes it home, uses it, and reports back to

Management Memo

Factors affecting customers response to promotions and their degree of effectiveness:

Price	20%
Creativity	35%
Timing	100%
The offer	200%
Target the customer	500%

As can be seen, hitting the right target is the key to success, then providing the right offer and at the right time. Creative advertising may stimulate interest and amusement, but is not always the best approach to take. [50]

the team about it.

- Give a talk to consumer groups about the product.

- Cross network displays of the new product with other retailers in your area who do not sell the same category.

- Write about it in relevant hobby or special interest magazines.

- Have your staff use it themselves so they can say, with complete honesty, 'when I first used it…'.

- Send out flyers in your catchment area.

7 Select new product lines carefully.

The world is full of new products that fail. This is primarily due to the manufacturer not doing sufficient homework. Select new products with caution. Do not buy because it is new: buy because it is proven and fits your targeted customers.

How to set up a shop window

The small shop was once the workplace for family-run businesses. Large windows were put 'in the front' to provide more light to the cobbler or weaver who worked in the front room. As businesses evolved they started selling from the front room and the window then became an area to display products. At the same time a facia was erected above the window to promote the business. Thus were the origins of today's shop window. Its aim—to grab the customer's eye and to promote the business, products and services…

1 Look on your window as a canvas.

UK shop window consultant Alan Wheeler stresses that an excellent shop window is a marriage between creativity and scientific principles. Look on your shop window as an artist would look on a painting:

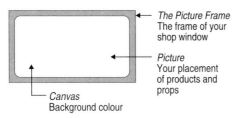

← *The Picture Frame*
The frame of your shop window

← *Picture*
Your placement of products and props

Canvas
Background colour

As a general rule, if you wish to create a down market image, then set up a window where customers can look into your store. If you want a more upmarket image, then an enclosed window may achieve this result for you. In either case, you are the artist and, from outside, it is your canvas.

2 Select a style to suit your business.

Windows can be contemporary, traditional, trendy or used to sell volume products. What style of window would reflect your business?

A final decision will depend on your position in the marketplace and the demographics of your customer base. This may mean you will need to do some customer research prior to deciding on a window style.

3 Group your products for effect.

The way you group products has a major effect on the appearance of your window. The skill is in arranging product and props in an interesting way that catches the eye. The majority of displays are based on the triangular shape.

Consider whether the display should be symmetrical or asymmetrical. Symmetrical displays allow for no variation, and give a formal, predictable look to your shop window. The eye is usually drawn towards the centre of a symmetrical display:

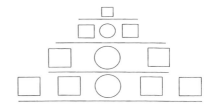

Terry Curry of Predictions in Melbourne says that asymmetrical displays still have balance, but products and props are displayed in a number of ways:

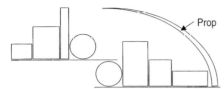

Prop

4 Create a colour theme.

Colour creates mood in your shop window—sexy, modern, innocent, nostalgic, sombre, trendy, or fresh. The general rule is to use a lighter background colour that complements your merchandise.

5 Plan your window well ahead of the event.

Planning is essential. If you plan the shop window display as you build it, you're likely to end up with a jumble of products and send a confusing message to the customer. Plan shop windows at least six months ahead. Develop a planning sheet for each window with these headings: Date, Theme, Merchandise, Risers Required, Props Required, Background, Signage Required.

6 Manage your shop window.

Managing your window displays is critical to your success—after all, they are, to the passers-by, the eyes of your store. The following ten tips will help you dare to be different:

- It takes four seconds to walk past the average size shop window. What does the customer remember when they walk past yours?

- Create emotion with colour and props, not the stock.
- Brainstorm what props you need with your team and how you can create the effect you want.
- Plan six months ahead.
- Dead blow flies and moths in shop windows show you do not care. Check the windows each day.
- Change your shop window to entertain your customers. A dress shop might change dresses in the window every other day to keep passing customers interested.
- People need personal space at the store entrance. Do not clutter this area.
- Your shop window is a 24-hour advertisement. Make sure it 'sparkles' in the dark.
- Link your shop window displays to your internal power displays and hot spots.
- Signage is essential in shop windows.

How to create movement in your displays

Retail competitiveness demands that you make your displays stand out from the hundreds of others seen by the public every retailing day of their lives. The great majority of displays are static. If you want to try something different, and stand out from the crowded marketplace, consider creating some moving displays—and here are some ideas...

1 Give a ripple or wave effect to banners.

Machines are available which allow you to hang banners containing your message and to give a ripple and wave effect to the hanging. The ripple machine is used with soft material and the oscillator works to give a waterfall effect.

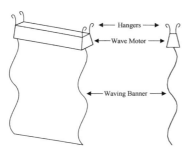

A wave machine oscillator provides a wave effect and is best used with stiffer banners. Both systems are very effective when combined with an adventurous use of lighting.

2 Put your product on a swing.

Many products lend themselves to display on a swing. Low generator motor systems are available to provide a swinging action to products.

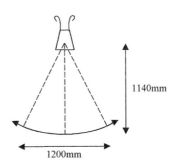

Remember:
    Movement + Interest = Sales

3 Place your promotions on a turntable.

Turntables are guaranteed to attract your customer's attention to a specific product, and are ideal for primary promotions where you believe movement is required to focus the customer's eye.

A typical turntable has a diameter of 500mm and upwards, and uses a low voltage motor with a gearbox. It can be switched to go either forwards or in reverse.

Small 500mm turntables are capable of taking up to 30kg central weight while larger ones can accommodate a motor vehicle.

4 Use rise and fall in your display.

Rise and fall machines are electrically operated and suspended above your display. Signage, banners, products, or other promotional material can be hung from the machine using nylon, and the item/s can be displayed at the same level or at different levels. The machine creates an up and down movement which gives a three-dimensional effect to the display.

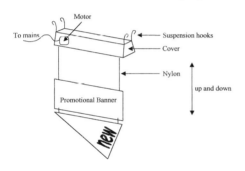

5 Get a balloon to jump out of a box.

Simple ideas are often the most effective—and getting a helium

Management Memo

R esearch in the United States has revealed that 43 per cent of people could recall products on static displays in stores. When movement was introduced to the display 94 per cent could recall the display and a staggering 80 per cent could name the product as well! [52]

balloon to jump and move around is just one of them. Balloon jumpers work using two small cell batteries and a nylon loop. Balloons can be decorated to look like flowers or faces or have the product name represented on them.

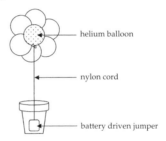

Displays with Movement are available from Robert Stockwell Associates, 20 Twixtvears, Tewkesbury, GL20 5B7, United Kingdom.

Managing your Store

The art is to be where the ball is going to be, not where it's been.

Sam Walton
founder of the world's largest retailer, Wal-Mart

How to maximise your customer flow

Retailers would like to get 100 per cent of customers to see 100 per cent of their product. But recent research into one retail sector in the United Kingdom found that 75 per cent of customers only saw a maximum of 20 per cent of product. Imagine how sales would improve if the customer flow encouraged all customers to see all product. Your aim should be to direct customers around your store, with clear direction, and the following suggestions will help you to maximise that customer flow...

1 Create a layout to reflect your needs.

Store design is the province of the professional store designer who knows that layout is determined by a consideration of the way the retailer would like customer traffic to flow. This usually reflects the needs of particular retail sectors and the image a store hopes to achieve.

There are two extreme styles of layout:

The Grid Layout
Supermarkets are the experts at implementing this design. It is a simple layout that attempts to ensure that 100 per cent of customers see 100 per cent of product:

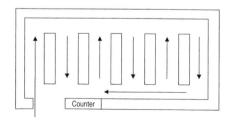

Informal or Boutique Layout
This design is common in smaller stores. The leading clothing retailers are very skilled at getting consumers

to flow around an informal layout:

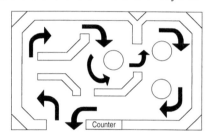

Between these two extremes there is a range of variations in layout, all of which work for different styles of retailing.

2 Locate your checkouts to direct customer flow.

The position of checkouts is critical in establishing how customers will flow around your store. When entering a store the general reaction is to walk away from the checkout. If the location of the checkout is wrong, you may find that you have obstructed half your products from the customers.

As a general rule in Australia, New Zealand and the United Kingdom, we are accustomed to keeping to the left. It is therefore advisable to try to establish a clockwise customer flow, finishing with a service counter at the entrance.

The worst scenario is to place a service counter in the major sight line which creates a direct runway to the checkout and reduces browse shopping considerably.

3 Bounce customers around your store.

Your aim should be to encourage movement of customers throughout your entire store. The placement of products or departments is the key to doing this. Here's how…

Review your customers' shopping lists—what are the most common items purchased? It is these that you should place at regular intervals around the store. In this way you force customers to visit all parts of the site. For example, consider the strategic placement of the following basic shopping list items—often referred to as 'anchor' products:

1. Milk	4. Toilet paper
2. Bread	5. Detergent
3. Sugar	6. Coffee

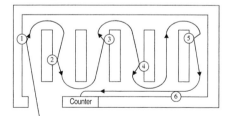

4 Maximise the use of sight lines.

Sight lines are essential in all styles of layout, but are far more important in a boutique layout than in a grid

design. Positive, appealing sightlines will draw customers around your store. Sightlines should use colour,

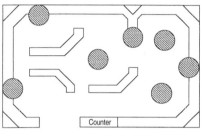

 Critical sight lines throughout the store

lighting, and product effectively to attract the customer throughout the store.

5 Develop destination departments.

Entice customers to various parts of the store by developing and strategically placing destination departments in the corners of your store and at the furthest points from the entrance and exit. Promote these departments and become famous for them—The Power Tool Department (hardware store), The Seedling or Bedding Plant Department (garden centre), The Ski Department (sports clothes), The In-house Deli (supermarket).

How to improve your 'first impression' image

In the eyes of the customer, perception is reality and your store's first-up image is important in this regard. Research shows that a customer captures up to 70 per cent of a store's image as a result of those first impressions gained at that initial shopping encounter—and those first impressions are absorbed within the first ten seconds! Which is why retailers should take steps to ensure that first impressions… quality impressions, are lasting impressions.

1 Understand the meaning of 'image'.

A leading authority on image, Bobbie Gee of Bobbie Gee Enterprises in California, has worked extensively with many retailers throughout the world and has standards by which customers can identify and judge a company's image. She claims that customers make their assessment on such factors as, in priority order:

- Your team's appearance
- First impressions of the store from outside
- First impressions of your displays
- The quality of your product
- The way your team approaches the consumer
- Checkouts
- Hygiene in your store
- The advertisements you use in the marketplace
- How you answer the telephone
- How you deal with complaints
- How you are perceived in the community
- Customers seeing your product before they get to the display.

2 Set your store's standards.

Bobby Gee encourages all retailers to set standards in each of the above areas and to ensure that all staff are familiar with them and abide by them.

Standards are always set at the top by the management team. The rest of the team will meet these requirements, although few will excel them. This means you must set your company's standards for behaviour and dress code reasonably high. Remember, too, you and your team will often be judged outside of work hours as well as during trading hours.

Do not put anything down to chance when it comes to an individual's perceptions. You should aim to have a consistent image and this can only be achieved through a written, disseminated image policy.

3 Develop your own image wheel.

Working on the principle that
Image + Reputation = Profit
is the key to a retailer's success, Bobbie Gee in her workshops with

retailers develops 'the image wheel'—if you want to influence the way customers look at your business, you will need to focus positively on these areas:

Your self image
Product quality
Corporate communications
Training programs
Customer relations
Development of standards
Your recruitment practices
The emotional condition of your business
How you get involved in community affairs
Your dependability
Visual image
Personal image
The owner's ego.

 ## Work from an image checklist.

By reference to your policy standards, develop a checklist which focuses on different image issues within your store. Refer to it on a daily basis. See 'How to make a positive impression in ten seconds' on page 18 for details.

 ## Always see your store as your customer sees it.

In terms of your store's image, always remember these three vital points:

- The impressions we gain from the world around us are based on our

Management Memo

Elophanto do not bite, mosquitoes do. It is not the big things that ruin us. It is the little ones. That is definitely true of image. It is all the little things we fail to give attention to that rob us of success. [54]

five senses. Research tells us that customers' first impressions are gained through:

Sight	83	%
Hearing	11	%
Smell	3.5	%
Touch	1.5	%
Taste	1	%

- A customer's first impression is gained in only ten seconds. The customer may give you, the retailer, a second chance. You will rarely get a third chance if you don't get it right!

- Customers always remember vividly the worst impression, not the best impression. You, as a retailer, always have to improve on that worst first impression. Your challenge is to know what must be improved upon.

The key is to see and think like your customer. Put yourself in your customer's shoes. Through your own senses, absorb what's on offer as you enter and move about your store daily. What you note may not at first seem important in your eyes because it's all so familiar to you, but it may well be a different image to a customer.

How to improve your 'last impressions' image

One of the most critical aspects of your business is what impresses a customer upfront, immediately upon entering your store—their 'first impressions'. Indeed, research shows that 70 per cent of store impressions are first impressions. We also know that 20 per cent of store impressions are 'last impressions'—gained as the customer leaves the premises. For this reason, it is important for retailers to set image standards at the checkout and on the customers' journey to their cars...

1 Set standards that your team can adhere to.

You must set staff guidelines for last impressions, just as you should for first impressions. Commit such standards to print and produce a checklist so that you can monitor these requirements. Once you have set standards, these become the levels of quality that all the team must consistently achieve.

There are a number of areas that leave a lasting impression on consumers. Your 'last impressions' policy should address them...

- Hygiene at the checkout
- The number of products you promote at the checkout
- Price strategy for products at the checkout
- How customers are greeted at the checkout
- How you add-on sell at the counter
- The visual appearance of your business behind the register
- Appearance of staff
- Services offered at the checkout
- How you provide extra services to the disabled, the aged and parents with small children
- How you gift wrap
- How you bag fill
- Cleanliness of the car park.

2 Make somebody accountable.

The key to success is to ensure someone is made accountable for standards of housekeeping at the checkout. The accountable person should check the counter on a regular basis during the day. If this area is neglected, you will find that clutter will accumulate around the counter until the close of trade. For the customer—these are last and lasting impressions!

3 Ask customers what they want at the counter.

Customers, of course, require space at the checkout to handle the products they have purchased, but may also have other needs. Have you ever surveyed your customers on their checkout needs? Those retailers that have, found that people wanted:

- Aisles wide enough for wheelchairs
- Express lane checkouts
- Alternative checkouts as full-service checkouts, e.g. wrap facilities, cheque writing facilities
- Some checkout points that don't have magazines on display nearby.

- Checkouts where children's products are not available—especially confectionery.
- Help in getting bulky items to their cars.

4 Promote one product at the counter.

Every counter should have at least one product, and no more than three, at the counter that might be proactively promoted by a person at the checkout. The key is to find a product that the majority of people want or need at that particular time. We tend to underestimate the value of the counter as a profit centre.

5 Have a specific management policy at the counter.

Australian Supermarketing magazine provides the following guidelines:

- View the checkout as a separate profit centre. Recognise it is one of the more important departments in the store.
- Use the 'space to share' method to allocate space. Assign space to categories based on their sales and profit contribution in a particular season, e.g. chocolate bar sales increase during cold weather and therefore require more promotional space at this time.
- Take full advantage of the sales potential of confectionery and magazines which account for 78 per cent of checkout volume.
- Merchandise similar items together, thus making it easier for your customers to locate what they are looking for. So, for example, position batteries next to battery-powered items.
- Put your best sellers in the best locations within their categories.

> ## Management Memo
>
> The two commandments for maintaining your image are:
> 1. Remain true to your beliefs. They are responsible for the success you are now enjoying.
> 2. Never sacrifice long-term image for short-term gain. [55]

Take advantage of their customer appeal. Place them in a sight line.

- Merchandise consistently: do not alternate. Customers only go through one checkout per visit.
- Focus on your program, not your fixtures. Think 'Categories and Merchandising' first— then select fixtures that accommodate your program.
- Emphasis in-store maintenance. Assign one person to the responsibility of maintaining the checkout area.

6 Stress the need for consistent housekeeping at the counter.

It is critical that the checkout is kept clean and tidy at all times, for last impressions are lasting impressions. Accordingly:

- Do not store products at the checkout.
- Keep the checkout dusted every day.
- Do not clutter with coffee mugs, litter or irrelevant products.
- Never eat at the checkout or in view of customers.
- Never leave traded-in or returned products sitting at the counter.
- Check counter three times daily.

Image is the name of the game. Every customer sees your checkouts. Be confident that they leave a good impression.

How to keep your store clean

Stores such as McDonalds and the Disneyland enterprise have built much of their reputations on cleanliness. Customers judge retailers on how clean their stores are. The key is not being clean—but consistently clean.

 Commit your team to cleanliness.

Your staff must be committed to keeping the store clean. Everyone needs to be involved. Develop a policy statement on the level of cleanliness you require in the store and ensure all staff know of their responsibilities in this area.

 Focus on critical areas.

The role of the manager is to ensure the aisles are free of clutter and litter, and safe at all times, and that displays are secure alongside the aisles. Monitor also those other untidy troublespots—behind counters, in corners, visible storage areas, restrooms, the parking lot, corridors, and so on. In particular, the level of cleanliness is critical in those areas where food is involved. Regularly check toilets, walls, floors, working surfaces and windows…

Toilets

There are those customers who judge a store on the cleanliness of its toilets. To show the customer you care, make sure you have a visible worksheet displayed in the toilet area:

Date	Name of cleaner	Time toilets checked	Signature of checker

Walls

In food areas, walls should be cleaned using hot water (above 60°C) and a recommended detergent. Scrub the walls to remove any dirt, rinse the wall using warm clean water, before applying a sanitiser solution to areas where food comes into contact with the wall. Leave this to react on the wall for the recommended contact time, and then rinse the wall again and allow the wall to air dry.

Floors

Floors must be safe for customers to walk on. Check daily for potential hazards and slippery surfaces. As a rule the floor should be cleaned each day when the store is closed. Food areas should be cleaned according to Food Safe Regulations.

Working surfaces

Again, these areas are critically important in food outlets, especially in areas where food is prepared.

A Cleaning and Sanitation Worksheet is essential in food outlets and desirable in other forms of retailing. An example of a typical worksheet is provided below from the Johnson and Johnson Safety and Hygiene Manual.

Windows

The first feature a customer sees is usually the store windows and door. Who hasn't been put off by fingerprints on windows and glass door panels, and blow flies, moths and other insects lying dead at the base of the window? Check your windows daily to ensure they create the correct first impression for customers.

3 Implement a best practice philosophy.

Make cleaning an accepted habit in your retail store. Best practice means that you:

- Have an established cleaning schedule that is adhered to. This

Management Memo

Research into cleaning programs carried out in the United States revealed the following:

97% of stores empty litter/trash bins
66% wash their windows once a week
52% clean their toilets daily
49% mop their floors daily
21% wax their floors once a month.

The opportunity exists to impress the customer with your cleanliness. [56]

includes sweeping, vacuuming, mopping, and waxing relevant floors, and washing windows and emptying litter bins on a set rota.

- Straighten displays every day and walk the store to check on its safety.
- Promote cleanliness in store meetings and staff newsletters.
- Repaint surfaces when the store begins to look stale. This may mean you may have to repaint your front door very frequently.
- Keep floors dry and use non-skid mats. If you must clean when the store is open then use caution signs to warn the customer.
- Check that the outside of your store is safe and tidy.

CLEANING AND SANITATION WORKSHEET

Location	Mon	Tues	Wed	Thu	Fri	Sat	Sun	Required frequency
Week commencing:								
Walls								☐ Daily ☐ Weekly ☐ Monthly
Floors								☐ Daily ☐ Weekly ☐ Monthly
Windows								☐ Daily ☐ Weekly ☐ Monthly

Insert name here.   Insert signature here.

How to walk the floor and talk to customers

The role of a retail manager can be compared with that of a maître d'hôtel. You should meet the guests—your customers, welcome them, and ensure they leave with a positive feeling about your business. Retailers should set aside at least one hour a day to walk the store and talk to customers. It is the most under-used of skills, but one of the most important and rewarding parts of the job...

1 Break the ice— and start talking.

Many owners are reluctant to walk the floor and to talk to customers because they find it difficult or get embarrassed about starting a conversation.

The simplest way to overcome this problem is to take out a sample of products and ask customers to try them. This is always a good discussion-starter and can easily lead to other matters, such as what they think about your store or the service.

An alternative approach is to meet customers where the action is— try cleaning the tables in a restaurant or working on bag filling at the checkout—ideal locations for starting up a conversation.

2 Be open about your intention.

When walking the floor, be candid about your mission—introduce yourself to customers as the owner and that you're seeking their views about the store and its operation. You'll find that most of them are

happy to provide you with ideas on how you could improve service.

3 Vary the time of day you walk the store.

Owners traditionally walked the store at opening time. This is still a strong tradition in Japan where retailing continues to be a very formal arrangement. However, you will gain more from varying the time of day that you do your rounds since you will more likely gather a more disparate slice of customer views.

4 Share your findings with your team.

Your team will be interested in the comments you have gathered. Make sure they are aware of why you walk the floor and be sure you talk to them as you do so. This will relax them and make them feel you are part of their team. Remember also, if your feedback warrants praise of individual performances, do so in public, but reprimand in private.

WINNING
OUR CUS
MANAGING
YOUR STORE
OMOTING
PRODUCTS
NAGING
BUSINESS
NDEX
125

AISLES
See also: 116, 238, 240

How to manage your aisles

The aisles are the areas of 'pathway' or floor space used by customers to reach the products in your store. Customers expect you to provide this access in a safe condition.

1 Make your aisles customer-friendly.

The aim of the aisle is to facilitate customer movement and to encourage customers to reach all departments and access all products in your store. The minimum width of the aisle should be one metre, and it should be kept clear of stock and clutter at all times, especially when shelf filling has to take place during opening hours.

2 Ensure your aisles are safe.

The role of the manager is to ensure the aisles are free of clutter and safe at all times. Walk the aisles on a regular basis during the day to ensure that they are indeed safe. Check also the safety of the displays alongside the aisles. Take steps to ensure your staff also know their responsibilities in terms of maintaining clean and safe customer passageways and that they do not store products in the aisles during trading hours.

3 Maintain standards via a checklist.

Compile a checklist similar to the sample below which focuses on aisle safety. In your walks around the store, regularly complete the checklist, and report your findings back to staff members:

IMPROVING OUR CUSTOMER FLOW IN THE AISLES				
	Needs lots of work	Needs some work	Looks good	We've got it right
1. The aisles are well-defined.				
2. The aisle width is correct.				
3. We keep the aisles clear at all times.				
4. Customers can visit all parts of the store.				
5. Our side aisles are the right width.				
6. We don't clutter the racetrack or aisles.				
7. The floor is vacuumed/swept daily.				
8. The racetrack and aisles are safe.				

How to make sure your displays are safe

One of the common devices used by retailers to shift product is the stand-alone display, built to catch the customer's eye. Often, however, the more eye-catching the display, the more risky it can be in terms of customer safety. The last thing you want is a display capable of collapsing if a shopping trolley or basket accidentally hits it. As well, customers come in all shapes and sizes, so that you need to ensure your displays are especially safe where the less-able and children are involved.

 Remember that safety overrides cleverness.

A display may look clever, even ingenious, but if it is not safe you could end up, at best with a mess to clean up, at worst with serious injury, or even legal action against the store. Be advised: safety is a priority with store displays.

 Become a bricklayer.

When building displays using boxes or cartons of product, you should do so in the same way that a bricklayer places bricks on top of each other. Bricks, like cartons, are overlapped so that each brick is securely bound to the next one. This gives extra strength to the total structure. Use this principle when constructing your product displays.

 Undertake regular safety checks.

Make sure you regularly and methodically check your displays for safety—at minimum every morning before the first customer arrives. Never leave unsafe displays in position with customers around. It is your responsibility to provide a safe working environment for your team, and a safe shopping experience for your customers.

Consider your own safety.

Too often retail staff are seen standing on boxes and unsafe structures to build displays. Health and safety regulations demand that safety steps or platforms be made available for team members to use and that they are advised as to why such aids are made available.

  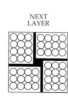

CUSTOMER'S VIEW   BOTTOM LAYER   NEXT LAYER

How to introduce texture into your displays

The majority of retailers rightly consider placement of products, lighting, and what type of props they need when it comes to building displays. Leading retailers, however, consider all aspects—and one area that is never overlooked is that of texture...

1 Know the impact texture can create.

According to Terry Curry, Managing Director of Predictions in Victoria, Australia, texture in displays can be suggestive, reinforce the message you are trying to get across, create a mood, help define the target market, impact on the colours you are using, and interact with your lighting system. Clearly, it's important when thinking about displays, to think texture.

2 Know what textures to use for effect.

If you want your display to be feminine and sensuous, then silk and satin are some of the best background materials to use. If you want your product to look expensive, then velvet is one material that will provide this desired background effect.

Many stores will require a masculine or outdoor feel to their product displays. In such cases, you should consider using burlap, course linen, nobbly wools, and tweeds. And for a more natural look try roughly sawn wood, mulch, sawdust, pebbles, gravel, sand, stone, brick, or ground up cork.

3 Match surface to the colour of your product.

Remember that smooth and shiny surfaces will make the products look lighter as such surfaces reflect the light on to the displayed items. Rough surfaces will absorb the light and make the products look heavier and darker.

4 Allow your staff to experiment.

Textures change, as they are part of fashion—for example, the 'bamboo' look may be very much in vogue for a period and becomes a texture commonly used throughout the entire industry. A year later, another texture will be in fashion. Allow your team to experiment using different textured materials.

How to manage product placement in your store

To maximise sales across the entire store, retailers must learn to position products strategically. Placement is based on an understanding of their classification. Products can be grouped into a number of categories based on their positioning in the store. Those categories include Known Value, Non Known Value, Purpose, Browse, Impulse, Link, Male/Female Products...

1 Be familiar with product categories and how to place them in your store.

Known value products.
These are products where the customer believes they know the exact price. Petrol, cigarettes, milk, and newspapers are typical known value products. If price is a major motivator for customers to visit your store, then known value products should be placed in primary sight lines. If price is not your major drawcard, then place these products in secondary sight lines, i.e. positions in the store that are not noticed when the customer walks into your store.

Non known value products.
These are products where the majority of customers do not know the exact price. They make their primary buying decisions based on wants, quality, benefits, and service. If you are not a price-motivated business, then you should be placing non known value products in the sight line.

Purpose products.
Purpose products are those on your

customers' shopping lists. They are the reason customers come to you. Some purpose products will also be known value products.

In a supermarket, for example, purpose products would include:

Tea	Baked beans	Bananas
Coffee	Cornflakes	Milk
Lettuce	Dog food	Eggs
Tomatoes	Toilet Paper	Carrots

These products should be positioned in the store in such a way that customers are forced to 'bounce' around the entire store to encourage customer spending in other categories.

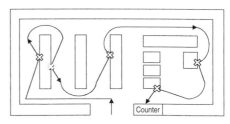

Counter

∷ 'Purpose products' positioned to bounce customers around the store.

Browse products.
Browse products are those items where customers need time and space to make a buying decision. Common browse products include:

Books
CDs and videos
Birthday cards
Seeds

Herbs
Power tools
Magazines
Paints

Such products should ideally be placed away from the major customer racetrack and in areas where the customers can take their time and have the space to browse-shop. Aisles need to be larger around browse products to ensure customers feel comfortable while they are shopping, and are not jostled by other shoppers.

Impulse products.
These are the products that customers do not plan to buy when they go shopping but can make up 60 per cent of a purchasing spend. To maximise sales, these products need to be placed in major sightlines. Due to the quantity of impulse items most retailers stock, it is important to rotate impulse lines on a regular basis to ensure all products are seen by customers and have a chance to sell.

Link products.
Link or cross-merchandised products are allied products and are ideal 'add-on' sale items. Examples of this category of merchandise include:

Flim alongside cameras
Razor blades alongside razors
Video tapes alongside video players
Plants alongside pots
Strawberries alongside cream
Batteries alongside toys.

In managing cross-merchandised products, you will often take two products from different product categories and place them on display next to each other. Cross-

> ## Management Memo
>
> Retailers must convey the message they intend. If you have chosen an upmarket product range, your store must reflect this. It must be clear to the customer who you are, what you are selling, and in what price bracket you operate. [57]

merchandised displays show the customer you understand their needs and care for them.

Remember these key points associated with link selling:

- Cross-merchandising should use a minimum of two selected products.
- Cross-merchandised displays must have signage that clearly links the products together.
- Displays must be topical and seasonal.
- Whenever possible, price specials should be linked to add-ons.
- Displays must be kept simple to ensure all customers understand and get the same message.
- Words used on cross-merchandised displays should be positive (i.e. 'Remember: you will also need...', 'Secrets of Success'...).

Cross-merchandised products should increase sales by at least 30 per cent.

Male or Female products.
Very strong female and male categories should be clearly separated. Males especially can get embarrassed if they find they have strolled into a female department by mistake.

How to use vertical merchandising to maximise your sales

Vertical merchandising is a form of shelf layout that allows items to be displayed in product categories in a vertical arrangement…

1 Display products for maximum customer impact.

Customers like to get into a position where they can view the entire range of a product category from one position. Vertical merchandising provides customers with that opportunity…

COFFEE	TEA	OTHER HOT DRINKS

But, within the vertical presentation, there are advantageous positions for products. Research shows that the majority of products sell at a sight-and-take position. The sight-and-take position is between chin and navel of the average-height shopper. The typical customer in most retail stores is a woman, which means that the sight-and-take position is between 150cm and 180cm from the floor, and its superiority as a selling position is apparent from the following research findings:

Position	Units sold
Stretch shelf	70
Sight-and-take shelf	100
Bend shelf	55
Floor level	20

Research shows if you take the same product at the same price and move it vertically into the sight-and-take position, then sales can improve dramatically.

2 Making vertical merchandising work for you.

Adherance to some basic rules can increase your sales through vertical merchandising:

- On the premise that you cannot sell air, construct your shelving to provide the minimum gaps at the sight-and-take level. Whenever you identify gaps, fill them as soon as possible or, if you do not have adequate stock to fill the gaps, space the product evenly across the category. Leave no air.

- Topical and seasonal products

should be displayed at the sight-and-take level to sell them faster.

- Display the most profitable sizes of specific products at the sight-and-take level.
- Purpose and best-seller products may need to be displayed on the stretch and end shelves.
- If out-of-season products need to be displayed, then display them at floor level.

3 Break the rules when you have to.

There are times when you will need to break the rules of vertical merchandising. Such instances include:

- Display products that say 'Caution. Keep out of the reach of children' at least 1.2 metres above ground level if they don't have child-proof caps.
- Bring children's products down to their eye level.
- Keep heavy products on the lower shelves to facilitate safe lifting of the product.

4 Be aware of security and size of stock.

Security and size of stock must be considered when positioning stock on shelves. For example, in retailing the greatest amount of stealing occurs along cosmetic aisles in supermarkets. These products need

Management Memo

It is vital for fixtures not only to be safe but also to look safe. Fixtures or displays that look unsafe will deter customers from selecting goods from them for fear of the fixture or goods falling. The fixtures should also be maintained in a safe condition. This includes checking for sharp edges, cracked or damaged shelves, particularly glass, and also for loose or damaged supports. [58]

to be positioned near the counter or within a major sight line. Smaller products are best located higher on the shelf in a sight line and larger items nearer the ground for easier lifting.

5 Adjust shelves to maximise sales.

Slatwall shopfittings allow you to adjust the shelving to the height you require to maximise sales.

The following example of a typical slatwall 'island' fixture allows you to adjust shelving to suit product size:

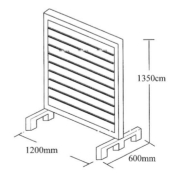

1350cm

1200mm

600mm

How to use horizontal merchandising to maximise your sales

Horizontal merchandising is a form of shelf layout that allows products to be displayed in a horizontal arrangement...

1 Be aware of the drawbacks of horizontal layouts.

There are two obvious problems associated with horizontal merchandising. The first is that the customer has to walk along the gondola to see one range of product, do the same to see the next range, and so on.

As well, one product range will be in a prime selling position while others, positioned high up, or low down on the shelving, are in disadvantaged selling positions.

COFFEE	⟵⟶
TEA	⟵⟶
OTHER HOT DRINKS	⟵⟶
MORE HOT DRINKS	⟵⟶
OTHER BEVERAGES	⟵⟶

2 Know when to use horizontal merchandising.

Horizontal merchandising is best used when you have one product that can only be displayed on one level due to its weight or unique characteristics. Typical products that are displayed horizontally include palletised items, indoor plants, large outdoor plants, bulky products, and furniture.

3 Design horizontal systems that sell.

Progressive plant retailers have developed display tables for plant material and their techniques may be adaptable for other retailer situations.

Hexagonal indoor plant tables make an attractive indoor plant display area.

Slimline sloping display tables are ideal narrow units where space is at a premium.

Octagonal units are practical and interesting displays for shrubs, alpines or other merchandise according to season. They can be made with or without a point of sale ledge, irrigation-carrying structure, and mesh windbreak.

Traditional display carts feature an eye-catching style with spoked wheels and canopy.

Management Memo

Some points on merchandising fresh product, using horizontal merchandising techniques:

- Produce should be displayed in family groupings.
- Colours should be used to maximise the effect.
- The level of fill along the bench should be consistent and even.
- Price tickets should be used to 'sell!' the product
- Supplier point of sale materials create interest and provide customer information. [59]

If you build your own merchandising tables, however, remember the following points:

- Make the tops separate from the legs if possible, so that the tables can be displayed at varying heights by using legs of different height.
- Ensure you provide a ledge for point of sale material.
- If timber, use treated timber. If metal, use galvanised material—you want the table to last.
- Do not make the table too large. Every product should be within an arm's reach of the average-height customer.
- Use materials that are easy to keep clean. The less maintenance required the better.

 4 ## Consider the use of merchandising tables.

Retailers can now purchase a variety of horizontal merchandising tables, made out of wood or galvanised metal. They can be purchased as ready-made items or to be assembled by the retailer.

How to manage relays

Retailing requires that products be presented to customers in a way that invites purchase. Products are usually arranged on shelves in relays, where one category of product is displayed within its grouping along the shelf (e.g. breakfast cereals). Experience and skill are required to manage these relays and in presenting product on the shelves in retail stores. The aim is to set up the shelf so that, logically, it makes sense to the customer and, strategically, it maximises the return per linear metre to the retailer...

Ensure logic dominates.

The key to shelf management is to place products in categories that make sense to the customer. The question is—what makes sense? For example, you may place breakfast cereals together and display grapefruits in the fresh produce area. The customer may be purchasing for breakfast—and the placement of cereals with grapefruit could seem, to the customer at least, a logical category arrangement.

For this reason, before setting up a category it is important, within reason, to think like a customer—which is why there are three accepted styles of relay management used in retailing today...

Consider like-by-like relays.

A like-by-like layout is where the retailer groups products together across the whole block. For example, all the 'beef' cat foods from different suppliers are placed next to each other, as are 'chicken', as are 'fish'.

The adoption of like-by-like relays saves time for retailers when filling shelves, and they look good. Retailers can layout the block based on gross profit return and have some control over the customer flow.

This layout allows the consumer to price shop relatively easily and, if the retailer is out of stock, the shopper is still able to choose similar products.

The disadvantages to the retailer are that the customer price shops and does less browse shopping. The consumer may find the layout boring as all similar products are together, and often misses new lines and alternative choices.

3 Consider like-by-like in a corporate block.

This style presents manufacturers in corporate blocks and then the like-by-like layout is superimposed. This system is easy for the retailer to manage, looks good, and allows the retailer to allocate specific space to a manufacturer. It is more difficult for the customer to price shop and the retailer's image can be upgraded or downgraded, depending on the positioning of the manufacturer's products, e.g. high gross profit items displayed at ends of gondolas.

These days, consumers are trained into brand shopping so this layout may be convenient for them. The opportunity also exists to highlight products within a brand. The disadvantage here is that customers may keep selecting a brand that has a low return to the retailer and the positioning of manufacturers means some get an excellent placing while others miss out.

4 Consider corporate company blocking.

This is where the manufacturer decides how their product will be displayed (often called 'book and order' category management).

The advantage to the retailer is that the manufacturer will provide the full merchandising kit and total professional backing by the supplier. The consumer can easily find promotional products and gets a good feeling about the image of the store because of the professionalism of the presentations.

The disadvantage is that the retailer relies on the company representative (some are excellent, others are variable). The manufacturer or supplier has a monopoly on the position and if retailers are not careful, they may become overloaded with stock.

If manufacturers or suppliers are developing corporate company blocks you may also find that as a retailer your return is lower, as the supplier will take a larger return.

5 Focus on... when laying out a category.

A category is a 'distinctive manageable group of products or

> **Management Memo**
>
> There are four types of products within a category. These can be classified as impulse or opportunity goods, company and consumer image builders, convenience items, and consumer destination items. Consumers and retailers perceive them differently: [60]
>
> | | Consumer Perception | Retailer Perception |
> |---|---|---|
> | Opportunity Goods | Low | Low |
> | Image Builders | Low | High |
> | Convenience Products | High | Low |
> | Destination Products | High | High |

services that consumers perceive to be inter-related', e.g. breakfast department, the bathroom, or patio garden. When laying out a category, consider the following:

- Segmented share of each product within the category (% sales of bath rugs versus shower caps)
- Trends within the category (colour, style)
- Trends in your local marketplace
- Publicity and promotions for specific products, e.g. in lifestyle magazines read by your customers
- What you want to promote.

6 Establish rules for product presentation.

Set a standard for presenting products on shelves and ensure that all staff are aware of the need to be consistent in meeting these guidelines. For example:

- Position price tickets uniformly.
- Face all products the same way.
- Ensure all products are spotless.
- Keep the shelves clean.
- Remove damaged products immediately.
- Maintain all products within date codes.
- Position all products correctly.
- Leave no gaps visible along the shelf, especially in the sightline.
- Allow no gaps between shelves, especially in the sightline.

How to face products correctly

In relay merchandising, facing is the way products are presented on the shelf to the customer by the retailer. The aim of merchandising is to maximise sales per linear metre of shelving and, for this reason, how well products are faced will have a significant impact on sales and stockturn...

1 Face forward.

Most products have a front and a back. For a number of reasons, products should always be faced labels to the front:

Firstly, the manufacturer has gone to a great deal of effort and research to ensure that the 'face' of the product has 'eye' appeal. It has been designed to entice the prospective buyer to pick up the item.

Secondly, many products have user instructions on the back of the item. Prospective buyers need to look at these instructions to make a buying decision. If you face forward, the reasoning is that the customers have to pick the product up and reverse it to read it—and once the product is in their hands, they are more likely to put it in their basket or trolley than put it back on the shelf.

Finally, a uniform shelf looks more pleasing to the eye and more likely to be browse-shopped than a shelf that looks like it has been stacked randomly and with little thought.

And, of course, facing forward improves your store's image.

2 Get the minimum length of facing correct.

If you wish to promote a product on the shelf, the width of facing on that shelf is critical and, in this regard, two theories are currently in vogue:

Theory One: If you wish to sell a product you must, as a minimum facing, have the width of facing the same as the height of the product.

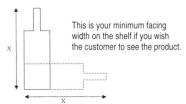

This is your minimum facing width on the shelf if you wish the customer to see the product.

Theory Two: If you wish to sell a product you must, as a minimum facing, present three of the products if you want the prospective buyer to select it. UK research has shown that, if you drop the facing down to two or even one product, then its sales decline dramatically.

3 Get the maximum length of facing correct.

Research in the United States and the United Kingdom reveals that, with the majority of products, if the facing exceeds more than eleven identical products on the shelf, the prospective buyer becomes suspicious, assumes you have bought incorrectly, or something is wrong with the item, certainly the product is not selling very well—and the result is that sales drop off. This theory of eleven facings does not apply to products purchased every day (e.g. toilet paper) or very topical promotional items (e.g. launch day for a smash video like *Titanic*).

 ### Vary facing when appropriate.

Most retailers do not have enough shelf space to put every product at a minimum of three facings. The practical reality is that you may have to utilise varied facings to maximise sales...

Face fewer than three of a product when:

- the product is out of season.
- you are running down your stock levels of that particular item.
- you wish to promote another product over this product.
- the item is out of fashion.
- it is such a bulky item that it does not need a facing of three to catch the eye of a prospective buyer.

Face more than three of a product when.

- it is a trendy item.
- the product is in season.
- the item is featuring in the media.
- it is being promoted by your store.
- suppliers are doing a major promotion.

 ### Compile planograms.

In the early days of facing it is very much a trial-and-error exercise to get it right. Once you have settled on a

successful facing ratio, you can then draw up a plan for your faced shelving on paper or computer. This is often called a planogram.

However, remember that in retailing what is correct today will not necessarily be right tomorrow, so you may have to keep changing your facing ratios to maximise sales.

Facing ratios will change when:

- you are in a seasonal industry sector such as gardening.
- consumer habits and fashions have changed.
- the media mentions products in a positive or negative way.
- manufacturers and suppliers undertake promotional campaigns.
- you widen or narrow the range of products you have on offer to the consumer.
- the life of the product on the shelf matures in relation to its shelf life.

 ### Consider indenting.

Indenting is the process where the retailer physically removes a product from the shelf to give the impression that some customer has already purchased an item from this range. The theory is that, if the relay is depleted, then customers are more confident to shop the range. In other words, indenting encourages shoppability. The practice normally involves removing one product, in a slow moving line, about every three metres along the length of the shelf.

How to manage your product range

One of the most challenging areas of retail management is dealing successfully with the product range. The most profitable businesses understand the market and select a range of products to meet the demands of their customer base. Given that four out of five buying decisions are made in the store, it is important for retailers to get their range right...

1 Understand the meaning of range.

Product range is usually considered in terms of 'width' and 'depth' of products held in your business. Width is the number of categories held by your particular retail store. For example, in a menswear shop, your width may cover:

Shirts	Trousers	Suits
Ties	Sweaters	Underwear
Socks	Jackets	Shoes.

Depth covers how deep you deal within each category. Depth covers areas such as:

Brands	Colours	Price Points
Number of Sizes		Number of Styles.

If your width were shirts, your depth would include:

Makes of shirts stocked
Colours of shirts stocked
Price points stocked
Styles of shirts stocked
Patterns of shirts.

2 Know how to manage your range.

The challenge for retail managers relates to stock rotation and identifying when things are going right or wrong with the range.

The majority of companies tend to get the width right, and even if the category is wrong, it is usually identified very quickly in most businesses.

When things go wrong, the problems normally relate to the depth of the product range, and it often takes longer to identify where this problem is.

If depth has become a concern, ask if you have become too shallow or too deep. As a general rule you should be deep in your core range and shallow in allied products.

For example, if a garden centre is well regarded for selling plants, it should be deep in the plant species it sells, the sizes it sells, the varieties, and so on. An allied product handled by such a garden centre would be slug and snail control. In this retail sector, this item is a companion product and not the core product—and the customers prefer you to be shallow in this area, i.e. they do not want depth in slug and snail control items; they want the one you believe to be the best for doing the job. The customer would also expect your team to promote this specific product.

VINNING
OUR CUS

**MANAGING
YOUR STORE**

MOTING
R PRODUCTS

NAGING
BUSINESS

NDEX

139

3 Always be prepared to change.

Retailing is a changing industry—it changes with seasons, fashions, events in the calendar, and trends. Your range needs to change with customer habits. Accept that as a fact of retailing life.

4 Keep your range performance under review.

Successful retailers analyse their range constantly to make sure they are in tune with customer requirements.

Various approaches may be taken to such analysis. Some retailers analyse stockturn rates, or sales per square metre, gross margins, or stock levels, and so on.

Whichever system you use, the key is to reduce the space demanded by products that are not performing and to increase the space for those that are performing.

5 Be prepared to bring a new product into your range.

The challenge for many retailers is how to introduce a new product into the range. Some guidelines for introducing a new product include:

- Talk to competitors, colleagues, and suppliers, and read trade magazines and product reviews so that you are fully advised of what is happening in the marketplace and what new products are available or in demand.
- Shop the competition and see if they are selling the new product.

Management Memo

Whether or not you decide to stock certain products depends on the current thinking of your customer base. Remember...

A fad is something that is in vogue for a few weeks. Fads may be based on the latest film, pop star, television program, or news item.

A fashion lasts about two years. The clothing industry survives on fashion and changes in the way we accept colours and cuts, how we dress ourselves and decorate our homes.

A trend develops over a decade. Trends could include changes in home construction and furnishing, gardening and landscaping, and social habits. [62]

If they are, monitor how well it is selling.

- Have a 'Requests Book' to monitor whether your customers are asking for the product.
- Consider whether the new product will add a fresh dimension to your width and depth. If it does, you may need to consider deleting a slow moving item from your existing range to accommodate the new product, otherwise you could run out of space.
- Ask relevant questions:
  - Is the price competitive in your marketplace?
  - Has the product a proven track record?
  - How will the supplier be promoting the product?
  - What sales backup is the supplier offering with the product?
  - Will it create more profit for you?

How to get the most out of best sellers

Each product category in your store has a best seller. The product will not necessarily be the cheapest or lowest gross profit item, but it will be the favourite product purchased by your customers in that category. You can use the best seller concept to your advantage if you introduce some simple management strategies...

1 Identify your best sellers in each category.

To take advantage of the best seller concept, you'll need to know the best seller in each category. For some categories, for example, beer, the best-selling product will probably stay the same throughout the year. For other products, such as fruit in a greengrocers, the best seller will change with the seasons and you would need to analyse your sales results on a monthly basis.

2 Position best sellers strategically in the category layout.

Do not use the prime location in the category layout for best sellers because they will sell anyway. Put your best sellers in what would normally be a lower selling position in the layout. They will help you increase sales in the overall category.

Customers need to see your best sellers, and shelftalkers will help you achieve this. Use your prime selling positions for impulse sales.

3 Have your team promote the best sellers.

Hilary Kahn, the Melbourne-based retail consultant, suggests you can increase your bottom line by getting your team to recommend the best sellers...

Compile best seller lists for staff.
If yours is a large store with many categories, prepare a list of best sellers each month and make it available to all team members. This gives them the extra confidence and the opportunity to sell in categories other than their own.

Train the team to sell best sellers.
When customers are unsure about what product to select within a category, get your team to promote best sellers as one of their selling options. A great selling opener is always 'Our best seller is ...'. It will give the customer confidence in the salesperson as it shows they have knowledge of the products.

One outcome of this is customers start to trust your team member and will then readily accept that person's advice.

Train your team to sell up.
In many situations customers will purchase the best seller simply on a team member's advice—or allow the team member to sell up to one of the store's more profitable lines.

 Educate your customers.

Consumers like to buy best sellers. If they do not know a product category very well, they are happy to purchase best sellers since, when they are unsure, they seek comfort in conforming.

Use shelftalkers or general point of purchase signage to highlight best sellers. Such signage could say:

'Our best selling *x* this month is…'
'Our best seller!'
'The top selling *y* in our store'
'Our customers' favourite *z*'.

The important thing is that you are honest with your customer.

Management Memo

Best selling strategies work brilliantly in some retail sectors and are under-used in others.

The book and record industries have used this technique for many years with merchandising strategies that show the Top 10.

I recently worked with a retail client where we introduced the best selling strategy for the first time. Prior to my visit they were unaware of which products were their best sellers. Once we introduced the strategy and used shelftalkers, their sales of best sellers increased four-fold.

What was even more interesting was that the overall sales within the category also increased. I believe this was due to the consumer gaining more confidence and trust in the retailer. [63]

5 Match promotions with fact.

When introducing a best selling strategy, make sure your advertising, internal promotions, and sales team are giving the same message to the customer.

How to manage slow-moving products

Slow-moving products are often called 'dogs'. They are those items that just will not sell. Leave them on the shelf and they move out of date code, or become unfashionable, or just gather dust. You must become proactive in shifting slow-movers or they will eat into your bottom line...

1 Identify your slow-movers in each category.

Every product category has slow movers, where the stockturn is slower than planned. It is important for retailers to identify slow-movers because:

- in the food industry, they could cause food poisoning when they move out of date code.
- in the perishable non-food industry, they could cost you more money to maintain their shelf life than to throw away.
- they become dusty and reflect poorly on your store's image.
- they could become dated or old-fashioned, giving the customer the perception that you are not keeping up with trends in your industry sector.
- they will affect your overall bottom line if you do not sell them.
- they may become unstable or will not do the job they were intended for. This is common where chemicals are involved.

2 Manage your existing slow-movers.

Once you have identified your slow-movers, it's time to take action.

If in any way the product is not going to perform to the customers' expectations, then it should be taken off the shelf and recorded as shrinkage to the business.

On the other hand, if the product still has some value to the customer, then consider the following actions:

- Move the item to another location and monitor its sales. Perhaps the product is fine, but the location was wrong.
- Promote it using signage or, if it is already promoted with signage, change the signage. It may be the sign is sending out the wrong signals.
- Alter its price. The customer may perceive the item as being too cheap or too expensive. We often reduce the price when we should have increased it. So, try changing the price and monitor what happens.
- Promote the product to your loyal customers as an extra benefit.
- Try selling two for the price of one.
- Promote it to someone interested in that product range; for example, if you have stamp albums that do not sell, promote them to existing customers who you know collect stamps.
- Gift the product to customers who spend over a certain amount of money with you.
- Place the item in a dump bin—but for a limited time only.
- Offer the product to people collecting items for charity.

WINNING
OUR CUS
MANAGING
YOUR STORE
MOTING
R PRODUCTS
NAGING
BUSINESS
DEX
143

Vol. 1: 198, 340

- If none of those work, take it off the shelf and replace it with a money-making product.

3 Manage your products so you no longer have slow-movers.

Every product has a birthday. Your objective is to make sure no product celebrates a birthday in your store!

Compile a product life cycle strategy.
Plan a 'product life cycle' strategy for your store (see below) and take steps to ensure that products listed are sold within the stated time frames.

Make buyers responsible for slow-movers.
The critical person in this strategy is the store buyer. A buyer's role is to make three basic decisions:

How many products should be bought?
What retail price will we set?
What will be the stockturn of this product?

For example, for *Product x*

Units purchased:	100
Retail selling price:	$10
Product x life cycle:	10 weeks

On the basis of such considerations, the buyer passes the details on to the merchandiser who then manages the sale of the product. The merchandiser's objective is to have no product from this buying cycle in stock on the last day of the tenth week. By implementing a realistic product life cycle strategy you should eliminate most slow-movers.

4 Actively support your life cycle strategy.

To prevent a product continuing as a slow-mover, or to turn around its sluggish sales, your life cycle

> ## Management Memo
> You might think best selling categories would sell in poor locations. In my experience stores who have tested this by putting best selling categories in poor locations decimated unit sales, and changes were soon made to put the best sellers back into the best positions. [64]

strategy might be supported in the following way:

The first five weeks of the cycle should be based on merchandising considerations:
- Change the location of the product in the store.
- Change the signage.
- Change the display style.
- Check the product knowledge of the team.

Hopefully those initiatives will start moving the product.

If those actions prove ineffective, then the second half of the product life cycle should focus on financial decisions:
- Put the price up.
- Sell two for the price of one.
- Reduce your gross profit.
- As a last resort, sell at cost.

If any product is left on the last day of the final week, remove it from the shelves to make way for more profitable lines.

5 Empower people to make decisions.

Retail stores have 'dogs' on shelves because management is sometimes reluctant to empower their category supervisors to make decisions on moving the product. We should care less for the product itself and more about managing the product. Our objective must be to maximise sales per square metre. To achieve this, your team must be made responsible and given responsibility.

How to manage counter displays

The counter or checkout area is a key position in any retail store. It's a location visited by every customer. Unwisely, many retailers look on this facility as the final port of call for a customer who has already decided on a purchase and sees the counter as a position where the only operation that needs to take place is the transfer of money. But the counter also provides an opportunity to sell and reinforce your store's image...

1 See the counter as a profit centre.

Look at the counter as a department in its own right. Indeed, see it as a profit centre, an ideal location for selling since every customer who has purchased products will come to this location. For this reason, the counter presents a great opportunity to sell another item or two.

2 Select the right products for the counter.

Research carried out in the United States has shown that, if the correct product is displayed and promoted at the counter, sales can increase by as much as 40 per cent. The key to selling, as always, is to display the right product, in the right place, at the right time, at the right price.

The mistake is to try to sell too many products from the counter. You will overwhelm the customer if you display more than three items. Some stores have considerable success by limiting the customer's focus to one carefully selected product.

Selecting the right product is the challenge. It should probably be:

- Seasonal
- Topical
- An ideal tie-in product to the majority of purchases
- An impulse line for the majority of customers
- Small
- Inexpensive, something customers can purchase with their change.

The more of these criteria your selected product covers, the more sales you will make. In petrol stations, chocolate bars have become the favoured counter product. In supermarkets, it is often magazines.

3 Train the team to sell counter products.

Train your team to see the counter area as more than simply a place to take customer's money. Encourage them to start a conversation and to promote the product on display. The style of conversation will vary depending on the product or situation, but examples could be:

'Have you seen our new...? They arrived today, just in time for Christmas.'

'Those seedling plants are a lovely choice. Do you have any snail control? With the weather getting warmer, you'll need it to keep them looking at their best.'

'Have you stocked up on… yet? They're on special at only 60 cents at the moment.'

Melbourne-based Hilary Kahn of Kahn Retail Solutions conducts a workshop called 'Expanding the Sale', an ideal program to improve selling skills using the above techniques at the checkout.

 ## Do not clutter the counter.

The biggest mistake made by many retailers is that they forget about the importance of image at the counter. Over 20 per cent of customers will remember, as a lasting impression, the counter area above all else in your store. For that reason alone, it must be kept uncluttered, clean, and tidy.

Keep your prime counter display well stocked, with a neat 'reminder' sign on it to encourage customers to make that last purchase. The sign could use such words as:

'Remember, only… days to Christmas'; 'St Valentines Day is February 14th. Remember your loved one with a few chocolate hearts'; 'New'; 'We recommend …'; 'Don't forget…'

Look past the counter.

Retailers usually get the image right on the counter, but forget what's behind the checkout personnel. Customers look in the opposite direction to your sales team and often the sales team are blind to the clutter the customer sees when facing the counter.

Have a company policy which says the only messages behind the counter that are visible to the customer are those that are relevant to the customer. Take down those

calendars, notes to staff, schedules, memoranda, price checks, and other irrelevant pieces of paper.

 ## Make somebody accountable.

Put someone in charge of the counter and make them responsible for keeping the counter display well stocked and the counter area tidy. While we all tend to be guilty of messing up counters, one person should be responsible for monitoring counter cleanliness. Do a daily check to ensure that the behind-the-counter area is kept clean and tidy.

Introduce housekeeping regulations at your checkout.

Remember, last impressions count. It is critical that the checkout is kept clean and tidy at all times. Therefore:
- Check the housekeeping standards at least three times a day.
- Keep the checkout dusted every day.
- Do not clutter with coffee mugs, litter or irrelevant products.
- Never eat at the checkout or in the view of customers.
- Never leave returned /exchanged products sitting at the counter.
- Give the customer space on the counter to pack and rest purchases.

How to manage stands provided by suppliers

To help them maximise potential sales in a retail establishment, many suppliers will provide stands for the specific purpose of promoting their product. In return for the retailer's goodwill and assistance in selling the product, the supplier is able to offer a range of advantages to the retailer. But what is needed is a genuine win-win partnership between the retailer and supplier on how these stands should be used...

1 Consider the opportunities.

By working in partnership with suppliers who provide display stands for their product, the retailer is able to take advantage of the situation in a variety of ways:

Large suppliers can link mass media promotions with the retailer.
The stand could well be part of a large marketing campaign. The retailer can then be seen by the consumer to be 'on the ball' and to be networking with the supplier to provide a professional image for the product.

Your supplier may take responsibility to maintain the stands.
Some suppliers are prepared to manage the stand, or shop space, on behalf of the retailer. This includes refurbishing the stock on display.

Discounts and allowances can be negotiated.
Discounts and allowances that can be negotiated may include discounts based on target sales, free product, shipping to store paid by the supplier, trade deals, or seasonal discounts.

Promotional assistance is often available.
Promotional assistance can come in a number of forms, including new product allowances, display allowances, advertising allowances, group funding, demonstrators, or PA promotions.

Some suppliers may offer financial assistance.
Major suppliers may be prepared to pay for shop fittings on the understanding that their product would be in a prime position. They might also offer a loan lease agreement or extended credit.

Other benefits. Many companies also supply sales training, merchandising programs, sales literature, and consultancy.

2 Seek protection.

Prior to working with a supplier you may need to agree on some form of protection for you as a retailer. This can come in the form of written agreement, return allowances, reorder guarantees, rebates, exclusive agreements, and resale price management programs.

3 Choose an appropriate position for the stand.

Every supplier wants the prime position in your store. Your challenge is to negotiate a location to their satisfaction and, in so doing, to increase your overall sales per square metre.

As a general guide, suppliers who provide stands in excess of 1.5 metres high should have them positioned against a wall, preferably along the customer racetrack. Stands below 1.5m high may be used in central areas of the store, preferably in the product category area.

Stands supplied must be in keeping with the image of your store. For example, you might resist using a stand that clashes dramatically with your colour scheme.

4 Develop a win-win relationship.

Be fair to the supplier. The majority of suppliers spend a great deal of research, time and money in developing stands for their product. You, as retailer, should therefore respect this and only use the stand for the relevant products provided by that supplier.

Look on the relationship as a long-term partnership with both players equally involved in promoting the product strongly to the benefit of both parties.

5 Monitor the performance of supplier stands.

The prime objective of a supplier stand is to sell more products than would be sold if that item were displayed on one of your store's standard merchandising units. As a retailer your role is to measure the performance of the product on the stand and to compare its sales results with past records. If sales have not markedly improved, then you should advise the supplier and return the stand.

How to manage perishable products

Many customers prefer one store over another because of the freshness of its products. This is particularly so in the case of florists, greengrocers, butchers, fishmongers, delicatessens, bakeries, and garden centres. If you must deal in products for which freshness is important, then the following advice will prove invaluable…

1 Be constantly vigilant in maintaining standards.

Customers find it difficult to compare company images on non perishable items. Perishable items are another matter altogether. If the department looks good and the product looks fresh, then the customer invariably assumes *all* the products you sell are of a similar condition. The reverse also applies.

2 Adhere to food hygiene standards.

For fresh foods, hygiene is critically important. Regulations may vary from place to place, but as manager you must ensure that your store abides by the food hygiene code as it applies to your business.

Set specific quality standards for perishable products and do not deviate from them. If quality deteriorates, you should not reduce the price or you'll be reducing your reputation for freshness as well. You are far better to remove from your shelves the deteriorating product and retain your image for quality.

To give assurance of quality to customers, display food hygiene certificates in full view of shoppers.

3 Monitor the shrinkage.

Profits can easily be eroded in perishable departments via shrinkage—the difference between actual sales and projected sales. Loss can be due to a number of reasons:

- Faulty storage temperature
- Waste disposal records not kept up-to-date
- Staff/customers eating the profits
- Bad cutting procedures resulting in high wastage
- Unacceptable stockturn/stock rotation
- Lack of care for product, e.g.watering of plants
- Poor handling, e.g. bruising of fruit
- Poor hygiene procedures
- Lack of staff training
- Crisping/Trimming procedures with vegetables
- Arrangement construction, e.g. by florists
- Inappropriate adding-value costing procedures
- Inefficient interdepartment transfer procedures.

4 Understand the needs of customers.

Customers tend to want more written information about perishable products than for other items. They want to know, for example, how to keep it fresh, cook it, eat it, plant it, or arrange it. Fresh food is often purchased for health reasons. Consumers want to know about the vitamin levels, what are the health benefits of the produce, and how best to cook the produce to retain those benefits. Are the staff responsible for your perishable products fully briefed in such areas?

5 Remember: managers are managers.

Certain specialist retail sectors employ skilled technicians—such as the florist, baker, horticulturist, butcher—to deliver expertise to the consumer. Such businesses also require managerial expertise—often a skill that does not reside in the trade 'expert'.

Retail managers sometimes leave the management of specialist departments to the skilled technicians, fearing they lack the technical expertise themselves. Even if they do lack the technical expertise, this relinquishment of management responsibility is a major mistake and often results in a poorly operated department and a technician who has lost all respect for the manager as a manager. Managers of stores must play as active role in specialist departments as in any other.

6 Foster an image for freshness.

Retailers use various techniques to portray to customers a 'freshness'

Management Memo

Some technicians dealing with fresh products believe they are better than their equivalents in other areas. They often justify this by saying they have had to dedicate a lot more time to training than people in the same position in other departments. This is often true and needs to be taken into consideration, but what you must not do is turn them into prima donnas. This will result in a less than happy team and an overall decline in team morale. [67]

image. As examples, consider these strategies:

- Adopt a 'farm shop' merchandising theme, creating the feeling that the product has come straight from the field. This is accomplished through the use of canopies and rustic farm equipment.

- Install lighting above certain products, including meat and vegetables, to enhance the appeal of such items to the customer.

- Publicise a merchandising policy where you, as a retailer, sell out of fresh produce before the store closes for the day. Around closing time, the customer sees empty shelves—and shelves full of fresh produce the next day.

- Consumers possess strong visual images of what a butcher, gardener, baker, greengrocer, or fishmonger looks like. To maintain this image, the dress code of individuals working within the perishable produce sector becomes an important consideration. One useful idea is to provide technicians with the look of the trade (e.g. the butcher in blue and white stripes)—reinforcing the impression that the person is skilled, knowledgeable in this area, and giving added assurance to the customer seeking a guarantee of freshness and quality.

How to manage shopping trolleys

Shopping trolleys have been designed for reasons other than just carrying products—they've been designed to carry *more* products! In their evolution over the years, the base of the trolley has become larger, because researchers have found that a larger based trolley results in an increase in the average sale per customer. Customers spend more as they are enticed to put more products in the trolley to cover its base. Shopping trolleys are an essential item in supermarkets and it's important to manage their use effectively...

1 Be aware: the trolley is a customer's first contact.

Often the first exposure a customer gets to your business is your shopping trolleys. They expect them to be in the right location, readily available, and clean. And, of course, they must work properly—there is nothing that draws more frustrated criticism from a customer than a trolley with a 'will of its own'.

2 Train your trolley assistants.

Many companies employ young people to manage their trolleys. They are key personnel, because, for most customers, these people are the first and the last ambassadors to represent your business during the shopping encounter. Often they are ill equipped to do the job. They should be recruited as trolley assistants and greeters—and trained accordingly.

The role of a trolley assistant is to:
- ensure trolleys are kept clean.
- keep trolleys well maintained. This involves daily checking of the equipment and, for this, they should have a tool kit and oil available.
- ensure trolleys are in a safe location and retrieved regularly from car parks.
- collect trolleys, in batches of ten, using special straps—not occy straps.
- clean trolleys at the end of the day before storing them in a secure location overnight.
- welcome and farewell customers to and from your business. In this regard they should be recruited because they can make eye contact, smile, and have the confidence to verbally greet and farewell the customer.
- look professional. Provide them with a staff uniform, even safety waistcoats, rain gear, hats and sunscreen for use when required.

3 Include trolley assistants in the team.

Too often trolley assistants are not considered to be part of the team. If this is a practice in your business, you will find that in time the service they offer customers will decline. By involving them in team meetings, in sales training along with the rest of your staff, you could discover untapped potential, talent which can be applied elsewhere in the business.

WINNING
OUR CUS

**MANAGING
YOUR STORE**

OMOTING
PRODUCTS

NAGING
BUSINESS

NDEX

151

4 Select a trolley suited to your needs.

Supermarket trolleys have been designed for a wide range of purposes—as the following selection, available to customers of the UK hardware supermarket retailer, Sainsburys Homebase, indicates:

Small wire basket trolley

Designed to carry:
• small DIY articles

Children are not to ride in or on the trolley.

Wire basket trolley with toddler seat

Designed to carry:
• packets
• bottles
• tins

One child to ride only in seat provided.

Disabled trolley attachment

Designed to carry:
• packets
• bottles
• tins

Wheelchair users only.

Flatbed trolley

Designed to carry:
• slabs, bricks,cement
• aggregates, plaster, peat
• compost, heavy bagged materials to 250kg max.

Children are not to ride on the trolley.

Management Memo

Shopping baskets also need to be located around the store. These handy baskets are often stolen and need to be replaced, although a client of mine found that, when he introduced red baskets, his pilferage rate decreased.

And in the war against vanishing shopping trolleys, a new UK magnetic device, the Radlock, attached to trolleys, jams the wheels when a trolley crosses a magnetic strip encircling supermarket carparks. [68]

Tubular frame trolley

Designed to carry:
• furniture, board, fencing
• trellis, doors, worktops
• sheet materials
• timber, plasterboard

Children are not to ride in or on the trolley.

Wheelbarrow trolley

Designed to carry:
• terracotta pots
• peat, compost
• outdoor ornamentation

Children are not to ride on the trolley.

DIY trolley

Basket:
• packets, bottles, tins
Side section:
• mops, brooms, parasols
Base:
• peat, compost

Children are not to ride on the trolley.

How to write signs that sell

Research carried out in the United States by LEK Partnership in the early 1990s showed the value of signage in the retail trade. When products had no signage they were monitored at a base of 100 units sold per week. When handwritten signs were provided, they sold 170 units a week and, when printed signs were used, sales increased to 265 units a week. Signs are an essential ingredient in any merchandising strategy...

1 Delegate the preparation of signs to one person.

Signs can be handwritten, or printed inhouse using computer software programs, or outsourced to signage specialists. If your policy is to handwrite signs for your store, then you must insist on consistency in the way they look. You can achieve this by delegating the signwriting to one person who can then ensure a uniformity in writing style.

2 Use lower case to promote your product.

Use capital letters sparingly. Resist the temptation to write messages in capital letters, although a single word in capitals is acceptable, e.g. NEW! or SPECIAL. Your reader will find a lower case message, in serif type style if composed on computer, far easier to read than one in capitals.

3 Use colours that create impact.

Colour attracts attention. We're told that red is associated with savings and therefore red price ticketing will give the perception of a bargain. Dark green gives the perception of

quality and therefore can be used for non price-sensitive lines.

4 Have your staff trained in the art.

If you prefer to display handwritten signs, send your staff signwriter to a workshop on 'one brush' signwriting. The course will provide instruction on the basic skills needed to produce more professional-looking signs.

5 Catch your customer's eye.

The average customer spends 1.4 seconds looking at each product in your store. The aim of signage is to make the eye linger longer.

According to a customer buying habits survey conducted in 1995 by the Point of Purchase Advertising Institute, 70 per cent of brand purchase decisions are made in the store—and 42 per cent of all brand decisions are made when point of purchase signage is present.

6 Promote products not signs.

Often a sign can be so dominant that all the customer sees is the sign and no product. Remember, the aim of a sign is to draw your customer's attention to the product you are promoting, not to assume the centre stage spotlight. The product must be the focus; the sign points the way.

7 Use words that sell.

In compiling a sign's message, always use words that increase sales by increasing your customer's interest. Such attention-gaining words include:

At last	Attention
Check out these	Exclusive
Finally	For the first time
Good news	Huge savings
Hurry	In a class by itself
It's here	New
New low price	Now you can
Save big	State of the art
Switch to…	Take a look at these
The smart choice	Urgent

It's all here for you at…
Back by popular demand
For those who insist on the best
Only… can give you…
Reasons why you should…
Take the… challenge
The… advantage
Quality does not have to cost you.

Use positive words to sell products. Donald Caudill from the University of North Alabama suggests using power words from his 'Power Word Alphabet':

A Action, accomplish, ahead, anybody, achieve, answer, announcing, amazing, at last
B Benefit, best, bible, big, bargain
C Can, calm, care, career, clean, comfort, challenge, compare, cash, control
D Discover, deliver, destiny, definite, dynamite, decide
E Easy, earn, effective, efficient, entertain, extra, exciting
F Free, famous, full, fancy, fun, future, facts, friends, fast, found

G Guarantee, get, glamour, great, gold, give
H Health, happy, heart, heaven, help, home, 'how to', hurry, honour, hot, hope, honest
I Introducing, intelligent, invention, invite, innovate, incredible, interest, improve, immediate, important, instant
J Join, jewel, jumbo, joy, just arrived, juicy
K Know, key, king, keep, knowledge, kind
L Love, land, liberty, luxury, look, last chance, life, lasting, listen, learn
M Money, magic, more, maximum, minute, modern, miracle, most, mind, mine, many
N New, now, need, nude, nice, neat, never before
O Opportunity, occult, open, on, original, occasion, own
P Proven, power, positive, promote, protect, payoff, pro, pleasure, profit, performance
Q Quality, quick, quiet
R Results, respect, revive, right, rich, revolutionary, remarkable, record
S Save, safe, sale, satisfaction, self, service, sensational, special, smile, super, startling, secret, suddenly
T Today, take, taste, thanks, time, true, try, total, tempting, think, trust
U Urgent, unique, understand, ultimate, useful
V Victory, vitamin, vacation, VIP, value, valour, volume
W Win, wise, wanted, worth, willing, wow, which, when, why, who else, wonderful
X Xanadu, Xavier, x-ray, X
Y You, your, yes, young, youth
Z Zest, zodiac, zip, zenith, zeal, zero

How to manage signs in your store

Signage needs to look fresh and professional. Indeed, a well presented sign could be considered as an extra salesperson in your store. Unfortunately, many stores do not realise the sales opportunities that signs can offer, with the result that signs are often managed quite inappropriately. To take full advantage of signage in your store, consider this advice...

1 Reflect on the size of your signs.

While the size of a sign is important, you must remember that your products are more important. Signs are only selling devices and their size will vary depending on their position in the store. Gondolas and relay management positions, for example, need smaller signs, end caps larger signs, and large free-standing displays can use larger signs again. As a guide, use 25mm x 88mm signs for relay management positions, 90mm x 120mm signs for end caps, and up to 1000mm x 750mm for island displays.

2 Select the correct typeface for your signs.

Typeface is important. It should vary in style—for example, hardware products are promoted using a bold type face, while a softer, lighter type face is used with expensive products for women. It should vary for legibility—lower case is often easier to read than capitals, and, if your customer base is getting older, you may need to use larger print to help shoppers with fading eyesight.

3 Be consistent.

The appearance of your signs does much for your store's image. To maintain or raise your image, delegate the responsibility for preparing your signs to one person, particularly if your signs are handwritten. Consistency is important.

4 Calculate the costs of producing your signs.

Handwritten signage is expensive. A typical sign (product name, price and three benefits) takes about six minutes to produce. In other words, a typical person, when writing non known value product signs can produce about ten an hour. Known value signs can be produced faster, about twenty an hour, as benefits don't need to be listed. With these figures, you can calculate the cost in labour to produce handwritten signs for your store. Compare that with the cost of using computer-based signage systems—some of which can create 40 signs an hour—and you are then in a position to explore the possibility of reducing your costs considerably.

WINNING
OUR CUS
**MANAGING
YOUR STORE**
OMOTING
PRODUCTS
NAGING
BUSINESS
NDEX
155

5 Develop a policy on vendor signage.

Suppliers are often keen to place their signs around your store, often at the expense of your image. Their signage should be part of a planned program and linked only to product promotions. Make it clear to these suppliers that you have a policy on signage—if you haven't, get one. It is *your* store, not the supplier's, and *you* should be in complete control of signage on your premises.

6 Always review your signs once a week.

Store walks should concentrate on signage at least once a week. Develop a checklist for your store tour and produce an action list as a result of your weekly findings. The checklist

below, as proposed by Sonja Larsen in *Signs that Sell*, should help.

7 Review your signage strategy every year.

The technology of signage changes rapidly and recent innovations could mean you are soon out of date. You should therefore review your entire signage strategy once a year and decide how you wish to develop your silent salesperson in the future.

WEEKLY SIGNAGE REVIEW CHECKLIST		
ACTIVITY	GOOD IDEAS	PROBLEMS
Review this week's sale signing Are all advertised items signed? (list) ☐ Do any advertised items have traditional problems, such as always needing two sides for back-to-back signing etc.? ☐ Are all advertised items easy to locate? ☐ Are there problems with customers confusing sale merchandise with adjacent non-sale merchandise?		
Review general signing policies ☐ Are there any out-of-date signs still up? ☐ Are there enough signs, per agreement, per fixture, gondola, etc.? ☐ Are there too many signs in any area? Too few?		
Review general sign quality issues ☐ Are signs consistent—legible and neat? ☐ Are the benefits well presented? ☐ Do the signs, in general, enhance the appearance of the store?		
Review trend signing ☐ Is what's new proudly out in front for the customers to see and is it properly signed? ☐ Are there any trends without signs? ☐ Does the customer understand the trend?		
☐ *Review any problems identified by store managers and associates.*		
☐ *Communicate this checklist to buyers and sign personnel.*		
☐ *Check sign department and store to make sure proper signing has been prepared and sent.*		

How to write a known value sign

Known value signs are used on products where it is assumed the consumer knows the price—and if your store varies from the expected price, you will be perceived as too expensive or too cheap. The price of petrol is a good example. In other words, the product is a basic item, a 'price sensitive' product, and as such warrants your special attention as a retailer...

1 Know the impact of your known value products.

Common known value (KV) products include petrol, cigarettes, newspapers, toilet paper, lettuce, sugar, milk, bread, and bananas. KV products can be used to give the public a price image of your store. If your products, within the KV range, are more expensive than those in your competitor's store, you will be perceived as being more expensive across your whole stock range. If your KVs are cheaper, the reverse view will be true.

2 Keep your KV signs simple—and sell.

With KV products, your objective is to maximise sales. The key to doing this is to keep things simple. In essence, all you need with a true known value product is:
• the name of the product
• the price of the product.
The product name should be at the top of the sign and the price in the centre. If you wish to show monetary saving, then write the old price in the right hand side of the sign and then

cross through it. This is far more effective than giving percentage savings.

Bananas

$1.25

Store logo

KV signs work if you apply the KISS principle—Keep It Simple, Sells.

3 Keep your KV signs large—and sell.

Put the price in larger print, and invariably the customer perceives the product as being cheaper, even if it isn't.

4 Get your KVs upfront.

Try to limit your KV products to a minimum of a dozen in your store. And if you want to foster an image of being price aware in the eyes of your customer, then put your KV products in your store's primary location.

WINNING
OUR CUS

**MANAGING
YOUR STORE**

OMOTING
PRODUCTS

NAGING
R BUSINESS

NDEX

157

NON KNOWN VALUE SIGNS

See also: 78, 128, 156

How to write a non known value sign

Non known value products are those where the average consumer is not at all sure what the exact price for the product should be. Usually their decision to buy is based on more than simply price. Signage is a key to selling non known value products...

 Identify customers' needs and wants.

Prior to writing a non known value sign, you should identify the key benefits to the consumer. The best approach is to brainstorm your ideas amongst a small group within your team and then identify the three key benefits that you believe are the most important to the customer.

 Design a sign that sells.

Research by Sonia Larsen in the United States and by Hilary Kahn of Kahn Retail Solutions in Melbourne, has identified that the customer needs to know, in sequence, what the product is, the three key benefits, the price, and finally a motivator to buy.

Design your sign with these details in mind. Again, keep it simple. If you give your consumers too much information, they will get confused, even discouraged, and the sale opportunity will be lost.

 Make bullet points do the job.

Do not assume your customers know as much as you do about the products you sell. The majority of us need memory joggers to encourage us to purchase. Your listing of customer benefits can become their memory joggers.

But, in doing this, many retailers make their signs far too complicated. Keep it simple. For example, to get benefits across to your customers, bullet points prove most effective:

Chrysanthemums

- Ideal Autumn garden colour
- Can be grown indoors or outdoors
- Come in fashionable colours

$1.50

Ideal to decorate your home

Check all your signs regularly.

Signs reflect your image. You need to monitor the appearance and effectiveness of your signs on a regular basis, and the checklist on page 155 will help in this regard.

How to use signs effectively

Since the introduction of the self-service concept into retailing, the application of promotional aids for point of purchase sales has increased greatly among retailers. Research by the US Skaggs Institute has revealed that a price-only sign increases sales when compared with no signage, but price-plus-benefit signage is the most effective. The evidence suggests that effective signage can become a silent salesperson and can have a dramatic effect on your average sale per customer...

 Write effective signs.

Signage should change in style depending on whether the item being promoted is a known value or a non known value product.

Signs for known value products— well used items usually purchased on price alone—need to be simple to be effective:

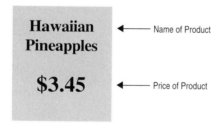

Signs for non known value products are most effective if prepared with the focus being price-plus-benefits...

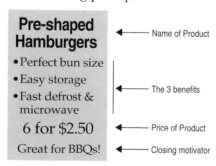

2 Adhere to the rules of product signage.

Although writing signs is an art, anyone can write one—provided they abide by a dozen simple rules:

1. Be specific in what you want to say to your customer.
2. Make the price easy to understand.
3. Sell the romance and sizzle.
4. Write facts, not fiction.
5. Don't state the obvious.
6. Explain what is not obvious.
7. Help the customer buy the best product.
8. Help the customer comparison shop.
9. Remind customers of logical needs.
10. Always state what they will save.
11. Stay positive and sign-friendly.
12. Break the above rules—if it fits your strategy.

3 Adhere to the rules of store promotion signage.

While signage can be used to promote products, it can also

promote your business. Again, follow some simple rules to ensure you use signs to promote your business effectively:

1. When you have something to say about your business, say so through your signage.

2. Promote the services your business provides.

3. If you have a strong policy statement, repeat it a number of times. The prime example is a prominently displayed sign in a Stew Leonards' store, Connecticut, in the United States:

   Rule 1: The customer is always right.
   Rule 2: If the customer is ever wrong, re-read Rule 1.

4. Place services signs in the relevant merchandise category departments.

5. Use signage to ask for customer feedback.

6. Promote store activities and occasions, prior to the events, via signage.

7. When changes are taking place in the store, always apologise for any inconvenience to the customer via signage.

8 Make sure permanent signs always look professional.

9. Your signs are part of your public image. Make sure you look on them in that way.

⁴ Invest in a complete signage package.

To be effective and to look professional, you need a complete signage system in place, not just scattered signs. Sign display systems are available in a variety of styles.

Management Memo

When writing company procedure signage always write it in customer-friendly language. Examples of positive signs include:

☐ If you bring bags, parcels and prams into the store we know you will understand we are obliged to check their contents when you leave.
Thank you.

☐ If you are lucky enough to look as though you could be younger than 18, you will understand that we are legally obliged to ask to see your ID before selling you alcohol/cigarettes.
Thank you for your co-operation. [71]

For example:
Velcro T Stands—normally steel stands fitted with velcro hooks on both sides.

Chrome ticket holders—usually adjustable stands with hooks to accommodate signs with holes in them.

Clear acrylic hanger signs—ideal for eye level merchandising.

Basket grip stands —for attaching to display baskets.

Velcro hook and loop fasteners—ideal for relay management and to prevent your team using staples or sticky tape to put signs up.

⁵ Rotate your signs regularly.

Signs should be placed next to the items you are promoting. As a general rule, sign about 10 per cent of the stock in your store and then rotate the signs on a regular basis to ensure that, over time, you expose all your products to the customer.

How to use background music in your store

Background music can influence the mood and spending habits of retail customers. Store silence can be unsettling for many. It can be embarrassing. Music is increasingly being used in retail stores to overcome this problem. Retailers have also found that music can enhance sales—and, if incorrectly chosen, that it can also drive customers away. To take full advantage of background music in your store, consider the following points...

1 Be convinced— music matters.

Research studies have revealed that the playing of background music in retail stores can have a sigificant effect on sales:

- Research in British supermarkets shows an 18 per cent increase in sales when the music from familiar television advertisements was played in the store.

- Leicester University researchers found that when French accordion music was played, Gallic wine and cheese outsold German varieties. When German oompah bands were played the situation was reversed.

- Sydney University research in 1999 found that:

  - Only about one-third of shoppers are aware of the music wafting down the supermarket aisles.

  - All are encouraged to undo purse strings or 'linger longer' by the tempo and style of tunes.

  - The faster the music, the faster people moved down the aisle.

  - More money was spent when slower music played. Indeed, nine weeks of slow music yielded an average $16,740 in daily sales in supermarkets, compared with $12,112 for fast music—a 38.2 per cent difference.

- US research shows that sales increase by 38 per cent when music is slowed from 108 beats per minute to 60 beats per minute.

2 Play music to relax your customers.

Relaxation music is now widely available and is ideal background music for the majority of retailers who want to lull customers into a spending mood. The key word is background, however. Whatever music you select, it must be in the background and not overwhelm the shopper in your store.

Play music when the store is quiet. When you are busy, your customers may be making so much noise that you may find you do not need any background music at all.

3 Tailor the tune to the tastes of your customers.

Do not play music simply because your staff like it. Play music your customers like. This may mean that you play different types of music at different times of the day or week. For example, if you have retired people as your main shopper group on Thursday mornings, you will need to play nostalgic '40s and '50s music, not '90s music. When the baby boomers shop, play Elvis Presley tunes. If you have a young customer base on Saturday mornings, then play contemporary music.

4 Experiment to find your solution.

Taste in music is, of course, linked to type of music. Australian research has shown that, in a bottle shop or liquor store, for example, different shopping behaviour resulted when different music was played. People bought more expensive bottles when classical music was playing—they moved from the $8 bottles to, say, the $15 bottles—than when Top 40 tunes were on offer. Classier music generated classier purchases.

Banks found that classical music and instrumental jazz encouraged a sense of trust and seriousness in customers, and music retailers found that bass-heavy music with broad appeal made customers more willing sales targets.

Experiment in your store to determine what's best for you—even consider other sounds. The sound of water, for example, can be an alternative to consider. For many years, a fashion shop has successfully used a water feature in one corner of the store to focus attention, to break the silence, and to soothe customers.

5 Feature music— not singing.

If you use background music with singing, you will find that customers will start relating to the singer. Since we all have artists we enjoy and those whom we dislike, you will find you are bound to upset some customers. Play it safe and use only music in the background unless it's a special season such as Christmas.

6 Play music to suit the season.

During traditional festivals, play music that is associated with these festivals. In these cases singing is acceptable. The festivals that come to mind include Christmas, St Valentine's Day, and Mother's Day. In a garden centre at bulb time, you might play 'Tulips from Amsterdam'.

7 Remember: tempo counts.

And get the beat right. Slower music doesn't force people to buy more, but it can make them linger longer. The music you play should have the same beat as a pulse beat. In hardware stores and supermarkets, music with fewer than 60 beats per minute—roughly the tempo of an average ballad—is recommended.

8 Do it properly, and legally.

If you choose to make music part of your retailing environment, quality counts. Invest in good quality audio equipment, and you will reap the rewards.

Finally, in many countries around the world you need a licence before you can play recorded music in public. Check your local regulations to ensure you are abiding by the law.

How to use aroma in your store

The aroma of freshly baked bread, the smell of freshly ground coffee, the sweet fragrances of cut flowers —these are the naturally occurring store aromas that attract customers. But no longer is it just the smells you sell that create sales. Today aromatherapy—the practice of generating artificial aromas—is becoming big business. Retailers are increasingly employing organisations to create smells for their stores in the hope of attracting customers and increasing sales...

1 Identify the aromas in your store.

Your store must smell attractive to your customers. Customers find the aroma of bread, coffee and flowers appealing while they find the odour of fertilisers, fish and manures generally offensive. Undertake a 'smell audit' in your store—only then will you be able to build on the positive and reduce the negative.

2 Position negative aromas away from customers.

Products with negative odours need to be carefully located. For example, fertilisers and manures may need to be merchandised outdoors or at least in a roomy and airy part of your shop. Alternatively, you may wish to install an extractor fan in the vicinity of such products.

3 Position positive aromas at the entrance.

The location of positive aromas at the entrance of your store can be achieved by using one of three methods:

• Position the more positive aroma products near the entrance, for example, locate your cut flower display near the door.

• Use a pipe system and channel a positive store aroma to the entrance; for example, the smell of bread in the bakery.

• Purchase perfume making machines and small cartridges of oil. These machines warm the oil and pump it out into the store...

4 Consider the advantages of artificial aromas.

We are told that artificially generated aromas can:

• enhance your store's image through the creation of a 'signature' aroma, which sends a strong message to your customers to ensure they associate that aroma with your store.

• increase browse shopping.

• promote a particular product.

• heighten customer perception of the quality of a product.

• lessen, in the customer's mind at least, the time spent in a queue.

• trigger impulse buying.

- build an image of quality, freshness, dependability, vivacity, or sophistication.

Research by Dr Susan Knako of the Marell Chemical Senses Centre in the United States shows that customers will browse longer if a store has a positive aroma. In fashion shops, she found rosewood, lavender and vanilla aromas increased sales. Men and women stayed longer in jewellery shops where there was a fruity, floral aroma. She found a positive aroma encouraged customers to feel more items—and the more they felt, the more products they purchased.

5 Investigate the use of artificial aromas in your store.

If you have a natural smell in your store—coffee, scents, baking bread etc, then let that permeate your premises. However, if your business is 'on the nose' for some reason, it may pay to investigate the use of artificial aromas.

Australian aroma marketing specialists Ecomist offer over 180 different fragrances ranging from freshly cut grass, to steak and onions, to roses. The aromas are dispensed from small wall units programmed to spray at regular intervals to create a pleasant smelling environment for customers to shop in.

To enhance the environment of

his premises, the manager of a timber-flooring retail store in Sydney, for example, located beside a busy inner city road, uses woody fragrances including pine, cedar and eucalyptus to combat outside car fumes—and to get up the nose of his competitors at the same time.

6 Do not overdo the aroma.

While the pulling power of fragrance is becoming the latest retailing tool for getting customers to part with their cash, the Centre for Chemosensory Research in Sydney cautions retailers to curb their enthusiasm.

Director Graham Bell warns: 'You don't want customers thinking they're walking into a brick wall of odour the moment they walk into your store. The fragrance must be subliminal, almost below the level of awareness to have most effect.'

How to make best use of colour for effective merchandising displays

The focus of all the merchandise planning in your store should be your product and your product displays must be designed to attract customers. Well-planned lighting and thoughtful use of colour will make these displays more effective, and in turn will create more sales...

1 Attract the eye of your customer.

To attract the attention of your customer, your merchandise displays should form a series of focal points throughout your store. The displays are your focus areas, and the goods are the primary features. Displays and product should always be clean, fresh, bright, well-lit, with a blueprint for merchandising and colour usage carefully shaped in advance.

The colour of your merchandise is the fixed element in your planning and, for this reason, colour selection for your displays should be based on the colour of the merchandise itself.

Where the merchandise is one dominant colour, then the background colour for the display should either contrast or complement your merchandise.

Where your merchandise colour varies, and a number of individual displays are called for, then the overall surrounds in your store should be a neutral colour. In this case, colour emphasis will be added to the immediate background of the displays, again to contrast with or to complement the colour of merchandise in those individual displays.

2 Create points of interest.

Whenever possible, displays should be built with strong primary colours as points of interest, then contrasted against cool, subtle hues for the background. This contrasting of colours makes the displays stand out and attract the attention of the customer.

When choosing colours, always test the colour samples in the light and in the environment in which they will be seen. Light colours can appear more intense on a wall, and the hue can vary depending on the light source, so an on-site test of colour suitability is essential.

If your products lack impact in form or colour, such as reading glasses in an optometrist's store, then a bright primary colour as a background to the display will highlight an otherwise uninspiring product.

3 Use contrasts of colour and form.

If you have dark objects in your displays, then display them against light objects to make them stand out. If your products are in warm colours, then set them against a background

WINNING
OUR CUS

MANAGING
YOUR STORE

OMOTING
PRODUCTS

NAGING
R BUSINESS

NDEX

165

of cool colours to add emphasis to the product. The secret is in the contrast between merchandise and your props.

If you use form in your displays, such as a cart, or a rickshaw, then surround the form with space. The way to highlight form is to surround it by unfilled space—do not give it a backdrop, just space. This works particularly well in window displays.

 ## Aim at variety.

Aim at variety in your displays, but take care not to overdo it. Use texture in your displays, for example wood, hessian, stone, rope, or straw, to create contrast and interest. This texture can sometimes be provided by the merchandise itself.

 ## Create a buying mood.

Your aim in building merchandise displays is to provide points of interest and attraction through the skilful use of colour and form, to create presentations that your customers comprehend and can relate to. Your ultimate goal is to create the ambience that will put your customers in the buying mood.

 ## Know how a colour wheel works.

If you use colours that lie opposite each other on the accompanying colour wheel (they're called complementary colours), you can create a dramatic effect, because each colour makes its partner appear more intense. Complementary colours are excellent in merchandising displays.

Colours that lie adjacent to each

other on the wheel, or tints and shades of the same colour, are called harmonious colours. Used together, these are more relaxing and subtle in their effects, and are useful if you want your customers to slow down and spend more time in your store.

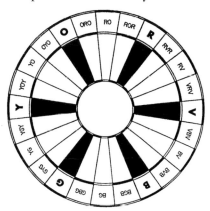

THE COLOUR WHEEL
Y = yellow, O = orange, R = red
V = violet, B = blue, G = green

The colour triangle below reveals that, when white is added to a full colour, a tint is achieved. When black is added to a full colour, a shade is achieved.

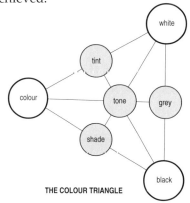

THE COLOUR TRIANGLE

Ref: E. Danger, *Using Colour to Sell*, Gower, London, 1968.

This topic was written by Linda Stanley, John Stanley Associates, Perth, WA.

How to make best use of colour for the store exterior

Colour is an emotional factor and a psychological tool that can be used to help create an ideal retail environment. Used wisely, colour can attract customers into your store; used carelessly and it can repel would-be shoppers. The external appearance of your store—and colour plays an important role here—should be in harmony with the type of product or service you sell, and the environment...

1 Use colour appropriate to your trade.

Your store exterior is your advertisement to passers-by. Make it clear to the passing public what it is you sell, and choose colours that are appropriate to your product or service. If you are in baby goods, then paint your store in pastels—racing green and checkered flags would be inappropriate. To decorate your store in this way would not communicate to the passing motorist that you are a baby goods retailer, no matter how much you love motor racing in your private life.

2 Identify, then market to, your customer base.

Determine who your typical customer is—age, gender, race, class, religion, and interests. Choose colours preferred by that market. If your customer base is primarily elderly, choose subtle colour tones, such as pastels, as elderly people prefer subtle colours; if they are sophisticated, use high fashion, sophisticated colours; if your customer base is working class, then you can use louder, primary colours,

since working class people are generally attracted by these. If you have a large ethnic group within your customer base, ascertain what their traditional cultural colour preferences are, and consider how you can use those colours to the best retail advantage. Choose colours that will attract your typical customer.

3 Promote your company image.

Your company image may be the determining factor for the exterior colour of your store. Choose hues that are appropriate for your image. For example, one shade of green may scream out to the passing public that your store is down market and cheap, while another shade may subtly say that you are upmarket and expensive.

The secret is in the hue, and the perception differs from culture to culture as to what that hue symbolises. Use of Harrods Green, Navy Blue, and Royal Purple may indicate a conservative, traditional, or even up market store in Britain. However, in another culture, those colours may indicate a down market, old fashioned, or poor taste store.

In most western countries, hot primary colours, such as red, indicate activity, or fast service. This is why most fast food outlets in the west use a large amount of red in their company colours—consider Kentucky Fried Chicken, Pizza Hut, and McDonald's. Freshness in the west is often symbolised by a bright green, symbolising countryside. Woolworths vegetable departments in Australia are an excellent example of this belief. The company's vegetable departments are a strong green colour which, along with very carefully placed lighting, accentuates the freshness of the products.

Carefully consider what your image is, then choose colours that will portray and enhance that image.

4 Harmonise with your local environment.

If your store is in an historic street or setting, then maintain that heritage image on your store exterior. Choose traditional colour harmonies that are appropriate to that era in history. Painting the walls in psychedelic colours, for example, will not only offend your customers, but your store will be completely out of step with the environment.

If your store is in an ultra modern shopping block, maintain that ultra modern image. If your store is a country store, keep the country image, and maintain the harmony of your surrounds. Your customers choose to live where they do because their environment appeals to them, whether that be ultra modern, country, forest, or heritage. Keep your customer happy. Harmonise with your environment.

Management Memo

Hot Colours refer to the red, orange and yellow hues. They are called hot colours because they stimulate the autonomic nervous system, increase blood pressure and heart rate.

Cool colours refer to the blue, green and violet hues. They are called cool colours because they have a calming effect on the autonomic nervous system, decreasing blood pressure and heart rate.[73]

5 Use colour to highlight architectural features.

Use harmonious combinations of colour to highlight any attractive architectural features your store may have. If the building and these features relate to a specific historical era, use a blend of colours appropriate to that era to detail the features. If the features are unattractive, then a single, pale, cool, colour painted over the whole area will help to send the features into the background. Cool colours visually recede.

6 Ensure the store exterior sends the right message.

In the retail store, colour is often limited to the facia which usually promotes a company colour, name and logo. In many stores this is the only visual panel available to attract shoppers, so plan it carefully to ensure it is giving the right message. If company colours are not used on the facia, then a hot colour would gain maximum attention.

Facades can be in the company colour also, the same as the facia. Alternatively, use a neutral colour to harmonise with the local culture.

This topic was written by Linda Stanley, John Stanley Associates, Perth, WA.

How to make the best use of colour for the store interior

First impressions are vitally important in attracting your customers' attention and, once attracted, in holding their focus, and encouraging browse shopping. Your store must first be inviting to enter, must create points of interest to encourage the customer to look around, and must stimulate customers to buy. In other words, your store must be designed to give to the product or service you sell a strong visual impact and appeal—and colour plays a major role in this regard...

1 Use colour appropriate to your trade.

It is vital that customers be put at ease in your store. Soft floral colours may make male customers in an automotive business feel uncomfortable, but would be expected by customers in a florist shop. Badly designed interiors can confuse customers, and leave them unsure of exactly what it is that you sell.

2 Use colour appropriate to your customer.

Determine the race, gender, age, religion, income bracket of your typical customer and use colours appropriate to that market whenever suitable. Children love bright primary colours so, if your primary target market is children, then paint your store in bright primary colours to excite these customers. If your market is primarily men, use masculine colours; if your market is women then use feminine colours. The emotional comfort of your customers is an important consideration, and colour is an emotional tool. Use it thoughtfully.

3 Keep the focus on your merchandise.

The background colours in the store set the stage for your merchandise displays. If your merchandise is one basic colour, then the store's internal decor can be chosen to complement that colour. A complementary colour is the opposite colour on the colour wheel.

If the colour of your merchandise is varied, then individual displays are necessary. In this case, the overall surrounding colour in the store should be a neutral hue with colour added to the immediate background of each display. Your customers' attention should always be focused on the merchandise and never be distracted by the surroundings— after all, it is the product that you are wanting customers to buy.

4 Use colour to create the atmosphere.

Bright, hot colours (red, orange, yellow hues) are stimulating to the nervous system. They encourage activity, so they are often used in fast food outlets and children's stores. Cool colours (blue, green, violet

WINNING
YOUR CUS

**MANAGING
YOUR STORE**

OMOTING
PRODUCTS

NAGING
BUSINESS

NDEX

169

hues) increase mental concentration and calm the nervous system. They are appropriate colours for doctors' surgeries, schools, and for background contrast in merchandising displays. Light, clear, warm hues create a welcoming atmosphere, and are suitable for restaurants and other meeting places.

5 Keep your image fresh with in-vogue colours.

The colours that your customers are painting their homes reflect the current colour fashions in your area. These fashion colours produce positive emotional responses in shoppers and create a stimulating environment that inspires customers to buy. If you require a particular colour for practical purposes, then choose a variation of that hue which is currently in vogue. This will keep your store and your merchandise looking up-to-date and fresh in the customers' eyes.

6 Make colours welcome your customers.

Consider the following points:

- Use colours and lighting that flatter your customers' appearance. Warm colours in medium tones are both welcoming and flattering to your customer.
- Avoid very light colours as they can create glare and excessive brightness which is harsh and uncomfortable on the eye.
- Consider the customers' comfort, and welcome them with warm colours.
- Avoid using a single colour throughout the store. It can be boring. Colour harmonies are much more inviting and friendly, and certain

> ## Management Memo
>
> **Warm colours**
> - make an area look smaller
> - bring forward distant walls
> - reduce visual size in lofty areas
> - are cheerful in cool or cloudy regions
> - are advisable in long narrow areas
> - work well in areas where there is little natural light
> - provide a welcoming atmosphere.
>
> **Cool colours**
> - make an area look larger
> - add distance, cool colours recede
> - give a cooling effect in warm areas
> - are good for contrast in the background of displays
> - work well in first aid rooms
> - create a calming effect. [74]

colour combinations are more effective than others.

- For expert advice on colour combinations, consult *Colour Image Scale* by Shigenobu Kobayashi, published by Kodansha International.
- Alternatively, seek the assistance of an interior decorator, or your local paint store.
- You can also get a lot of ideas on colour combinations from the many 'home beautiful' type of magazines available.

7 Contrast architectural features.

Make the most of any attractive architectural features inside your store. Use contrasting hues to add emphasis and interest to these aspects. Don't highlight ugly features, however. Instead, use one cool light colour to make the features visually recede.

This topic was written by Linda Stanley, John Stanley Associates, Perth, WA.

Managing your Business

The person who has had a bull by the tail once
has learned 60 or 70 times as much
as the person who hasn't.

Mark Twain

How to develop a retail business strategy

As a successful retailer, you need to work 'in' your business to generate a return on your investment today and to work 'on' your business to ensure that you generate a return on your investment in the future. This means it is critical that you take time to stand back from the business, to analyse it objectively, and to develop a plan for the future...

1 Do a SWOT analysis on your business.

Most consultants will tell you that it is critical to examine your business at least once a year by carrying out a SWOT analysis—where you explore your **s**trengths, **w**eaknesses, **o**pportunities and **t**hreats. The 'think tank' process should be undertaken away from the workplace so that you are not distracted by the day-to-day operations of business, and with the assistance of up to half a dozen key team members...

2 Identify your strengths.

The first step is to clearly identify the strengths of your business. As a group provide answers to the following questions:

- What do we do really well?
- What sector of our retailing adds most to the bottom line?
- What are the areas of our business where we outperform our competition?
- What parts of our retailing endorse how customers perceive us with positive recognition?

3 Identify your weaknesses.

In identifying your weaknesses you need objective answers to the following questions:

- What areas of our business operation provide the most frequent complaints?
- In what situation are we most vulnerable as a retail operation?
- What products or processes provide the most problems?
- What products or processes bring in the lowest returns?

4 Analyse your opportunities.

Once you decide on what your strengths and weaknesses are, you can then start planning your future direction. Again, start with the positive and look at the opportunities that might be available to you by answering the following questions:

- What opportunities exist to improve the internal running of our retail business?
- What current marketing opportunities should we exploit?

- What changes are taking place that are external to our business, that will allow us to operate more effectively?

5 Analyse the threats to your business.

The final part of your SWOT is to analyse the threats to your business. You need answers to the following questions:

- What are the main factors that create a potential threat to our retail operation?
- Which threats are the most serious to our future retailing operation?
- What changes could take place that could threaten our business?

6 Prioritise your actions.

Having carried out a SWOT analysis on your business, and explored the possibilities for and implications of future development, you now need to prioritise your findings. Make your decisions based on the response you believe you will get from your customers, your team and their capabilities, and on a consideration of your economic situation and technical skills and abilities...

7 Consider staff reaction to proposed changes.

How will your team respond to any proposed changes, how will you measure their responses, and how will you involve them in implementing the changes? Consider as well the extent to which you will need to involve your customers in the process. You will need to adopt a professional approach when addressing these issues.

Management Memo

When analysing change in your retail business, you need to look at the internal aspects of your business, and to develop a Positioning Statement...[75]

Our customers are............. They come to us for.................... because................ We are better than...............for the following reasons: ....
Customers prefer us because..................

8 Consider your financial position.

How will the changes affect your retail business? Know precisely why you should be making the changes, how they will reduce costs, increase profits, or both, and to what extent they will increase your market share. Do you have the resources to make such changes?

9 Understand the technical implications.

You need to evaluate how technical and technological developments will enhance your business, especially as far as the customer is concerned. Do you have the internal resources to deal with such changes and does your team have the knowledge, understanding and motivation to deal with the changes.

10 Examine critically the final strategy.

Finally, you must critically examine each envisaged change in detail. Critique all the information available to you, to conclude with answers to the following: What?, When?, Where?, Who?, How?, and Why? Only then will you be fully prepared to implement your new strategy.

How to benchmark your store

Successful businesses need to monitor what they are doing. The old saying, 'if you can't measure it, you can't manage it', is very true of retailing. But not only do you need to measure within your own business, you also need to measure your enterprise against other businesses in your retailing sector, especially the leaders in your field. This is the process of benchmarking and it is undertaken so that you can become as good as, or better than, your competition...

 Aim above the average.

It is easy to fall into the trap of gathering measurements from an industry, averaging them, and then comparing your figures with these 'average' statistics. This can be misleading since those average figures also include the businesses that are failing. What you need is to benchmark against the top one-third of performers in your retail sector. By using these as your yardstick, you will get a truer picture of how you are performing in your industry sector.

 Know why you measure.

In benchmarking, you measure key profit indicators within your retail sector. If you find you are performing below standard, then the process will force you to ask questions about your performance. Perhaps your figures are unique because of your location, demographics, unique product mix, or management style. Perhaps your store is simply performing poorly. Benchmarking will not normally give you answers. Instead, look on the

process as a management tool, never as the answer to your problems.

 Know what to measure.

In retailing there are some common benchmark areas that relate to all retail sectors. These include:

- Sales per selling square metre
- Average sale per customer
- Sales per full time team member
- Sales return as a percentage of sales
- Markdowns as a percentage of total sales
- Shrinkage as a percentage of sales
- Labour cost as a percentage of sales
- Stockturn during the year.

Other figures can be analysed, but an exploration of these benchmarks can help you in a practical way to improve your business.

 Know how to measure.

To obtain a benchmark figure in the key retailing areas, apply the following equations:

Sales per selling square metre

$$\frac{\text{Total dollar sales}}{\text{No. of square metres of selling space}}$$

Do not include car park, office space or other non retail areas in this equation.

Include aisle ways. It is exceptionally valuable if you can do this in each product category as it allows you to identify your profit and loss merchandise areas.

Average sale per customer

$$\frac{\text{Total dollar sales}}{\text{Number of customer transactions}}$$

This tells you how good your merchandising and selling strategy is. The information should be available to your whole team.

Sales per full time team member

$$\frac{\text{Total dollar sales}}{\text{Number of full time members equivalents}}$$

The key is to look at full-time equivalence, so group causals' hours into full-time employee equivalence. If you do not, it is very difficult to compare one store's figures against anothers.

Sales return as a percentage of net sales

$$\frac{\text{Returns in total}}{\text{Total of transactions}}$$

This will provide you with a customer satisfaction report based on return of goods, not on human relationships with your team. For example, a high goods return may reflect on your quality control.

Markdowns as a percentage of sales

$$\frac{\text{Markdowns}}{\text{Total sales}}$$

Shrinkage as a percentage of sales

$$\frac{\text{Inventory shrinkage}}{\text{Total sales}}$$

This will provide a shrinkage figure that then needs to be marked against customer theft, team member theft, or administration errors.

Labour cost as a percentage of sales

$$\frac{\text{All payroll expenses related to selling}}{\text{Total sales}}$$

This tells you the cost of doing business with your present team.

Stockturn during the year

$$\frac{\text{Total retail sales per year}}{\text{Retail value on inventory held at any one time}}$$

This tells you how often you turn your products during a twelve month period.

You should contact your trade organisation for assistance and information relating to benchmarking within your industry sector.

5 Interpret your findings.

The value of benchmarking comes in knowing how to interpret the figures, and the following table will act as a guide:

BENCHMARK	ABOVE TOP THIRD IN INDUSTRY	BELOW TOP THIRD IN INDUSTRY
Sales per selling square metre	Well done	You have opportunities. Review your product mix, merchandise, display and signage strategies.
Average sale per customer	Well done	Review your sales training. Your team are not add on selling, selling up or communicating with the customers as well as others.
Sales per full time equivalent	You may need more team members. They may eventually burn out.	You could be overstaffed, or have the wrong people selling, or your training program needs reviewing.
Sales return as a percentage of sales	Customers are dissatisfied. Find out why as a matter of urgency.	Well done
Markdowns as a percentage of total sales	Are your price strategies correct? Are team members selling professionally?	Well done
Shrinkage as a percentage of sales	Analyse your shrinkage policy as a matter of urgency.	Well done
Labour cost as a percentage of sales	Is your training effective?	Do you have enough team members to service customers properly?
Stockturn during the year	Well done	You are overstocked or have the wrong merchandise mix.

How to maintain standards in your store

Success in today's retail world is not about achieving perfection, or even excellence. Realistically, it is about achieving consistency. Customers accept that perfection is elusive and that few stores will be excellent. What they will not accept is a retailer who is inconsistent. A successful business ensures consistently good standards in customer service, hygiene, merchandising, and general safety. To maintain such standards, consider the following advice...

1 Walk the floor regularly.

Management needs to be visible, actively involved in retailing and maintaining retail standards. This cannot be achieved by staying in the office. Walk the floor once a day— and be seen to walk the floor. During that walk you should have a checklist and use it to prioritise tasks that need to be carried out during the day.

2 Walk in your customer's shoes.

When walking the store you should do so as if you were a customer. Start outside the front door to the shop and take the route your average customer would take. Go through the checkout and leave the store. If you do not, you will miss the obvious. Never assume anything.

3 Remember: retail is detail.

Detailed retail stores are admired by their customers. Always check:

- finger prints on the front door (especially if it is glass)
- the condition of the floor
- toilet paper in the restrooms

- the cleanliness of worktops and the checkout
- posters that are out of date or ripped
- cobwebs
- dead flies in the store window.

A survey of small stores carried out by Arthur Andersen in the United States found:

Emptied litter bins daily	97%
Washed windows daily	66%
Cleaned the toilets daily	52%
Mopped floors daily	49%
Waxed the floors daily	21%

4 Devise a standards listing for your store.

To maintain consistency, prepare a list of questions which will guarantee you are projecting the image you want your customer to have of your store. Your list may comprise such items as these, compiled by Rod Pickworth of Home Owners Warehouse:

- Is your store front clean and inviting to the customer?
- As you enter your store where does the customer's eye focus? Is this what you want as the focus?
- Are the key locations in the store supporting the correct product? Is this product at the correct stocking level and is the signage clearly visible?

- From the entrance is it easy to locate all the departments in the store?
- Can you see strong promotional signage related to the specific products you are promoting in the store?
- Is the race track easy for the customer to follow, is it uncluttered, clean and safe?
- Is the store inviting to the customers when they take the first five steps into the store?
- Are all the lights working? Are they all on and located in the correct locations and at the correct angles?
- Do products on display make a strong statement to your customers and are they inviting the customer to buy?
- Does the merchandise reflect the image of your store?
- Does your store reflect a personality to your customers? Does it reflect the name on the outside of the store?
- Are the familiar brands that customers ask for in the correct locations around the store?
- Do the shop fittings and fixtures for promotions reflect the image you are trying to create?
- Have you 'lifestyle' statements around the store that your customers can relate to?
- Are you using the upper walls correctly? Is the consumer's eye brought down on to products or are you encouraging them to look at the ceiling due to misplaced signs and products?
- Is all the cross merchandising in the store relevant to your customers?
- Have you the correct ratio of signs in the store and are they relevant to your customers and the products next to them?

5 Devise appropriate checklists.

The following checklist is typical of one which you could adapt/compile for use with your store:

Management Memo

Do not delegate store walks. They are a key part of the role of management. The team must see them being done and they must be done daily. Management 'swooping' down from Head Office to do store walks every three to six months can demotivate teams and are not good for your business culture. [76]

WEEKLY STANDARDS CHECKLIST
How good are we?

— ⟸ Extremely | Quite | Slightly | Neither | Slightly | Quite | Extremely ⟹ +

PHYSICAL APPEARANCE

	Extremely	Quite	Slightly	Neither	Slightly	Quite	Extremely	
Dirty	☐	☐	☐	☐	☐	☐	☐	Clean
Unattractive decor	☐	☐	☐	☐	☐	☐	☐	Attractive decor
Difficult to shop	☐	☐	☐	☐	☐	☐	☐	Easy to shop
Slow checkout	☐	☐	☐	☐	☐	☐	☐	Fast checkout
....	☐	☐	☐	☐	☐	☐	☐	....

STAFF

Discourteous	☐	☐	☐	☐	☐	☐	☐	Courteous
Cold	☐	☐	☐	☐	☐	☐	☐	Warm
Unhelpful	☐	☐	☐	☐	☐	☐	☐	Helpful
Inadequate Numbers	☐	☐	☐	☐	☐	☐	☐	Adequate Numbers
....	☐	☐	☐	☐	☐	☐	☐	....

ADVERTISING

Uninformative	☐	☐	☐	☐	☐	☐	☐	Informative
Unappealing	☐	☐	☐	☐	☐	☐	☐	Appealing
Unbelievable	☐	☐	☐	☐	☐	☐	☐	Believable
Unhelpful	☐	☐	☐	☐	☐	☐	☐	Helpful
....	☐	☐	☐	☐	☐	☐	☐	....

PRODUCTS

Narrow selection	☐	☐	☐	☐	☐	☐	☐	Wide selection
Depleted stock	☐	☐	☐	☐	☐	☐	☐	Overstocked
....	☐	☐	☐	☐	☐	☐	☐	....

PRICING

Comparatively low prices	☐	☐	☐	☐	☐	☐	☐	Comparatively high prices
Average dollar spending low	☐	☐	☐	☐	☐	☐	☐	Average dollar spending high
Large number of specials	☐	☐	☐	☐	☐	☐	☐	Low number of specials
....	☐	☐	☐	☐	☐	☐	☐	....

How to work with percentages

To allow comparisons to be easily made between stores and for benchmarking to be more realistic, many retailers prefer to talk in percentage terms rather than in financial terms. For this reason it is essential for retailers to understand the basics of percentage calculations—although it is important to remember that you bank money, not percentages, and it is money that eventually is counted as profit and pays the expenses.

1 Know how to calculate simple percentages.

A percentage is a part of a hundred and working out a percentage is a simple mathematical equation.

For example, 59 per cent (%) is 59 parts of a hundred.

$$\frac{59}{100} = 0.59 = 59\%$$

$$Percentage = \frac{Part}{Whole} \times 100$$

Percentages allow you to compare figures within your retail business.

2 Develop an understanding of percentages.

It is important for retailers to understand percentages since it enables them to calculate valuable comparative statistics as:

Net Profit as a percentage of sales
Gross Profit as a percentage of sales
Wages as a percentage of sales
Shrinkage as a percentage of sales
Expenses as a percentage of sales

and so on.

Retailers need to be able to analyse such financial ratios to determine the health of their retail business. As a retailer, then, you need to:

Step 1. Gather accurate information and package it so you can see relationships

Step 2. Calculate financial ratios

Step 3. Record your industry standards

Step 4. Compare your results

Step 5. Analyse possible causes of problems

Step 6. Take action.

3 Be able to calculate percentage change.

In retailing we often need to calculate a percentage change between two figures.

The formula for this is:

$$Percentage\ Change = \frac{Change}{Original\ Number} \times 100$$

For example, if you have reduced the price of a shirt from $12 to $10 and you need to tell the customers on the ticket the percentage change to the original price:

WINNING
YOUR CUS

MANAGING
YOUR STOR

PROMOTI
YOUR PRO

**MANAGING
YOUR BUSINESS**

DEX

179

Percentage change =
$$\frac{2 \text{ (the change)}}{12 \text{ (the original price)}} \times 100$$
= 16.6% saving.

 Know how to work out discounts.

Suppliers and manufacturers are constantly contacting retailers with discount buying opportunities. These are often based on the amount of product ordered, reduction on list price, or an agreed payment contract. As a retailer you need to know how to calculate discounts so that you can confidently make a business decision...

A supplier telephones you and offers a 7 per cent discount on dog food. Your immediate task is to work out the saving in financial terms to

Management Memo

Discounting can be a major indicator your store is in trouble. Discounting should be used as a tool to manage stockturn, but if you become established in the customers' eyes as a discounter, you may never achieve the gross profit you are aiming for. [77]

your business. This can be calculated using the following formula:

Discount

= Discount Percentage x Normal Price

= 7% x $2000 (normal bulk price)

= .07 x 2000

= $140 saving on order

This order will actually cost you $2000 less $140. You will pay $1860.

How to work out mark up versus gross profit

Gross profit is your key financial guide for growing your business. Everyone in your organisation should be able to understand gross profit and how it affects the life blood of your retailing and their department. An understanding of gross profit allows your team members to make decisions that will improve the way your business operates...

 Understand gross profit.

Retailers generate a lot of money through the cash register. A large percentage of this money is used to pay for the goods sold, as well as the other expenses as a result of doing business. The aim of a retailer is to generate enough money from selling a product to cover the costs of purchasing that product, to cover all the related expenses—and to obtain a profit from entering into the venture. Gross profit is the dollars in profit from buying and selling a product. Put another way:

$$\text{Gross Profit} = \text{Sell Price} - \text{Cost Price}$$

The gross profit is used to pay expenses and to provide a return of profit. e.g.

$$
\begin{aligned}
\text{Gross Profit} \quad &= \text{Sell Price} - \text{Cost Price} \\
&= \$5.00 - \$3.00 \\
&= \$2.00
\end{aligned}
$$

2 Think in terms of gross profit percentages.

Although retailers bank dollars, not percentages, they often talk about gross profit in percentages terms.

$$\text{Gross Profit \%} = \frac{\text{Sell Price} - \text{Cost Price}}{\text{Sell Price}} \times 100$$

e.g.

$$\text{Gross Profit \%} = \frac{\text{Sell Price} - \text{Cost Price}}{\text{Sell Price}} \times 100$$

$$= \frac{\$5.00 - \$3.00}{\$5.00} \times 100$$

$$= 40\%$$

If you purchased a product for $3.00 and you sell it for $5.00, you will generate a 40 per cent gross profit.

3 Understand mark up.

Mark up is the profit obtained from the sale of a product when expressed as a percentage of the cost price.

$$\text{Mark Up \%} = \frac{\text{Sell Price} - \text{Cost Price}}{\text{Cost Price}} \times 100$$

Note: Cost Price, not Sell Price, goes below the line.

e.g.

$$\text{Mark Up \%} = \frac{\$5.00 - \$3.00}{\$3.00} \times 100$$

$$= 66\%$$

This shows that a 40 per cent gross profit is in fact a 66 per cent mark up. They are completely different percentages.

WINNING
YOUR CUS
MANAGING
YOUR STOR
PROMOTI
YOUR PRO
**MANAGING
YOUR BUSINESS**
DEX
181

4 Avoid costly mistakes through confusion.

Confusion can cause major problems for the retailer. By looking at the calculations below, it is readily understood that, if team members confuse gross profit percentages and mark up, the retailer can end up with some very misleading figures when analysing sales.

Schedule of Comparisons
between Mark Up Percentages
and Gross Profit Percentages

Mark Up %	Gross Profit %
10	9.90
15	13.04
20	16.67
25	20.00
30	23.08
35	25.93
40	28.57
45	31.03
50	33.33
55	35.48
60	37.50
65	39.39
70	41.18
75	42.86
80	44.44
85	45.96
90	47.36
95	48.73
100	50.00
105	51.22
110	52.38
115	53.49
120	54.56
125	55.56
130	56.52
135	57.45
140	58.33
145	59.18
150	60.00

Many people get confused in grappling with the terms mark up and gross profit. By considering the above chart, you can see why you mustn't.

5 Explore ways to increase your gross profit.

The bottom line for retailers is the size of their profits. If you hope to increase the size of your gross profit, then consider the following actions:

- Purchase your products at a lower price.
- Change your product mix.
- Reduce the number of markdowns.
- Charge higher retail prices.
- Price your services higher.
- Stock more seasonal items.
- Offer fewer Stock Keeping Units (SKUs).

According to research by Arthur Andersen in the United States, the best method of increasing gross profit is to change your product mix and to include high gross profit items of a non known value nature, which will allow you to use price pointing effectively. In addition, they recommend that retailers link this to more value-added services. Customers appreciate such service and are willing to pay more for it.

On the reverse side, it is important for retailers to be aware of, and take steps to minimise, those factors which can result in a decrease in gross profits. These include:

- Competition pressure.
- Too many retailers in your sector within your catchment area.
- Customer preferences change.
- Change in product mix.
- A lot of lower priced merchandise in stock which gives low gross profits.

How to set prices that sell products

A good pricing policy is a vital ingredient in any retail business and is the considered outcome of a range of factors—manufacturing costs, government charges, suppliers' costs, overheads, expenses, profit margins, customer needs, perceived value of the product, and so on. For the retailer, it also becomes a balancing act as the customer demands better quality products and better service, at acceptable prices.

Be aware of the two product types.

There are two types of product in the marketplace and both need to be treated differently by the retailer when setting prices.

Known Value Products
Known value products are basic commodities and are very price sensitive. Customers purchase them on price considerations— newspapers, dog food, toilet paper, cornflakes, tea, and so on. Some retail sectors promote relatively few known value products, but they are a major part of the product mix in supermarkets in particular, and trade in these items is very competitive.

Non Known Value Products
Non known value products are normally bought for reasons other than price—they are customer 'wants' rather than 'needs'—and include fashion clothes, toys, exotic fruit, most garden products, and sports equipment. With such items retailers have more leeway in terms of the price levied. To stimulate customer demand, such products are normally promoted on their benefits,

rather than price. This has been successfully achieved by the florist, wine, and chocolate industries.

As well, retailers can price such products on the notion of 'perceived value'. Clothes, toys, cosmetics, and plants are often based on a retail price that at times has no relation to manufactured price. Both the toy and clothing industries learnt long ago to base prices on perceived value.

Use price points.

The practice of price pointing is based on the price barriers that most customers subconsciously set in their minds when they go shopping. These price barriers are 50 cents, $1, $1.50, $2, $3, $5, $7.50, $10, $15, and so on.

The perception is that a 95c product is seen as acceptable—but at $1.05 it is perceived as expensive. Another product, priced at $1.29 is perceived as being cheap, having moved away from the $1 price barrier towards the next barrier at the $1.50 mark.

Price points used effectively can ensure you maximise profits and stockturns.

Avoid those price point barriers.

Every customer has a 'price barrier' when they shop—a pre-conceived, perhaps subconscious feeling of what is a 'cheap' product and what is the point at which that same product becomes a 'dear' product. Pricing your products with these barriers in mind can dramatically improve your bottom line with no other effort on your behalf. To defuse those barriers, refer to the accompanying Management Memo.

 Try lifting prices on a monthly basis.

One Australian retailer has a novel strategy for handling inflation via his computer-based pricing system. He increased prices by adding one percent at the start of each month. In this way he claims he eliminates the hurdle of confronting customers with large annual price increases and, being programmed into his computer, it happens automatically. This increase compounds to give a 12.6 percent increase for the year—yet the monthly price jump is negligible.

Other advantages soon become evident. Buyers, encouraged by the better price, purchase earlier rather than later. The well-proven marketing strategy of warning customers of pending price increases happens 12 times a year rather than once.

As well, he argues, manufacturers delay price increases because they fear market reaction and loss of business to other producers who have not increased their prices. They only discover the real extent of their problem 12-18 months later when annual accounts are finalised or when liquidity has dried up. The loss factor on lines that sell slowly due to a large price increase is minimised using this strategy.

To explore his strategy further, consider the effect, over one year, of a one percent monthly increase for a $3.65 product…

September	$3.65
October	$3.68
November	$3.72
December	$3.76
January	$3.79
February	$3.83
March	$3.87
April	$3.91
May	$3.95
June	$4.00
July	$4.03
August	$4.07

Management Memo

Avoiding those Price Point Barriers [79]

Major Price Barrier	Minor Price Barrier	Your Price Point Should Be
$ 1.00		$ .95 or 1.25
	$1.50	1.45 or 1.65
	2.00	1.95 or 2.25
	3.00	2.95 or 3.25
5.00		4.95 or 5.25
	8.00	7.95 or 8.25
10.00		9.95 or 10.50
	13.00	12.95 or 13.25
15.00		14.95 or 15.50
	18.00	17.95 or 18.25
20.00		19.95 or 20.50
	23.00	22.95 or 23.25
25.00		24.95 or 25.50
30.00		29.95 or 30.55
40.00		39.95 or 42.00
50.00		49.95 or 55.00
75.00		74.95 or 78.00
100.00		99.95 or 110.00
150.00		149.95 or 175.00
200.00		199.95 or 225.00

Ref: Ron Marceil, Garden Centre Consultant, California, USA

How to increase your prices

Retailers spend a great deal of time considering price reductions when they should in fact be considering how to put prices up. To understand how much you can increase the price of a product, it is essential to understand the principles of price banding. The price band will vary according to your location and demographics.

 1 Position the product.

Product positioning is basically your attempt to influence the perception a customer has of your product. Where you locate the product in the store, the promotion campaign you adopt, even the price itself, all play a role in influencing the shopper's perception. As a guide, the higher the quality profile a product has, the more a customer is prepared to pay for it.

Price positioning in relation to quality perception in the eyes of the customer is of paramount importance. Get the price point wrong and sales may be dramatically reduced. For example, the customer expects to pay more for an expensive-looking flower arrangement at a florist. If the item is cheaper than they expect, they question how long the flowers will remain fresh.

2 Consider the impact before increasing price.

Everything you do should be measured. If you increase the price of a product, you must know how it will affect sales. Raise your price only when you understand the impact of the increase. The table below is a

Ref: Results Corp, Queensland	If your present margin is...								
	20%	25%	30%	35%	40%	45%	50%	55%	60%
...and you increase your price by......	...your sales could decline by the amount shown below before your gross profit reduces								
2%	9%	7%	6%	5%	4%	4%	4%	4%	3%
4%	17%	14%	12%	10%	9%	8%	7%	7%	6%
6%	23%	19%	17%	15%	13%	12%	11%	10%	9%
8%	29%	24%	21%	19%	17%	15%	14%	13%	12%
10%	33%	29%	25%	22%	20%	18%	17%	15%	14%
12%	38%	32%	29%	26%	23%	21%	19%	18%	17%
14%	41%	36%	32%	29%	26%	24%	22%	20%	19%
16%	44%	39%	35%	31%	29%	26%	24%	23%	21%
18%	47%	42%	38%	34%	31%	29%	26%	25%	23%
20%	50%	44%	40%	36%	33%	31%	29%	27%	25%
25%	56%	50%	45%	42%	38%	36%	33%	31%	29%
30%	60%	55%	50%	46%	43%	40%	38%	35%	33%

useful tool for measuring the consequences of price increases. As the perceived quality of the product improves, the customer expects the price to move up. The motor vehicle industry does this exceptionally well.

3 Do your homework when setting prices.

Do not just put prices up or down without undertaking some basic research. You must link your price strategy to your customers' perception of value (what they would pay for it). This is often different from your perception of value. Indeed, in many instances, your perception will be lower than the consumers'.

US research by Arthur Andersen found that retailers, when setting a price, do so for the following reasons, in order of importance:

1. Expected gross margin
2. Competitor's price
3. Manufacturer's recommended retail price
4. Customers' perceived value
5. Perceived demand
6. Cost to retailer
7. Company image
8. The product is in fashion at present
9. Volume of stock on hand.

Always review your competitors' prices, your consumers' expectations, and your image before setting a price.

4 Vary your price according to the type of product.

When pricing your product, consider it in one of three categories:

Management Memo

Retail store managers mark down their products after having considered the following factors: [80]

End of season	72%
Sales movement	59%
Age of product	58%
Walking the store	55%
Rule of thumb markdowns	21%
Across board markdowns	10%
Predetermined markdown formula	4%

A Basic Product, e.g. cornflakes
A Fashion Product, e.g. grey dress
A Seasonal Product, e.g. sunscreen
Pricing strategies in general retail vary based on the category of the product. In the Arthur Andersen Research, they found:

	Product Range Pricing Breakdown		
Retail policy	Basic	Fashion	Seasonal
Everyday low pricing	59 %	10 %	31 %
Full price promotion	50	25	25
Consistently moderate price	48	26	26
High-low price	45	23	32

5 Cater for changed buying habits.

Research by Grey Advertising in 1991 and 1993 in the United States found customer buying habits are changing.

	1991	1993
Many moderately priced brands meet my needs today	70 %	77 %
Less expensive brands have equal or better quality	72	89
I will not go back to the spending I used to	72	83

Clearly, customers are shopping around and being more critical. For this reason, you would be wise to monitor the price changes of your key products in your competitors' stores and position your price accordingly.

How to set an advertising budget

Advertising, if done correctly, is a rewarding investment in your business future. Too many retailers look on it as an expense and prune it when the economy is weak. This is dangerous and not a strategy that will provide you with a profitable future. Before you can plan your advertising campaign, however, it is vital that you set a realistic advertising budget…

1 Adopt a proven overall approach.

Use one of two well tested budgetary approaches when considering the financial implications of your advertising strategy:

Objective Technique—planning an advertising budget to meet your previously set objectives. Here your advertising strategy can be systematically costed out, and is not developed on hunches; but the budgetary approach will only work if you have already planned a future direction for your business.

Percentage of Sales Technique. Many retail sectors have benchmark figures for companies to work on. For example, the standard for your sector of retailing may be that the average company invests 5 per cent of turnover on advertising. If your projected turnover for the next year is $100,000, then your advertising budget should be $5,000.

2 Consider the factors that matter.

When deciding on how to develop your advertising budget, you need to consider a range of factors that impact upon your business, including:

The age of your business. If you have a business that is fewer than three years old, you need to spend more money on advertising than the benchmarked business as you still need to get your name known in the marketplace.

Your location. If you are situated in a high rent area, you will need to increase the sales per square metre in your business—which means you will need more exposure through advertising.

Your size of retail outlet. If you have a large outlet, in comparison with other businesses in your retail sector, you may already have a successful operation and may need to spend less than the benchmark for your retail sector.

The business economy. If the retail trend is negative in your business sector, you may need to increase your investment in advertising so that you can increase your market share in tough times.

Merchandising policy. If your objective is to move product quicker than your competitors by using a lower price strategy, then you will need to increase your advertising budget to increase consumer awareness.

Special events. You will need to invest extra funds to advertise special events.

3 Check your profit pointers in the planning process.

Do not just plan your advertising budget across the whole business carte blanche. It's a lot smarter to identify your 'profit pointers' and let

WINNING
OUR CUS | MANAGING
YOUR STOR | PROMOTI
YOUR PRO | **MANAGING
YOUR BUSINESS** | DEX | **187**

Vol. 1: See 374, 376, 392

them point the way in terms of your advertising investment priorities.

- Analyse all departments over the last trading period and look for the peaks.
- Identify departments that are expanding.
- Find out if any manufacturers are planning any major promotions in the next twelve months.
- Investigate what your competitors have planned for the coming year or so.
- Determine the extent to which your competitors are investing in advertising their businesses.

4 Be systematic in your approach.

Budgetary planning involves analysis of your business and a consideration of future directions. A typical simple chart you might devise as a tool to help explore your options could be as follows:

Department	Sales last year	Target sales this year	Advertising budget available
1.			
2.			
3.			
4.			
10.			

5 Select the appropriate media.

Having determined how much money you have allocated to advertising, you now consider what means of communication will provide the best return on your investment. Again, the following checklist will help you to explore the options.

When advertising in print media, your aim should be to get the lowest cost per thousand of targeted customers. Evaluate the relative cost of each newspaper, for example, based on the cost per thousand

Marketing Communications Checklist

	Ideal for the Planned Promotion	Unsuitable for the Planned Promotion
Mass Media		
Television	☐	☐
Radio	☐	☐
Press	☐	☐
Magazines	☐	☐
Billboards	☐	☐
Mixed signage in the community	☐	☐
Target Media		
Catalogues	☐	☐
Direct mail	☐	☐
Telemarketing	☐	☐
Sampling	☐	☐
Free riders (Gifts)	☐	☐
Publicity	☐	☐
Sponsorship	☐	☐
Organised events	☐	☐
Instore Media		
Merchandising	☐	☐
Display	☐	☐
Point of sale	☐	☐
Brochures	☐	☐
Display packs/products	☐	☐
Personal Media		
Sales representatives	☐	☐
Retail staff	☐	☐
Demonstrators	☐	☐

Ref: Open Learning Advertising Manual, Capel Manor College, UK

potential customers reached:

	Advertising Investment	Circulation	Cost/1000 customers
Newspaper A	$500	10,000	$\frac{\$500}{10,000} \times 1000$ = $50
Newspaper B	$1000	50,000	$\frac{\$1000}{50,000} \times 1000$ = $20

6 Adapt your strategy as required.

Retailing is an ever changing scene. Do not set a budget for the year and leave it. Monitor your strategy and results, and change your emphases accordingly to changes in the economy or your business.

How to maintain a competitive edge

Retailing is becoming more competitive. Australia has seen dramatic increases in selling space per head of population and many pundits would argue that we are over-shopped. Therefore getting new customers and making sure they stay loyal to your business is a major challenge and requires specific strategies...

1 Plan a strategy to develop your staff.

In today's retail environment it is difficult to stand out from the crowd. Your competitors, more than likely, sell the same products at the same price. You therefore need a campaign that says, 'I really want your business'. A key to success in this area, of course, is that your whole team should be striving for new business. They must be trained in professional skills of selling.

2 Work on your promotional techniques.

You need to offer more than just basic product if you are going to grab the customer's attention. For example:

- A hairdresser could promote allied products.
- A fashion store could use perfumes as an add-on.
- A bookshop might start a book club.
- With any purchase, offer a free gift that will be treasured by the customer.

- A travel company might provide a complimentary leather travel wallet.
- Try the buy-one-and-get-one-free strategy. It's a stronger statement than 'two for the price of one' or 'fifty per cent off'. Free is a powerful word in this context.
- Try a banded offer. This involves coupling two products together and putting a band around them, e.g. four litres of paint banded with half litre of turpentine with a price reduction over buying them singularly.
- Try price reductions. Do not have more than two sales a year, or customers will only come at sales time. The best sales work when you maintain a money back guarantee. It gives consumers extra confidence.
- Try sampling. Provide samples to encourage sales. The Duty Free Shop at Auckland International Airport recently had a whisky sampling session. You can imagine what that did for sales!
- Try vouchers and coupons. These

are used by many retailers, especially the supermarkets who use it to capture your weekly loyalty.

- Insist on quality service—this is your best promotional strategy.

3 Manage your promotions.

Promotions need planning at least four months ahead if they are to be successful. Saatchi and Saatchi, the international promotional company, advocates the three month cycle for promotions. This allows your customers to get used to the promotion. You must have a calendar to plan such sales initiatives.

4 Make a sales promotion work for you.

A key to success is to read the consumer magazines, those related to your industry sector that your consumer reads. This will help you relate to your customers more closely. You should aspire to the same things they aspire to.

Keep your promotion relevant.
Keep it simple.
Keep it quality.

Management Memo

Don't be afraid of the competition. Remember, a kite rises against, not with, the wind.—*Hamilton Mabie*

Every time you succeed, I die a little—*Gore Vidal*

5 Get the contract signed.

If you are working towards the signing of a contact with your customer, be aware of the following:

- People often buy for greed, fear and laziness. Listen for these clues in your conversation.

- Get from a verbal agreement to a financial agreement.

- Agree on the little things before you start on the big ones.

- Keep the negotiations friendly.

- Finally, when you have closed the sale, do not close the relationship. You should have worked towards a win-win situation that allows you to continue the relationship.

How to develop sales promotions

Price reduction campaigns can work in certain locations and economic climates, but if you fail to plan carefully for such campaigns, you may find that you have cultivated a price-motivated shopper who only comes for discounts. Supermarkets have taken the lead in specific price promotions and the lessons learned from positive promotions in that retail sector can be readily adapted to other retail industries...

1 Consider Everyday Low Price promotions.

ELP promotions are common in supermarkets and home improvement stores. Here the company promotes its business as the cheapest in town on the products it supplies. To develop this concept as a strategy you must regularly review your competition and compare your prices with theirs. To develop ELP promotions, you will need to be a major player in the marketplace as you will have to buy in bulk to ensure you can maintain such promotions.

2 Consider using Bulk Purchase Discounts.

BPDs are another useful way of increasing the average sale per customer. One of the most successful sales promotions is the 'four-for-three' promotion on products. Try using the strategy during one month to increase sales, or on weekdays during one specific month to increase sales on quieter days. This can be successful as it increases your average sale per customer and ensures the initial purchase items are at full gross profit.

3 Consider a Variable Day Price policy.

For VDP promotions you make a business decision to vary the price on specific days of the week. You usually take your quietest day of the week and use reduced prices on that day to increase your customer traffic. Some companies call these days 'Pensioners' Day' or 'Ladies Day'.

4 Position sales promotions to increase total sales.

The objective of a sale is to increase your customer traffic and as a result increase your cash flow. To achieve this, many businesses place sales bins at the front of the store. Others hold the view that it is better to place a 'taster' of the sale at the front of the store and then place the major sale bin at the rear of the store, thereby encouraging the consumer to walk through the store and, hopefully, to pick up more product on impulse as they pass.

5 Be aware of the value of price banding.

Price banding is the band of prices in which a product will sell. For example, if the maximum perceived value is $30 and the minimum is $25 then this leaves a price band between $25 and $30 for flexible pricing. A retailer in a depressed area or in a lower economic group area may select a price nearer the $25 giving him/her the flexibility to increase prices in the future. A retailer in a more affluent area or higher economic group area may price the product near the $30 and achieve the same volume of sales.

6 Ensure promotional sales work for you.

In more difficult trading climates, the tendency has been to reduce prices and to have sales promotions to increase turnover. The result of continued sales promotions may be increased turnover, but can this increase in turnover justify the reduction in gross profit percentage?

Management Memo

Is it better to increase the rate of gross profit rather than sales? You may be able to achieve an extra 1 per cent gross margin without losing sales. How? By pricing according to what the market determines. Rather than sell at $9.95, go well past the $10 price barrier and sell at $11.99. In other words, once past the price barrier, it is better to move near to the next one which in this example is $15, rather than stay too close to the previous price barrier. Pricing below the next barrier gives the consumer the impression you are inexpensive, while pricing just above a price barrier gives the impression of being expensive.[81]

The table below, prepared by Results Corp, Queensland, is a useful guide when reducing prices. You may find that the turnover increase you achieve may not justify having an overall price reduction.

Ref: Results Corp, Queensland	If your present margin is...								
	20%	25%	30%	35%	40%	45%	50%	55%	60%
...and you reduce your price by...	...to produce the same profit, your sales volume must increase by								
2%	11%	9%	7%	6%	5%	5%	4%	4%	3%
4%	25%	19%	15%	13%	11%	10%	9%	8%	7%
6%	43%	32%	25%	21%	18%	15%	14%	12%	11%
8%	67%	47%	36%	30%	25%	22%	19%	17%	15%
10%	100%	67%	50%	40%	33%	29%	25%	22%	20%
12%	150%	92%	67%	52%	43%	36%	32%	28%	25%
14%	233%	127%	88%	67%	54%	45%	39%	34%	30%
16%	400%	178%	114%	84%	67%	55%	47%	41%	36%
18%	900%	257%	160%	106%	82%	67%	56%	49%	43%
20%	-	400%	200%	133%	100%	80%	67%	57%	50%
25%	-	-	500%	250%	167%	125%	100%	83%	71%
30%	-	-	-	600%	300%	200%	150%	120%	100%

How to manage non price sensitive products

Surprisingly for most retailers, price is not always the major reason people purchase a product. A recent survey of customers at a Melbourne garden centre found that their priorities for purchase related to, in order of importance—name of plant, its height, the colour of its flowers, the scent, its non-poisonous nature, and, finally, price. Indeed, the majority of products sold today are non price sensitive or non known value products. Understand the special nature of such items and you can improve your profit line...

1 Be aware of your non price sensitive products.

Non price sensitive lines are normally purchased on impulse. They are often a 'want' rather than a 'need' and are normally not purchased with price being a major initial motivator. These are the items that can grow your bottom line, since they should have a larger gross profit than price sensitive product lines. In the majority of retail situations, 80 per cent plus of products stocked will fall into this category.

2 Position non price sensitive lines carefully.

Positioning is based on image. If your customers come to your store because price is a major motivator, then price sensitive products should be displayed in major sightlines. However, if they come because of your range, quality and service, then non price sensitive products should be displayed in those key positions.

Obviously you cannot display all your products in prime selling positions, so you will need to adopt a procedure where you rotate products in sightlines. Decisions in this regard will take into consideration:

- Is the product in fashion at present?
- Is it the right season to promote it?
- Is the product currently topical?
- What is the life of the product? e.g. Teletubby toys had a 2-year retail life.

3 Produce special signs for non price sensitive lines.

Customers purchase non price sensitive products for reasons other than price and so, to maximise sales of such items, you will need carefully constructed signage to emphasise qualities other than price.

Research tells us we remember facts in groups of three and this is a valuable guide when preparing your signs. The following is a proven format for non price sensitive signs:

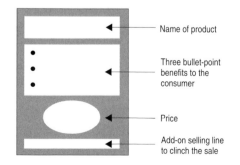

Name of product

Three bullet-point benefits to the consumer

Price

Add-on selling line to clinch the sale

Train the team to sell benefits.

Price may be an issue for your sales team, but it is normally not an issue to the consumer in terms of non price sensitive products. For this reason, sales people should listen to the shopper, identify the real benefits to that customer, explain these benefits —and finally get around to price. Training programs should include product benefits training and its importance in the role of selling.

 Understand customer needs—then sell.

Customers, when purchasing non price sensitive products, usually place other considerations over price. For this reason, you should:

Offer assurance. Your signs and selling techniques should erase any doubts they have. 'Stroke' them, so that they will feel like winners by making this buying decision.

Project quality. Be ruthless with your standards because, in today's retail world, quality is expected.

Inspire them to buy. Group products in themes, suggest uses for the products, show how easy they are to use, and demonstrate the benefits.

Offer a complete package. Always think 'link' and offer a complete package. The customer has come shopping for enjoyment and expects you to provide everything they need—including related items.

 Display products to maximise sales.

The aim is to encourage customers to shop the non price sensitive lines and search for the price sensitive lines. You may therefore need to reorganise your merchandising to achieve this objective.

Management Memo

Nowhere outside of the home furnishing department is it possible to group so many different types of merchandise together in lifestyle presentations. Lifestyle retailing allows considerable opportunity for cross mechandising. [82]

By placing the appropriate non price sensitive lines at the gondola ends and the budget lines in the centre, you can achieve extra sales along the whole gondola.

End of Gondola	Middle of Gondola	End of Gondola
Non price sensitive products	Budget lines	Non price sensitive products

Remember, finally...

Note these key points in managing non price sensitive product displays:

- Ensure the display is striking, yet in keeping with the style of the retail outlet.

- Communicate with your customers by providing information via leaflets, advertisements in newspapers, recorded messages in the store, literature near the cash register, promotions on cash register receipts, and promotions on trolleys and baskets.

- Let the display promotion spread into a storewide promotion. This is easily achieved with theme selling for spring, autumn, Halloween, and Christmas promotions, but more difficult with generic promotions by an individual company.

- Prepare a promotion plan and record all activities. You need to measure the success and failures of any activity.

How to 'open price' your products

Products are priced in one of two ways. The majority are now computer code-marked by manufacturers or the retail supplier using a 'number' code or a 'bar' code system. However, although in decline, the 'open pricing' system is still in use in many small retail stores, where the retailer must put the price on the product using a non-computerised system. If using this approach, be aware of the following guidelines...

1 Select a price label that best suits your business.

When adopting a technique for pricing your products, you would normally consider one of the following options:

- *Felt-tip pens.* These are usually a quick-fire solution for marking cardboard cartons and paper labels, for they are permanent and cheap. The markings do have certain drawbacks, however—they deface the product, are not easily erased or changed, and may also detract from your desired image.

- *Rubber stamp price markers.* These are also ideal for cardboard cartons and paper labels, for they are quick to apply. Unfortunately, they don't work on damp or dusty surfaces, and smudging can be a problem, often causing the price to be indecipherable.

- *Self-adhesive tickets.* These are ideal for any smooth, dry, dust-free surface. Tickets are cheap, easy to apply and can be printed with your name. Labels can be applied to the product via a small, easy-to-use gun and prices can be changed

easily. The drawbacks with this technique are two-fold—the price-guns need to be maintained regularly, and ticket switching can be a security problem, although this can be combatted by using tickets that are made so that they tear in half if ticket switching is attempted.

- *Tie-on labels.* These are ideal for plants and awkward items such as wheelbarrows. They are cheap, permanent and easy-to-apply. They come in various sizes and the tags can be easily changed. A disadvantage is that they can be easily switched.

2 Adopt a consistent labelling style.

Whichever method you select, it is important for the customer and your team that you are consistent. For example, always price in the same position on the product.

3 Adhere to the rules of product marking.

Basic principles apply in relation to the marking of your products...

- Prior to marking prices, always check the price against the price list.
- Ensure your price marking equipment is accurately set up and works correctly.
- Price marks must be clear, easily read, and legible, not only by the customer, but also by the checkout operator.
- The best positions for pricing are:
  - On the top of bottles, jars and cans.
  - On the top end of boxes and packages.
  - On the top right-hand corner of the front of paper sleeves and blister packets.
- Make sure that you put the price the right way up on all products. Prices placed upside down will slow down the checkout operation.
- When pricing cartons, the key is to be methodical, since accuracy and consistency usually follow. For this reason, keep to a proven routine, such as the following:
  - (a) Remove the outer wrapper and expose the goods.
  - (b) Select the correct price on the price gun.
  - (c) Mark one entire layer.
  - (d) Place all the marked goods on display.
  - (e) Price mark the next layer of products…and so on.
- Make sure the price is clearly visible. Staff and customers need to be able to see the price at a glance.
- Adopt a tagging policy that always prices the products in the same location on the item every

> ### Management Memo
>
> The prime function of the retailer is to maximise profit. Pricing is influenced by a number of factors:
> - Competition in the product category in your catchment area.
> - Characteristics of goods. Certain goods are expected by the consumer to be more expensive.
> - Availability of goods. Generally the more scarce the product, the more expensive.
> - Stockturn. A high stockturn means you can lower the price, increase the stockturn and make more profit.
> - Promotions. Both in and out of store.
> - Store Image.
> - Theft.. [83]

time. Consistency counts.

- Do not obscure vital customer information with a pricing label, for this is a sure way to annoy customers.

4 Be aware of security pricing strategies.

Security pricing can help reduce pilfering. A professional thief will often attempt to sneak products through the check-out by deliberately placing items inside others—for example, hiding smaller items at the bottom of pots, buckets, bins or similar containers.

If you price on the outside of products, chances are the cashier may not look inside the item, for example, the pot. On the other hand, if you price *inside* containers such as pots and buckets, the cashier has a reason to look inside the items and can then pick up the other products, recording them at the checkout without causing any embarrassment to either party.

How to buy effectively

Retailing is the process of buying and selling products. To be successful, you need a policy that enables you to buy the right product at the right price at the right time which then allows you to sell it as soon as possible at a profit. Many businesses work on a system where they calculate a 1 per cent increase on the buying price for every month the product sits on the shelf in the store. All of which means that the buying process is critically important for retailers. Get it wrong and the result can be a loss.

1 Develop a positive relationship with suppliers.

You are your suppliers' customer and the relationship you have with them should be the same as the one you have with your own customers. It is a relationship built on trust. So you should select suppliers you can depend upon when it comes to price, quality, value, and timely delivery.

2 Select your suppliers carefully.

Your customers select their retailers carefully and you should select your suppliers with the same care. You often have a choice between buying directly from a manufacturer or from a wholesaler. Whichever avenue you source, your decision should be based on such considerations as:
- the type of product you are buying
- the origin of the product
- the size of your business
- the proximity of the suppliers
- the supplier's policy on buying
- the financial status of the supplier and yourself.
- price.

Suppliers can be contacted in a number of ways—via the Internet, by visiting cash-and-carry wholesalers,

attending trade fairs, group buying or co-operative buying, central office buying, or through representatives visiting your store.

Retailers today have a wide choice of suppliers offering similar products. To help you make the right decision as to which supplier to use, a decision-matrix can prove useful. Consider the following example provided by John Berens:

	Your weighting	Suppliers' priorities as you see them					
		A	B	C	D	E	F
Suppliers can fill orders	5	3	4	4	2	0	1
Mark up adequate	4	2	4	3	0	1	2
Customer requests you stock it	1	1	2	4	3	0	0
Supplier supplies fashion changes	3	2	3	4	1	0	0
Supplier helps promotes	2	1	0	3	1	2	2
Supplier delivery policy	6	0	1	3	4	3	0

Journal of Retailing (71/7)

Score each supplier who you believe has the same priorities as you. The supplier with the closest weighting to yours is the one to select.

Plan your purchases.

Buying has to be planned and the astute buyer will use the following formula:

Planned Purchase at Retail Price =
Planned Sales + Planned Reductions + Planned End of Month Stock − Planned Beginning of Month Stock

Remember that Planned Purchase at Retail Price is not how much the buyer can spend. Once you have this figure you will then be able to calculate a buying price and a budget for your buyer.

The table below will help you plan your purchases.

 Ask questions before accepting bulk discounts.

Suppliers often supply discounts for early bird buying and bulk buying. Before taking up such offers, you will need to consider such questions as:

Is it a slow moving item for you? What extra costs of handling and storage will

> **Management Memo**
>
> Research in the United States shows that retailers look for the following in selecting a supplier:
> • responsiveness to specific retailer needs
> • commitment to follow through
> • flexibility
> • on-time delivery
> • integrity and honesty
> • good communication. [84]

you need to add? What is the financial cost for you to carry this stock for a longer period? Do you have the storage space? Will you sell the entire purchase? Will the supplier provide extended credit? Will the supplier guarantee the goods? What assistance will the supplier provide to help you move their product on to the customer?

Consider central buying.

Larger organisations often rely on central buying using specialist buyers who, in theory, should be able to select better deals as they are specialists in their field.

PURCHASE PLANNER	AUG	SEPT	OCT	NOV	DEC	JAN	SEASON TOTAL
1. Planned BOM stock	$197,919	$225,168	$243,811	$254,233	$243,880	$232,825	$251,500
2. Planned sales	48,273	54,919	59,466	55,268	87,100	44,774	349,800
3. Planned reductions (total of a+b+c below)	5,971	3,379	4,159	5,493	3,054	7,317	29,733
(a) Markdowns	5,247	2,915	3,267	4,664	1,748	6,645	24,486
(b) Shortages	483	549	595	553	871	448	3,499
(c) Employee/other discounts	241	275	297	276	435	224	1,748
4. Planned EOM Stock (BOM stock for following month)	225,168	243,811	254,233	243,880	232,825	251,500	-
5. Planned retail purchases (items 2+3+4-1)	81,493	77,301	74,047	50,408	79,099	70,766	433,114
6. Planned cost purchases (initial markup is 44.3%, so cost is 55.7% of item 5)	45,392	43,057	41,244	28,077	44,058	39,417	241,245
7. Planned cumulative initial markup (44.3% of item 5, or item 5-6)	36,101	34,244	32,803	22,331	35,041	31,349	191,869
8. Planned gross margin (item 7-3)	30,130	30,505	8,644	16,838	31,987	24,032	162,136

Ref: William Davidson, Daniel Sweeney and Ronald Stamp, *Retailing Management*

How to manage stockturns

Two companies in the same town sell the same product at the same price. One turns stock four times a year; the other sixteen times a year. The second retailer concentrates on stockturn in the belief that the customer should constantly be presented with fresh product. The second business makes the bigger profit. Stockturn is a key ingredient for succcessful retailing...

1 Know what you have in stock.

Before evaluating your stockturns you should have a best practice procedure in place for receiving stock. If you know what you have, you will not over-order and will turn stock more quickly. Plan ahead so that you can anticipate new deliveries and schedule displays. Storage is expensive so use specialised equipment to reduce manual handling and ensure you have a delivery receiving area. Make sure the receiving area is clean, well organised, secure, and has easy access for delivery vehicles.

2 Make buyers responsible for stockturn.

Successful stockturn begins with the buyer whose role is to:
- select the right product in the right volume
- obtain the product at the right price
- decide on the stockturn for that product.

For example, a buyer should plan each product's life in accordance with a simple formula, such as:

Buy 100 yellow cushions to retail at $12.95 and sell over a 10 week period.

This information must then be passed on to the merchandiser so that the product can be managed on a 10-week cycle.

3 Manage your stockturn.

Products therefore should have a lifespan in the store; the key is to manage that lifespan. Using the above example, the management program for the yellow cushions would be:

Product: yellow cushions
Retail Price: $12.95
Volume: 100
Stockturn: 10 weeks

Week	Units to sell a week	Accumulative total
1	10	10
2	10	20
3	10	30
4	10	40
5	10	50
6	10	60
7	10	70
8	10	80
9	10	90
10	10	100

With such a schedule, your task is to manage the product week by week to achieve the desired stockturn.

WINNING
YOUR CUS

MANAGING
YOUR STOR

PROMOTI
YOUR PRO

**MANAGING
YOUR BUSINESS**

DEX

199

 Focus on week one.

Many retailers leave management of stock too long into the life cycle, slow sales then aggravate the problem, and you end up with a poor seller. Your actions in the first week are critical as this is when you can monitor sales and take appropriate action.

If, for example, you planned a 10 unit stockturn that week and you achieve a 21 unit stockturn, that's good. You may even decide to purchase more product. On the other hand, if you planned to sell 10 units and you sell only three, you will have to become proactive in managing and monitoring the product.

5 Monitor the stockturn during the life cycle.

See the product's lifecycle in two halves. In each, you will require different management approaches.

In the first half of the product's life span, use merchandising strategies. If stockturn is low during the first five weeks, focus on product promotion and display. Change one thing and monitor it, if this does not improve the stockturn then change something else. Changes to consider might include:

- Move the position of the display
- Change the shape of the display
- Make the display more shoppable
- Change the signage
- Change the promotional literature
- Check the team have the product knowledge to promote
- Ensure that your staff are promoting the product.

If merchandising strategies fail to move the product, in the second half of the product life span introduce pricing strategies to bring your

Management Memo

Monitoring stock levels is vital in ensuring sufficient stock to avoid being out-of-stock. It makes a big difference in customers' perception. [85]

stockturn back on course. You might now consider such changes as:

- Increase or decrease the price
- Sell three for the price of two
- Reduce the gross profit
- Sell at cost
- Sell at any cost.

6 Be aware of the pros and cons of stockturn.

Turning products quicker means that the product is fresher, a particularly important point for retailers of perishable products. Fresher stock may be sold at a higher price and therefore the store not only achieves higher sales, it can also take extra profits. As well, in such situations the sales teams will usually become more highly motivated. Finally, the operating costs of doing business should be lower, cash should be more fluid in the business, and interest costs could be reduced.

There is a downside to increasing your stockturn, however. If your product moves so quickly that your stock becomes depleted in certain lines, your customers may go elsewhere. The business will need to incur higher transport costs due to extra shipments and the buyer is going to spend more time with suppliers. As well, your sales staff may even become stressed because they may have trouble with the pressure of keeping up with the pace of stockturn. Such a situation needs to be addressed through work planning priorities and training.

How to monitor departmental performance

Successful retailing demands that managers monitor the performance of all categories of products in the store. Smaller retailers are usually aware of how well the store is performing but fail to review how individual departments are performing. Often one department is generating twice as much profit as another or a department is negatively performing. If you know what is happening department by department, you can then focus your attention on and, in the end, more effectively improve overall store performance...

1 Manage departments or categories, not stores.

Category management is the buzz word for managing specific sections of your store. Delegate team members to manage departments or categories, with the responsibility to make decisions within their designated area. In managing a category, they will need to adopt a four-step approach:

Develop a financial plan.
Benchmark the category against leading retailers who have the same category. Set realistic sales goals in that area.

Undertake a competitive analysis.
Really get to know local demographics, who competitors are in your catchment area, and how to keep an eye on them. Identify and analyse the winners in your category, their strengths and weaknesses.

Develop a tactical plan.
Decide on your optimum product mix, pricing strategy, and promotion strategy, and develop planograms.

Compile an implementation strategy.
Who is going to do what and when is it going to be done?

2 Initiate departmental performance reporting.

Without a regular analysis of product performance in each department, it becomes difficult to set realistic retail prices and to achieve predicted profit levels. Some companies analyse departments weekly, monthly or every six months. The objective of these performance reports is to use them as tools to check on the health of each department. Without the evidence they provide, an action plan will lack credibility.

3 Compile performance reports.

Your staff member responsible for producing a departmental report for analysis undertakes this task in three specific stages:

Record all purchases. Once a decision has been made on how often reporting is to occur, record all purchases made by the store during the period leading up to the report. This should provide details of the supplier, invoice number, the date the product was delivered, and the financial amount on the invoice. On the same record should be any supplier returns.

Complete a stock count. At the end of the period, undertake a physical stock count of every product on the retail shelf and in the storage areas. (When you implement departmental reporting for the first time, remember to count the stock *before* the first period begins as well.)

Record all sales. Record all the sales made in the category over the selected period.

WINNING
YOUR CUS

MANAGING
YOUR STOR

PROMOTI
YOUR PRO

**MANAGING
YOUR BUSINESS**

DEX

201

Vol. 1: See 198

With all this information (see the accompanying sample pro forma), a departmental performance report can now be compiled.

Analyse the figures.

Your benchmark figures and your actual figures provide you with a valuable tool. You may find your gross profit is lower than you had planned. If this is the case, you need to analyse your shrinkage, buying procedures, markdowns, product mix, and selling techniques, and take appropriate action. If your gross profit is higher than you had planned, explore and capitalise on the reasons for this occurring.

Analyse a department's contribution overall.

It's useful to know how a department is performing, and what percentage of total store sales comes from that department:

Using the figure for sales in the department and your total store sales, you can obtain the Department Sales Contribution as a percentage of total sales. The next stage is to find out the Department Gross Profit

---

Management Memo

Decisions relating to store design, department location, product mix, and space valuations should be based on performance reports. Factors in locating selling departments include:
- Sales productivity of space
- Impulse versus demand lines
- Replacement frequency
- Adjacent departments
- Seasonal needs
- Size of department
- Physical characteristics of product
- Shopper considerations
- Merchandise arrangement. [86]

Contribution, as follows:

Department Gross Profit Contribution =

$$\frac{\text{Dept Sales Contribution} \times \text{Dept Gross Profit \%}}{100}$$

e.g., the electrical tools department contributes 15 per cent of total store sales at a gross profit of 25 per cent.

$$\text{Department Gross Profit} = \frac{15 \times 25}{100}$$
$$= 3.75$$

This number represents actual dollars that this department contributes to the store gross profit. If, for example, the store gross profit is 15 per cent ($15 in every $100), then your department is contributing $3.75 to the $15. The remainder comes from other departments.

DEPARTMENT PERFORMANCE REPORT							
Category:				Period:			
PURCHASES				RETURNS			
Date	Invoice	Supplier	Amount	Date	Invoice	Supplier	Amount
					GROSS PROFIT CALCULATION		
					Opening Stock	$	
					+ Total Purchases	$	
					− Total Returns	$	
					= Sub Total	$	
					− Closing Stock	$	
					= Cost of Goods Sold	$	
					Sales	$	
					− Cost of Goods sold	$	
					= Gross Profit $	$	
					= Gross Profit %		%
TOTAL PURCHASES					TOTAL RETURNS		

Ref: IGA, *Managing the Dollars* workbook

How to develop an open to buy policy

Stockturn and stock management are important concepts in any retail business. Many businesses tend to be overstocked, a situation which critically affects the profit line, because stock that is not being sold should actually be money in the bank. Smart retailers have in place a system where they buy when product is being sold, rather than buying and then trying to sell. This is often called an open to buy policy...

1 Set a budget and stick to it.

Many businesses find that, as sales go up, they purchase more product to sell—and sometimes discover that they are left with excess stock. If this situation continues over a period of time, the usual result is that the business runs out of money to buy stock that is *actually* selling. Stock purchases must relate to actual sales.

The solution is to have monthly targets. Set a budget for your business and stick to it.

2 Establish a monthly buying system.

Whenever possible, buy monthly, rather than quarterly, six-monthly, or yearly. To buy monthly you need to know:

- the actual sales for each month of the year
- the budget sales for each month
- the actual purchases for each month of the year
- the budget purchases for each month of the year.

Determine your buying program through the use of a profit and loss budget, a critical tool in your stock control management. Consider the following example:

Sales Situation

Actual sales for month	$80 000
Budget sales for month	$100 000
Difference	$20 000
Convert to Cost (100% – Target GP, e.g. 10%)	90%
Overstock position as a result of not making sales	$18 000

Purchase Situation

Actual purchase for month	$85 000
Budget purchases for month	$80 000
Difference ($85 000 – $80 000)	$5 000
Overstock position due to over ordering	$5 000

What This Means to You

Budget closing stock	$150 000
Stock adjustment not making sales	$18 000
Over ordering	$5 000
Actual closing stock	$173 000

In this situation, you would be overstocked by $23 000 against what you planned for the month. You are now able to plan a new budget for the following month, aware that your planned purchase budget will be pruned by $23 000 to ensure that your stock management is maintained at the appropriate levels.

WINNING
YOUR CUS

MANAGING
YOUR STOR

PROMOT
YOUR PRO

**MANAGING
YOUR BUSINESS**

DEX

203

 **Know your stars
and dogs.**

The key to stock control is—if it does
not sell, sell it! You cannot afford to
have products on the shelf gathering
dust. Slow movers, often called
'dogs', can cost your business profits.
So, think about your products in
terms of four categories, as
advocated by Peter Cox, FMRC
Business Development, University of
New England, NSW, Australia:

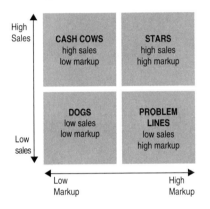

Prior to ordering stock, judge it first
in terms of where it would be placed
in the above categorisation. The more
'star' and 'cash cow' products you
have in your business, the happier
your bank manager will be, just as
s/he would be happy to have you
stock up with few, if any, 'problem
lines' and 'dogs'.

Buy for the seasons.

The open buy policy is more
important for seasonal retailing than
for non-seasonal retailing when
money can be tied up for longer
periods. For example, a garden

centre should aim for a situation
where in the slow winter period it
generates 1/15th of its annual sales
and in the active spring season half
of its sales for the year. Supermarkets
will normally generate similar sales
for each month of the year, making
their buying a far easier proposition.

**Ask the seven
critical questions.**

As a store or departmental manager,
you need to ask seven key questions
prior to buying. If you cannot answer
all seven with factual evidence, you
may well find you will have stocking
problems in the future:

1. How much should you invest in
stock?
2. When should the investment be
made?
3. When should stock levels be
decreased?
4. When should stock levels
increase?
5. What should you invest in?
6. Why invest?
7. Where should you invest your
money?

How to increase your average sale —and increase your profits

The secret of success for the great majority of retailers is not to open more and bigger outlets with the associated high capital costs; the key is to increase gross and net profits in their existing businesses. And rather than attempting to increase the number of customers, most retailers find that a more effective approach is to sell more products to their existing customer base. Using this strategy, profits can increase with very little cost by adopting a few simple ideas…

 Try 'selling up'.

Rather than offer the smallest product to the customer on every occasion, why not sell up? Most people tend to buy from the 'sight and take' shelf. For this reason, your displays should be designed to encourage customers to buy the large size before the small one (assuming the larger is more profitable to you).

In your displays, ensure the customer sees the large product before the smaller versions. All too often we put large products on the top shelf or small sizes in prime selling spots. If you do want to sell the small size, always place a large product in the centre of the display.

 Train your staff in the art of 'selling up'.

Familiarise your team with the principles of 'selling up'. When a customer comes in and asks 'Have you got an X?', do your staff:

- Show the customer the *largest* item X first?
- Select more expensive items in the range first to show the customer?
- Pick up the *large* size when simply talking about the product?

3 Try the price points strategy.

Everyone has a price barrier when they shop. If a product is above the price barrier, it is seen as being too expensive; too far below the barrier and it is perceived as being too cheap and possibly defective in some way.

You can increase gross profit by having your customers pay a little more for products they have already decided to buy. To make this work you need to understand how to use price points effectively, by relying less on price and more on value as perceived by the customer.

Does this theory work? A UK retailer altered its pricing policy using the price points theory—1986 gross profit: 29 per cent; 1987 gross profit using price points: 34 per cent. The firm increased sales by £53,000 while the number of units sold remained the same!

 Try suggestive selling.

Be suggestive. Give customers ideas. Use words on point-of-sale cards like: 'Ideal for…' or 'We recommend…'. This will encourage people to spend—particularly when they are desperate for ideas.

5 Try link or tie-in sales.

There is a tie-in item for many products we sell. When selling plants, it may be fertiliser, compost, stakes, or climber supports. When selling toys, it may be batteries; when selling cameras, it may be film or carrying case. Promote link selling through such strategies as:

- Verbal suggestion
- Point-of-sale reminders in front of, or with, the product
- Direct linkage via display
- Linked products packaged with the primary product
- Header boards suggesting links, i.e. 'Dont forget…' signs.

Train your staff in the nuances of link selling. Encourage them to use 'link-product closes' whenever appropriate.

On the reverse side of the tag, customers are reminded that, for maximum growth, their new plant requires water—and bonemeal, peat and fertiliser which can also be bought at this store.

6 Focus on your trolleys or baskets.

A company in California found that many customers stopped spending when their trolley was full. This raises a number of questions:

- Are your trolleys or baskets clearly visible?
- Does every customer pick up a basket or trolley?
- Are they the right type or can you get others that hold more products?
- When a trolley is full, do you approach the customer and offer to push the trolley to the till—while giving them an empty one?
- Do you use 'greeters' on busy days to hand out trolleys as people come into the store?

All these points will help you increase your average sales.

7 Use open questions upfront.

How often do you, as a customer, say 'No, just looking', when the sales staff say 'Can I help you?'? Rarely does someone walk into a store just to look. All are potential customers. And the first step to a sale is to use open or leading questions, with the aim of starting a conversation which leads to you identifying the customer's needs and wants.

8 Make the average sale value known to staff.

Staff can be motivated to increase their average sale per customer, but they must know the current 'average sale per customer'. With this information, employees have a standard to work to and can monitor their own progress.

Consider implementing an 'average sales competition' for staff in a retail store or as an intra-company competition. Working on an accumulating points system, at the end of the set period, the highest total of points wins a pre-determined prize. To ensure the system is fair, the product range should be specified at the outset and all staff should be trained in basic selling skills prior to its introduction.

How to calculate the margin of safety for your business

A retailer is in business to make profit. In more difficult trading times, this becomes increasingly a challenge. During such slow economic periods, some businesses tend to strive aggressively for market share, believing that if they increase market share during the 'bad' times, they will then reap more benefits during the 'good' times. There can be risks involved, however. At all times, both good and bad, a retailer needs to know how safe the business is, for this can provide either peace of mind or a call for action.

1 Understand the term 'margin of safety'.

Margin of safety is a ratio that tells you how risky your business is. It is wise to calculate your margin of safety on a yearly, quarterly or monthly cycle.

The margin of safety is a very important statistic for your business, especially in a changing market, where competition increases and when companies start reducing prices.

2 Calculate your margin of safety.

According to Peter Cox of FMRC (*Retail Globe*, Issue 9), you need to work out your margin of safety, you must know your Gross Profit and your Net Profit, and apply the following formula:

$$\frac{\text{Net Profit}}{\text{Gross Profit}} \times 100 = \text{Margin of Safety (\%)}$$

3 Interpret your margin of safety.

If your margin of safety is calculated to be, say, 20 per cent, your store can lose 20 per cent of its sales before you can no longer pay your expenses or provide a profit for the owners. If your percentage figure is higher, then your margin of safety is higher.

4 Compare your position with benchmarks.

It is valuable if you can compare your margin of safety with what is the norm in your retail sector. According to FMRC's Business Benchmarks Comparisons, University of New England, Australia, the following benchmarks may help:

	Margin of Safety
Auto electricians	50.09%
Book shop	28.57%
Coffee shop	28.57%
Small corner store	29.06%
Electrical retailer	28.20%
Shoe shop	36.00%
Furniture shop	28.41%
Gift shop	20.97%
Men's clothing store	40.11%
Milk & fruit juice retailer	46.15%

How to grapple with absenteeism

Team members who do not turn up to work cost your business money—do you know how much money? There are those who do not come to work for genuine reasons, but there are others who stay away for reasons of low morale and poor motivation. As a retail manager, your aim should be to develop a culture where people *want* to come to work...

1 Know what absenteeism costs your business.

Absenteeism is costly for your business. To calculate how costly an employee's absences are over a year, apply the following formula:

Cost to Business =

$$\frac{Salary + Employment\ Cost^*}{No.\ Working\ Days\ per\ Year} = \frac{Labour\ cost}{to\ business} \times \frac{No.}{Days}\ a\ day\ \ Absent$$

* It is generally accepted that 30 per cent of a person's salary is allocated as the 'employment cost'.

For example:

$$\frac{\$20,000 + \$6000}{240} = \$108.3 \times 10 = \$1083$$

This is the cost of a team member being away from work.

2 Work to reduce absenteeism.

Managers should be proactive in their efforts to reduce absenteeism, particularly in terms of their management style and their attitude towards younger employees.

Absenteeism often has links to management style. When the store is high in task-orientation and low in people management, absenteeism increases since team members assume that management does not care about them as individuals.

Young people are particularly vulnerable. According to research by Robert Tillman of Lowes, the US hardware retailer, 70 per cent of young people leave school to start their working life in retailing. Most of them become part-time employees. Of that 70 per cent, only three per cent really wanted a career in retailing.

Unless we show young employees the value of their retail experience, then it becomes simply a means of getting income; they will show little or no love for the business. They will think nothing of taking unwarranted days off. We should create career paths and demonstrate to young people how personally and professionally rewarding a career in retailing can be.

For other strategies to combat absenteeism, consult the companion volume, *Just about Everything a Manager Needs to Know*, pp. 268-9.

3 Introduce an absenteeism policy

Introduce and implement a policy where the team member must contact your business promptly to advise they will be absent on a particular day.

How to recruit effective salespeople

Many retailers are unshakable: they are no longer able to find good people to work in their retail outlets. They are convinced that the people they require just do not exist any more and lay the blame variously with education, lack of interest in retailing by young people, and the existing pay structures. In reality, however, nothing has really changed. Effective salespeople do exist, as they always have. It is just a matter of recruiting the right people in the right way…

 Analyse your needs.

Salespeople are recruited by retailers for one of three reasons:

- Their company is expanding and they need salespeople to provide customer service to an expanding customer base.
- The company has an incorrect customer-to-staff ratio which is resulting in a low average sale per customer.
- Someone has left the business and a vacancy now exists.

The golden rule should be not to automatically replace someone who has left. If someone leaves you have an opportunity to review the whole structure of your team. It may be time to rearrange the team, or their work times and duties to allow the business to operate more effectively.

 Write a job description.

If a vacancy does exist, then if you do not already have one for the position, the first task is to write a job description which covers the duties and responsibilities. It should be specific in identifying all the duties you would expect the salesperson to perform within your business. For example: 'Increase the average sale to $__ by using add-on selling techniques', 'Set out a relay product category', 'Handle complaints'…

3 Decide on personal specifications.

With the job description, you can then draw up a profile of what the successful applicant will be like. The job specifications will identify where it is *essential* the person is competent and other areas where it is *desirable* they are competent. Never recruit someone who is not competent in all your essential duties areas. The essential and desirable competencies should be listed as the following example shows:

Job: Salesperson

Essential Competencies:
well groomed, capable of identifying features and benefits, able to use effective open conversation, capable of closing a sale, able to deal with customer complaints.

Desirable Competencies:
capable of suggestive selling, able to do relay management, competent in sign writing, able to build a promotional display.

 Advertise.

Recruiting a new person means you will need to use some means of advertising. The most common methods are: advertisement in local newspaper or trade press, friends/relatives of existing team members, word of mouth in the local community, and promotion to school leavers. Some businesses find recruiting friends and relatives as the most desirable approach as this can quickly build a team spirit, but others are against this as they feel it can cause an increase in staff pilferage. Remember, you are not only advertising for a person; you also have the opportunity to promote your business to your market. As a guide make sure your advertisement covers three important areas: details of your business, details of the job, details of the person you require. By doing this you are being very specific with your targeting and will reduce the number of unwanted applicants.

 Employ personality over knowledge.

Retailing is a personality industry. It is extremely difficult, if not impossible, to improve a personality

> **Management Memo**
>
> To help you decide whether there is a vacancy, why not seek the views of the person who is leaving? After all, they know the job better than anyone else. In an informal interview, ask them:
> • Do we need to recruit, or can we handle the job in some other way?
> • Should we keep the job as it is, or can we improve it?
> • What sort of person should we recruit?
> • Do you know anyone for the job? [88]

through training. On the other hand, if the employee has the personality, it is comparatively easy to train them in product knowledge. So, your recruitment procedure should be aimed at selecting people with the right personality for your business. Consider using such personality checking strategies as:

• A surprise telephone call (to the candidate) to check their tone of voice and natural approach on the telephone.

• Passing a compliment to the candidate in the interview and gauging their reaction.

• Getting a fellow team member to show them around the store and to report back on their personality in the more relaxed setting.

How to interview potential salespeople

The purpose of an interview is to determine if the applicant has the knowledge, skills and personality to fit into your organisation. The interview, however, is more than a conversation. It involves a range of procedures and skills with which all retail managers should be familiar. The following advice will also prove useful...

 Conduct the interview.

You have two aims: to get the information you need to reach a decision; and to give the applicant the information they want, and to sell the job to them. Have these documents to hand:

- Checklist of essential requirements
- Applicant's details (letter or application form)
- Job breakdown, including terms and conditions.

Consider using the following interview sequence:

Office—Introduction

- Welcome applicant.
- Ask one or two informal questions to get them talking and put them at ease.
- Explain the stages: discussion/ tour/discussion.

Office—Opening discussion

- Work through the checklist of essential requirements, confirming points and asking questions.
- Ask open questions to get enough information to reach conclusions.

- Probe or challenge on any points of doubt to get them to open up.

Tour of the business

- Make a further check of essential (technical) requirements by questioning about the enterprise and systems as you tour them.
- Probe on any point of doubt, asking how they would solve particular problems, or do things differently.
- Explain the layout of the store.

Office—Concluding discussion

- Make a final check of your list of essential requirements, asking questions if necessary.
- Give any further explanation of the business and organisation.
- Discuss details of the job, using your written job breakdown.
- Negotiate pay and conditions, using your written job breakdown.

Office—Close

- Tell them how and when you will let then know if you are offering them the job or not.
- Arrange an expense payment. Thank them for attending.

2 Be professional in your approach.

It is essential that you appoint the right person to a job—which is why the hiring of staff is a major responsibility for retail managers. To be confident you appoint the best person, make sure you follow the appropriate interviewing procedures and that you brush up on your face-to-face interviewing technique. *Just about Everything a Manager Needs to Know*, on pages 146-7 and 78-9, will prove invaluable in this regard.

3 Check the applicant's personal qualities.

During the interview process, try to focus in particular on the personal qualities of the applicant in the following areas:

- Personality
- Reliability
- Attitude to retailing
- Ability to work on own
- Judgement
- Sense of responsibility
- Team attitude
- Communications skills.

In particular, you will require a person who has an outgoing personality, someone capable of holding a pleasant conversation with complete strangers. Listen carefully, watch the interviewee's body language, and pay attention to your intuition. Remember, once you hire people, you're stuck with them.

4 Plan your questions.

Questioning is a powerful tool and an essential ingredient in an interview of this type. Keep your questions simple and direct, and

focused on a specific topic. Start with general issues before moving into specific detail. Where necessary, probe and be persistent if the answer given is vague. Again, useful tips on questioning techniques appear in the companion volume, pages 220-1.

5 Never employ second best.

Never select 'the best of a bad bunch'. If you cannot find a suitable candidate from those you have interviewed, then you will be far better to not recruit at all and to readvertise the position.

6 Induct the new person into the team.

It is unfair to any person to put them directly on the retail floor without going through company policy, meeting the team, discussing your approach to customer service, or having a formal induction procedure. Induction should be formalised and carried out over the first week of employment.

How to get best value out of Generation X employees

Today's Generation X is a unique group of young adult employees and, so research tells us, should be treated a little differently to older groups of employees. They have a more negative view of the world, question authority, demand freedom, lack certain basic knowledge but possess expertise in other areas (such as computer technology), and need to be motivated and rewarded to get best value from them...

1 Motivate young workers to excel in your business.

Employing people is expensive and therefore you need to manage people in a positive way to produce the best results. The Generation X require special consideration.

Many of these youngsters come into retailing while they are looking for another job outside the retail sector. As a manager it is your role to motivate the team. If you are considerably older than the team, remember that your values will probably be very different from those of the Generation X. You will not change their value system; you will have to work with it.

To maximise their input, consider the following points:

- Meet with the team on a regular basis.
- Act like a parent until they feel comfortable in your organisation, but do not belittle them.
- Get to know them and be fair and consistent in your dealings with them.
- Ensure you communicate your standards in writing as policy.
- Evaluate their progress.
- Become a good listener and mentor.
- Ask for their ideas and input.
- Establish clearcut procedures.

2 Be aware of how your behaviour affects morale.

Your positive and negative behaviours can affect the morale of your team, especially the Generation X team members.

Common negative behaviour that should be avoided includes:

- Monopolising the conversation.
- Interrupting their conversation.
- Withholding normal social cues such as traditional greetings.
- Using non verbal put-downs.
- Not respecting their opinions.
- Refusing to negotiate or compromise on the way things are done.
- Making them feel guilty.
- Embarrassing them in public or in front of peers.
- Relating their ideas for them.
- Using crude, obscene or vulgar language.

You should embrace the following positive behaviours:

- Allowing the team members to express their views.
- Praising the team when it is due in a sincere way.
- Giving honest praise when it is warranted—particularly if they have tried but have failed at the task.
- Showing you care about the team.
- Keeping the confidence of team members.

- Using open questions that are straight forward and unloaded.
- Delaying automatic reactions.
- Confronting difficult situations in a positive way.

3 Appreciate the importance of rewards.

In many retail sectors today, the pool of available labour will come from Generation X. You therefore need a style of management that encourages this generation to become dedicated team members.

According to US research by Bob Losyk of Innovative Training Solution Inc, you can accomplish this through a rewards and recognition program. He raises these key points:

- Do not use monetary rewards alone.
- Reward must have a recognised value.
- Reward those habits in team members you want repeated.
- Always link rewards to performance.
- Vary the type of reward.
- Reward the team as well as selected individuals.
- Rewards must be immediate.
- Eliminate demotivators in your business.
- Individualise rewards whenever possible.

4 Initiate a program of recognition and reward.

Bob Losyk also suggests strategies for recognising and rewarding your Generation X staff for a job well done. Among the ideas you might consider would be the following:

1. Employee of the week, nominated by peers.
2. Supervisor of the month or quarter, nominated by employees.
3. Instigate special awards: Service Maniac of the Month/Year; Service Rookie of the Month/Year; Service Martyr of the Week; MVP Award (most valuable player); Idea of the Month; Spirit of the Company Award
4. Spotlight exceptional service people by

giving them extra responsibilities (helping in orientation or training).
5. Highlight top employees with photos on notice boards or in display cases. Or, give them a special parking space for a period of time.
6. Forward letters from owners/top management to the employee's home.
7. Place letters from satisfied customers on bulletin boards and mail home to the employee.
8. Use spoken or written praise and acknowledgment.
9. Say thank you, with a handshake (preferably in front of peers).
10. Give out yellow post-it notes or customised memo slips with positive comments. After an employee receives ten, they get a prize, bonus, or extra time off.
11. Issue praise points redeemable for money or some other prize. These are redeemable each month or can accumulate towards bigger prizes.
12. Provide rewards for service innovations, cost saving ideas and actions, and creative approaches to the business.
13. Instigate friendly competitiveness between units in the company towards a predetermined service-related goal.
14. Hold informal parties to say 'thanks'.
15. Develop performance appraisal bingo cards. Define your service related performance standards and place these on a (say, 5 x 5) bingo-type card. Five boxes in any direction earns an award or prize. If the entire card is filled up, the employee may receive a pay rise.
16. Refer a friend as a new employee. If the person meets certain standards of service in a certain time frame, the employee who referred the newcomer wins a pay rise.
17. Conduct social events—family picnics, Christmas party, bowling team, softball team, Halloween party, birthdays.
18. Reward the employee with the lowest number of complaints this month.
19. Send employees to seminars of their choice and reimburse the tuition costs. Continuing education is an important motivator.
20. Consider a time-off scheme, where each employee can bank time-off credits for achieving superior levels of service.
21. Begin a Mystery Shopper Award with prizes for those giving superior service.
22. Brainstorm possible staff prizes: Vacations, raffles, free dinners, gift certificates, gift baskets, plaques, lapel pins, TVs, sports or theatre tickets…

How to develop a mystery shopping program

Mystery shopping has become one of the manager's most effective tools in evaluating the customer's experience within a retail business. The process involves a 'secret shopper' visiting your business and recording the experience on a pre-determined report. The tool can also be used to coach and develop the team, as well as reward staff for high performance. And on a more strategic level it is an excellent tool to identify the customer service strengths and weaknesses of your business...

1 Make a commitment to the program.

Mystery shopping is not a 'one off' activity. It is a program of events that measures the journey of customer service improvement in your business. Introduce the initiative if:

- you seriously want to improve the customer's experience in your business.
- you wish to motivate your staff.
- you want to introduce the mystery shopping program on an ongoing basis.
- you're prepared to find time to review and improve the program constantly.

2 Develop the service processes.

Before you can develop the mystery shopping program you must break down the service processes in your business. For many customers, the service experience begins as they enter the car park to your store. You therefore need to ask yourself 'What would I want the customer to experience within the car park?' Your answers will be: Is the car park clean? Was it easy to park? Was it easy to find the store entrance?... Then take this process through your whole business and develop sub-sections under each area. For example, what is the process for a customer requiring help on the shop floor? At the check-out? Or for a customer with a complaint?

3 Compile the report form.

Having analysed the service processes you can now develop your report form. Take the processes you wish to measure and list the questions relating to each process. You will then have developed the mystery shopping report form. The form could have a few basic questions or a number of more detailed questions. Remember that someone has to carry out the mystery shop and too many questions can make the exercise a little daunting! Allow space at the end of each section for the shopper to make comments in support of their observations.

4 Introduce a scoring system.

When the report form is developed, devise a scoring system which allows you to identify the customer service strengths and weaknesses. For each correct answer give one point. Thus, if you have six questions relating to the checkout experience, give each question one point. To score 100 per cent, the shopper will mark 6 out of 6.

 Find a mystery shopper.

Now that you have your measurement tool, you need to find someone who can carry out the mystery shop. Since this person may also need to make some comments to back up their observations, they need to have the ability to describe clearly the experience in writing. Written observations allow the shopper to 'paint a picture' of the experience. This will help you to use the report as a coaching tool with your team.

 Inform your team.

It is important that you tell your team of your intentions. You have two options in this regard:
• You can wait until some visits have been carried out. The benefit of this approach is that you receive a true initial measurement.
• You can tell the team in advance—in which case the customer service standard immediately lifts as staff begin to treat every shopper like a mystery shopper!

Introduce incentives.

Incentives are very important. If a staff member or the team reaches a certain score, reward them for their effort with cinema tickets, a meal out, in-store publicity, certificates… If the whole team achieves the goal, then take them all out for dinner or a fun activity. It is important to ensure that all the team becomes involved in this activity.

 Develop a coaching tool.

Use your report as a coaching tool. Sit down in turn with each staff member involved in the report and take them through the shopper's feedback. At the same meeting, set some goals for the next visit. If you have an issue or wish to develop a particular staff member, ask the shopper to try and have a service interaction with this individual.

Establish an ongoing program.

Make mystery shopping an ongoing part of your business strategy. Depending on the size of your business, you may only have one mystery shop a month. With a larger team, you may ask for a weekly visit.

 Continually improve the program.

It is important to review the questions and the program every three months. As your team improves their customer service skills, then the measurement needs to become more demanding. This ensures that the customer service is constantly being developed and your staff are forever being challenged.

This topic was written by Jonathan Winchester, Shopper Anonymous, Perth, Western Australia.

How to maximise the benefits of team meetings

Are you one of those retail managers who believes that there simply isn't enough time to hold staff meetings and, even if you did, not everyone would be able to attend anyway? Team meetings are not as common as they should be. The result is that staff often feel alienated, they are unable to network effectively with colleagues, or to share ideas and plan for the future. Consequently, many companies are underperforming.

1 Encourage total team involvement.

To begin, try scheduling team meetings at least on a monthly basis. Retail hours often mean that such meetings will have to be held after-hours or before your store opens. Hold the meetings on a different day each month—for example, alternate between Tuesday and Wednesday evenings, to give the majority of your team the opportunity of attending. Rotate the chair between senior team members. A meeting chaired by the owner provides the opportunity for the owner to express personal views and opinions, but it won't help build a team if the other participants are reluctant to speak against those views. By rotating the chair on each occasion, you will open up the meeting, build the team and improve communication skills.

2 Set and circulate an agenda in advance.

Compile an agenda prior to the meeting so that everyone has the opportunity to think about the issues before the meeting begins.

A retailing team meeting could include topics such as:

- Sales achieved last month against target.
- Target sales for the next month.
- Ideas from the last month on how to increase sales.
- Department reports.
- Competition awareness activities.

3 Follow normal meeting procedures.

In this regard, consider these points:

- The chair should ensure everyone has the opportunity to participate. It is critical that the meeting is held in a positive manner with one aim—improving the business.
- The team meeting is an opportunity to praise, but not a time to reprimand.
- Keep notes of the meeting—one set for the file, and copies for all participants and those who were absent.
- Always focus on increasing sales and customer service. Don't allow the meeting to get bogged down in internal issues that should be sorted out by senior management.

4 Make the meeting a part of your culture.

Ensure you hold a meeting at least once a month. Even if the owner or senior manager cannot make the meeting, the scheduled event should proceed. It should be a welcome part of your company culture.

And while on this theme… A retailer in the United States agreed to hold staff meetings over breakfast and that the owner would pay for breakfast. The meetings were a failure. When analysed, it was found that team members felt they could not give 'honest' opinions and ideas at the meeting while the owner was paying for breakfast. Once they paid for their own breakfasts, the meetings started going exceptionally well.

The important lesson here is that, for team meetings to be successful over a period of time, you must first get the 'feel' and culture right.

5 Consider alternative approaches.

You may argue that the holding of different types of meetings is a more effective way of involving staff and ensuring the efficient running of your store—for example, departmental meetings or senior management meetings. The meetings that are most neglected, however, are the full team meetings, where all your people—including those at the sharp end who deal with the customer— are able to be kept in the full picture and can be made to feel an important part of the store team.

Management Memo

How effective was your team meeting?

1. Did members freely voice their opinions and vote according to their conscience?
2. Were ideas thoroughly questioned and examined before being either rejected or accepted?
3. Was good use made of meeting time?
4. Did members leave the meeting with clear direction on how to proceed regarding decisions made in the meeting?
5. Were differences of opinion resolved productively?
6. Did people listen to each other and build on each other's ideas during discussions?
7. Did a climate of trust pervade the meeting?
8. Did everyone speak up on every important issue discussed?
9. Did confidential discussions remain confidential following the meeting?
10. Do you agree with the way the meeting was run? [91]

6 Remember: follow-up is essential.

Brief minutes of the meeting should be typed and disseminated to team members. Meeting outcomes should be clearly defined—if a decision has been made to do something, state who will be responsible for doing it and by when. Follow-up later to ensure the tasks get completed by the due dates.

How to train the team

Retail staff need training in a range of areas—customer service, merchandising, product knowledge, people skills... But the long hours often make it difficult to get the group together in one place at the one time. In such situations where a training program is difficult to organise, a mix of different tools should be explored to ensure that appropriate training takes place...

1 Remember: training is essential.

Training is not only vital for imparting the skills of retailing to your staff, it also serves another purpose in a high turnover industry such as retailing. US research reveals that 70 per cent of school leavers start their careers in retailing—although only 3 per cent want to. For this reason alone, it is management's responsibility to offer training packages and encourage team members to participate. If your staff, particularly the younger members, become involved and enjoy the experience, they may then see retailing as a career, rather than a stopover, and become a valuable asset to your business.

2 Consider videos as a training tool.

There are many training organisations around the world that can provide video training on customer service and other retailing skills. Videos are easy to use, convenient and allow you to provide a professional training package with less input than having to prepare from scratch—

although you still have to do some preparation to ensure you are ahead of the team. If you use a video, do not just switch on the television set and leave your team to view the tape. You should also:

- have a hand-out prior to the viewing to get the group thinking about the subject as it relates to your store.
- preview with staff the key points in the video, prior to showing it, that have relevance for your store.
- provide a written questionnaire for the group to complete at the end of the viewing.
- let them watch the video.
- review the video with the team, and bring out the key points and what action should take place in your store as a result of watching the program.

3 Consider audiotapes as a training tool.

Audio magazines such as *Retail Globe*, along with others in the marketplace, provide the opportunity for training to take place while the listener is driving to work (or at any other convenient time). This style of training is ideal for managers and supervisors in particular, who usually have the motivation to train themselves.

4 Consider in-house workshops.

Getting the group together to train allows you to focus on specific subjects and to explore them in confidence and in depth with your staff as a team. To be successful, this style of training works best with an accredited outside trainer who knows the retail industry. To get maximum benefit, the sessions should be managed in an informal way with plenty of group participation.

5 Consider out-sourced workshops.

Most urban areas have 'open' training programs where anybody can attend. The value of these workshops is that they expose your team members to other retailing people who have similar challenges and concerns. The sharing of ideas with outsiders can enhance the training program and provide useful networking opportunities for your staff.

6 Consider open learning programs.

Open learning training is operated by colleges and universities. They offer accredited courses, and provide workbooks that are mailed to individual participants. In this way, the individual can undertake formal self-paced training at home, but to a specified level. On completing each segment of the course, workbooks are mailed back to the provider for assessment. Certification is usually awarded upon successful completion of the course.

Management Memo

The Second Cup is a speciality coffee retailer based in Toronto, Canada. They have training sessions where they train their team about the different types of coffee, how they are grown, where they come from, and how they differ from each other. The result is the customer's shopping experience is improved and team members come across as coffee experts. They are also trained in how to prepare coffee and selling skills. After training, team members are tested and given a certificate. The result is an increase in the average sale and team members who have pride in their skills.[92]

7 Consider remote-area training.

Countries like Australia are serviced by retailers in remote communities that are vast distances from training providers. Conventional training then becomes very costly. Increasingly, technology is defeating distance. For example, live programs can be beamed at once via satellite to television sets in hundreds of stores across the country. The up-link also allows trainees to interact live via telephone with the presenter. In this way quality training is provided to large groups in a wide territory at one time at a very cheap cost. Internet and intranet delivery of programs via computer is also on the increase.

8 Never forget: training is an investment.

Retailers must know their products and how to sell them. Along with other benefits, training provides the essential skills. This can be expensive, yet the leaders in the retail industry train their staff extensively because they realise it is an investment in their business.

How to develop a good relationship with the local press

If, as part of your strategy for building a loyal customer base, one of the aims of your retail business is to be depicted as 'the good guys' around town, then you'll need to develop a long-term relationship with the local print media—getting your store into print without investing advertising money. The key is to interest the press in the 'good news' stories about your organisation, and there are various strategies for doing this...

1 Know what might interest the press.

You can identify news leads for the local media in a number of areas, for example:

Team matters. If team members obtain a certificate for completing a training program, a team member gets promoted, or a long term member retires, you may have a story of interest to the press.

New products. If you are the first business in your area to get a genuine new product, you may be able to build a story around this. The new car industry does this very successfully at new model car launches.

Winning Awards. Every business should enter awards as a matter of course. Consumers love winners and an award winner in your industry has a story for the news media.

Writing columns. If you are the local hardware, garden centre, car dealer, dressmaker, or whatever, you can become the area expert with a newspaper column. Contact your local newspaper and see if they are interested in a 'handy hints' column from you. Your print visibility will reflect well on your business.

Prizes. If your local newspaper engages in competitions, offer prizes—but make sure they mention your company's name when giving credits.

2 Always be prepared for the unexpected.

You never know what opportunities can exist and, for this reason, always have a camera in your store (with film loaded) so you can take a photograph of any unexpected event. The press is always looking for pictures of the unexpected. Be ready. You never know what might happen tomorrow.

3 Write your own press releases.

Do not rely on the press to write a news story on your organisation. Write it yourself and give the newspaper the authority to modify it. In today's technical world, you are more likely to get a press release published if you email it to the

WINNING
YOUR CUS

MANAGING
YOUR STOR

PROMOT
YOUR PRO

**MANAGING
YOUR BUSINESS**

DEX

221

Vol. 1: See 398, 400, 402, 404

newspaper, along with your contact details, as they can easily and quickly edit it into shape.

 Do your homework.

Publications do considerable research into their readership and then tailor their style of writing to the target audience. You should do likewise. Before writing a press release, read the publication and identify its particular focus and style of writing.

Be aware of the FOG Index, or the Frequency of Gobbledegook. Different media have different standards in terms of the amount of technical jargon they use per 100 words. Aim to match the standard of the publication of your target interest.

Gunning's FOG formula is used in the United Kingdom to test written material for adult reading. The formula rates different media as follows, with the lower score indicating the less gobbledegook and the greater the 'understandability' of content. For example,

Women's magazines	25
Newspapers	26-39
Passport application form	45
Application for credit card	49
Government letters	49

The moral is: for a mass audience, keep your message simple!

Remember these basic principles...

- Always provide your contact name and telephone number.
- Double space the type and leave wide margins if you are sending by fax or mail.
- What you consider as

Management Memo

The relationship between a journalist and a source should be a position of mutual trust. The reporter trusts you to tell the facts and the full story; you trust the reporter to present the story in an even-handed and fair manner. But always remember: you can't promote a favourable image if your organisation is not well run, competent, ethical, and reputable. An organisation must always 'put its house in order' before undertaking a media relations program. Otherwise such a campaign will backfire badly. [93]

newsworthy, may not be what the press believe. And vice versa.

- Keep sentences simple and limit the amount of industry jargon.
- Provide facts to support any claims you make.
- Don't put pressure on the media; it will work against you.
- The media has its own standards and adheres to them. These may be different to yours. Do not challenge those standards.
- Refrain from including a 'do not publish until x date' on a press release. Release it when you are ready.
- Try not to be disappointed if the press change or do not publish what you have written.
- Be persistent. All newspapers have what is termed 'a slow news day', and that could just be *your* lucky day!
- The press prefer short, sharp stories—so keep them short. And make sure that in your press release you mention your USP (Unique Selling Proposition).
- Always be available. Remember, journalists often work shifts.

How to write a customer newsletter

Building relationships with your customers is an important way of establishing customer loyalty. One well-proven technique used by successful retailers is the production and distribution of a store newsletter. It is not a sales brochure or a direct selling tool. It is a communications vehicle which attempts to provide news about the store, its customers, staff and services, and to assure customers that they are an important part of your store's family.

 ## 1 Decide on a regular schedule.

Research shows that newsletters work most effectively if they are mailed out every 90 days. Any more frequently and your customer may start treating the material as junk mail; as well, you will put a lot of pressure on youself and your team to keep the initiative alive. If you leave it longer than 90 days, the customer will think you have forgotten about them and the impact is then lost. Remember, however, once you have committed yourself to producing a customer newsletter you must keep to deadlines or you lose credibility.

2 Keep it short.

Your customers are busy people, too. They do not have time to read lots of information about your business. Limit your newsletter to a maximum of four pages. Each page should have a specific theme of interest to your customers and be written in an interesting style. Consider this typical structure:

Page One. This is the page that should grab reader attention and encourage them to read the rest of the newsletter. Use key words such as *you* and *your*, and avoid words like *I*, *us* or *we*. Your customers are not interested in your business; they are interested in themselves and their lives and how your business might impact on them. Have a headline that is punchy and never more than twelve words long. You will need a 'lead story' that is relevant to your customers. New items, innovations and surveys are ideal topics for page one.

Page Two. This page can include news stories, a photograph of you, your team or a member of your team, and a signed editorial. Research shows you get more impact if the editorial is signed in your own hand writing—a time consuming activity, but it actually works and is effort well rewarded.

Page Three. Use this page for a key story you want to get across, but remember to write it in a style the customer wants to read. Use this page to promote how to use seasonal, topical or fashionable products that you sell. Recipes, how-to tips, and building and fashion ideas are ideal on this page. The page will read and look better if you provide several short stories rather than one long one.

Page Four. This is the relaxation page and should be full of short items. It can contain forthcoming events and promotions as well as community news. Do not forget to promote your business at the bottom of the fourth page—

including hours of business, phone number, and a map to remind people where you are.

3 Be on the lookout for newsworthy items.

When seeking attention-grabbing items, be aware of these four elements:

- *Human interest.* People want to read about things happening to people.
- *Timeliness.* An event has news value only if it is about to happen or has happened recently.
- *Uniqueness.* People want to read about things they haven't heard about before.
- *Novelty.* People love to read about the unusual.

With these points in mind, consider using the following regular features in your newsletter:

Local community events
A team member's/customer's favourite recipe, plant, book, clothes etc.
How to build, plant, care for...
Local good news stories
Global events that are affecting your business
Get to know a team member/customer
Children's column
New products being launched
Reviews of books related to your industry
Reasons why you care for products the way you do
Environmental issues.

Be selective about what's included.

Don't try to cram too much down your readers' throats at one time—if it looks too daunting, they'll drop it. It's better to limit your newsletter to a few concise, well-written, interesting items, along with adequate white space, than to jam-pack everything submitted for that issue. Sort and prioritise the items for maximum impact.

5 Pay attention to how you say it.

Has the content been written with a true knowledge of your audience? Remember the three rules of readability: simplicity, specificity and brevity. Use colourful and lively writing. Avoid trade jargon. Keep the language casual and informal. Polish until perfect and, before printing, an outsider should read the newsletter for clarity.

6 Don't let the layout smother the content.

Avoid the temptation to turn your newsletter into a masterpiece of design and decoration. If the art gets in the way of the message, to the point of distraction, then what's the point?

Seek reader feedback.

Is your newsletter really doing the job intended? To find out if your readers find it interesting, lively, informative, readable—you must *ask* them at least annually! Try a variety of approaches: a reader response coupon in your newsletter, a mini-survey, or an in-store feedback box.

How to become a sponsor

Sponsorship is an ideal avenue for you to get your name in front of potential and existing customers at events where those attending have the same values in life as those of your company. Increasingly, consumers want to purchase products from companies that share their values. By sponsoring the appropriate event, you have the opportunity of getting closer to your targeted customers, and, in doing so, confirm that you care about them and their lifestyle...

1 Understand what is meant by sponsorship.

Sponsorship is not a donation from you to those seeking sponsorship. Its aim is to provide a reward for the sponsor and the sponsored. The UK Association of Business Sponsorship makes this key point:

> The common interest between sponsor and sponsored demands that their relationship be based on mutual respect, candour and understanding, with each investing the necessary time and attention to define clearly the aims of sponsorship, the expectations of the deal, and the provisions for evaluating and publicising projects. They must also try to understand each other's motivation.

As a sponsor, you will want to know how your money will be spent by the sponsored group and how you will benefit from the relationship through either more sales, greater exposure, or both. Remember, the aim of sponsorship is to put both sides in a win-win situation.

2 Ask the appropriate questions.

Before accepting a role as sponsor, consider the advantages to you:
- What does the sponsored group want from your sponsorship?
- Do your values match those of the sponsored group and the event?
- How will the sponsorship affect you?
- How can you maximise your exposure?
- Will the sponsored have the people and resources to maximise your involvement and the return to your business?
- Is there evidence that they have done their homework on your business and personalised their invitation?

3 Be aware of the types of sponsorship.

Whether you envisage a 'one off' event or a long term relationship, give consideration to the type of involvement, which might include...

Sole sponsorship. The sponsor wants the event to be named after their product or name, e.g. The Whitbread Cup, The Coca Cola Challenge.

Graded Sponsorship. A number of sponsors are involved, their return based on the degree of sponsorship.

Special Event Sponsorship. A single event in the program is sponsored by an individual company.

Underwriting Sponsorship. Here the sponsor will fund any losses the event makes.

Endorsement Sponsor. To give the event credibility, the sponsor lends its name, but no money.

Sponsorship comes in many forms.

You may be asked for financial support, the provision of goods or a site, or to fund a coffee break at a conference, and so on.

4 Target the market.

An event will have a highly defined market. For example, a flower show will be aimed at keen gardeners and flower arrangers, while a trade show on hardware will attract the top handymen. Such events obviously provide a great opportunity for those retailers to promote their business to a specific market and ensure they get maximum benefit from their financial involvement.

Ideally you should aim at heavy users of your product, develop a strong association with the event, and get your name upfront—The *Coca Cola* Olympics, The *Greengrowth* Flower Show, The *Product x* Home of the Year.

5 Consider your products and sales.

Apart from linking your name and products to an event, you can also use this as an opportunity to launch a new product or revitalise your products and services. But you will need to check beforehand whether this is purely sponsorship, or if you will be able to promote and/or sell products at the same time. A camera retailer, for example, might sponsor a tea break at a conference on the clear understanding that it would have a sales booth in the conference hall on the day of the sponsorship. People are more inclined to buy at this moment than after the event when the euphoria has declined.

6 Ensure you embrace the target market's lifestyle.

Selling product is not the aim of sponsorship. Building loyalty is. For this reason, ensure that your potential customers at the event relate to you in their lifestyle. For instance, if you sold pool chemicals you would not sponsor a back-to-nature event, but a sporting goods retailer would find this an ideal opportunity for involvement.

7 Make sponsorship work for you.

How will your sponsoring of an event affect your company's stature?

• If it is an environmental, charity or educational occasion, it is an ideal public relations exercise.

• Sponsoring an event will involve you with customers in a non-sales relationship. It allows you to spend quality time with them, the result of which should mean future sales contacts.

• Sponsoring the right event will win you new friends *and* build employee relations. The New Zealand Post Office, for example, found sponsoring the New Zealand Olympic team was a major boost in building employee morale.

• Oddly, only 10 per cent of companies forge a marketing campaign around their sponsorship. Coca Cola, Nike, Reebok, and Telecom built excellent marketing campaigns around their Olympic involvement. Link your sponsorship to marketing.

• Forty percent of sponsors do not even advertise their involvement with an event. If you are going to spend on sponsorship, budget an equal amount on advertising and promotion linked to the event.

How to keep shrinkage under control

Shrinkage is the loss of sales due to a variety of factors—theft, error, damage, and so on. The benchmark for shrinkage in most retail operations is 2 per cent. In other words, if you purchased $100 worth of product at retail sales value and, after selling $95 worth at retail value, you had no product left to sell, your shrinkage would be $5 worth of product at retail value. A retail manager's aim should be to minimise such loss...

1 Know what causes shrinkage in your store.

US research reveals that the 2 per cent shrinkage in retailing results from the following:

Employees stealing product	51%
Customers stealing product	24%
Incorrect receiving procedures	9%
Damage to product	7%
Accounting errors	5%
Incorrect retail pricing	4%

Shrinkage through employee stealing occurs at the following locations:

Cashier station	44%
Service area	23%
Courtesy booth	12%
Back room	10%
Management and supervision	5%
Other	6%

2 Know what shinkage can cost you.

Shrinkage of 2 per cent may seem a small concern, but a 2 per cent saving over a year could well be equivalent to one week's turnover:

e.g.		
	Weekly sales	$5,000
	2% shrinkage	$100
	Annual $ shrinkage	$5,200

Think of this another way. If a product sells for $50 and has a gross profit of $5, and if one item is stolen or broken, then you need to sell 10 more items to break even.

Shrinkage is often looked at in percentage terms.

Shrink $ = Potential gross margin $ − Actual gross margin $

$$\text{Shrink \%} = \frac{\text{Shrink \$}}{\text{Sales \$}} \times 100$$

3 Focus on controllable shrinkage.

Some shrinkage can be controlled in your business, while other shrinkage, through accidents and damage for example, is uncontrollable.

Controllable shrinkage includes some theft by staff and by customers, some staff accidents, vendor theft, cashier dishonesty, throw aways, some customer accidents, markdowns, demonstrations, and incorrect wrapping. Your objective should be to focus on reducing the controllable shrinkage within your business...

4 Maintain security at the checkout.

The checkout is a notorious shrinkage area in your business and the following procedures proposed by Richard Burns of Intercept Security Services are critical in reducing shrinkage at this location:

- Always check the price of any merchandise with a damaged, missing or irregular ticket.
- Keep the cash register closed between transactions and locked if unattended.
- Inspect all merchandise that is tendered for payment, especially boxes or cartons into which smaller items could have been placed.
- Always block a checkout aisle when the checkout is unattended.
- Be careful when a large note is tendered for a small purchase. Always count out change to a customer before placing the note into the till.
- Wrap and seal purchased merchandise. Attach receipts to the outside of packages.
- If packaged goods are presented for payment in an unsealed or tampered carton, check its content.
- Put point of sale merchandise at the till in a position where the staff can observe the display.

5 Attend to housekeeping matters.

Shrinkage is difficult to eliminate, but it can be reduced by introducing some simple housekeeping rules into your business. For example, always keep aisles clear of merchandise for customer safety and so that anything dropped on the floor is quickly visible. Your team must be the eyes and ears of the store. Ensure they are familiar with products on display and keep small vulnerable items in their view.

6 Consider using deterrents.

Signs on doors — 'If you steal you will be prosecuted'— are not always effective deterrents because they accuse everyone of being dishonest and the thief rarely believes the retailer will prosecute anyway. Far more effective are strategically

Management Memo

You need two important ingredients working for you If you are to reduce your shrinkage. Firstly, the total workforce must be innoculated with the philosophy that they all bear the consequences of shrinkage if company procedures are not followed. Secondly, you must have a Shrinkage Improvement Program which should include key procedures, such as recording of purchases, sales, markups and markdowns, breakages and write-offs, plus opening and closing stock.[96]

placed security mirrors and cameras. Buzzers on doors work effectively, especially in self service stores where contact with customers is minimal.

7 Get your team on side.

Your staff have an important role to play in contolling shrinkage. The best deterrent is to ensure team members acknowledge all customers when they enter the store and can keep eye contact with them during the store experience. Lower gondola displays will allow shoppers to be watched across the store. Keep expensive items in locked display cabinets or anchor them to displays to ensure they cannot be easily carried away.

8 Try incentive schemes.

One of the world's leading retailers has identified that the majority of shrinkage is happening via team members. This company now has a shrinkage rate of 1 per cent—achieved by introducing an incentive scheme aimed at reducing shrinkage. If shrinkage drops below 1 per cent, the team share the benefits—as much as US$800 per team member per year.

How to reduce shoplifting

Shoplifting is, alas, an increasingly common occurrence in retailing and has a direct impact on the bottom line. Responsibility for reducing the incidence of shoplifting resides with everyone in your team. All staff members need to be vigilant and know what to do when they suspect a shoplifter is in the store...

1 Accept that shoplifting is a retailing hazard.

Shoplifting will happen in your store. It is simply a hazard of the industry. According to *Retailers Digest* (October 1996), the most common items stolen in retail stores are:

Cosmetics	23.6% of products stolen
Clothing	16.6%
Food	14.6%
Medicines	12.7%
Hardware	11.4%
Household Goods	5.2%
Miscellaneous	15.9%

For this reason, as a retail manager, it is your responsibility to implement strategies and procedures which will minimise shoplifting and reduce the inroads shoplifting makes into your profit line.

2 Commit your team to combat shoplifting.

Your obvious aim should be to deny the opportunity for theft, delay the opportunity, and deter the opportunity. Of course, your team has a major role to play in this regard. Key strategies in the battle would be:

(a) the better the customer service the more difficult it is to steal.

(b) position the most vulnerable products as listed above in areas where your team can observe them and customers clearly.

3 Compile and disseminate a policing procedure.

Your team need to know what your policing policies and procedures are as you attempt to reduce loss through pilfering. It is the role of management to develop a set of procedures and to ensure everyone is aware of them and is prepared to follow them. This means you must also do spot checks to ensure the policing policy is adhered to at all times.

4 Increase staff awareness.

Written procedures are one thing, but the team need to be trained in carrying out these anti-shoplifting policies. They need training in how to remove the opportunities to steal, how to watch customers without the customer feeling threatened or harrassed, how to read body language, and how to approach customers positively.

Vol. 1: See 266, 270, 274, 372

5 Implement a bag check policy.

One common method to reduce theft is to have a customer bag check policy. This must be implemented in a friendly, positive way, and embrace the following procedures:

- Display a bag check sign that is clearly visible at the entrance to the store.
- If the customer refuses to have a bag checked then you can ask them to leave the store and refuse to sell them goods.
- Carry out bag checks with discretion and sensitivity. Ask the customer to open the bag and let them handle products in the bag. You should not touch the bag or put your hand inside.
- If in doubt call a supervisor.
- If you believe a customer has stolen products, you may detain them (without recourse to physical restraint) and call your security organisation. You must of course be confident that an offence has in fact occurred.

6 Be aware that employees also steal.

Your staff members are also capable of stealing products, yet often do not think of it as stealing. Comments from team members caught in the act have included: 'You'd never miss it', 'You owe it to me', 'Everyone's doing it', 'I need it more than you do', 'It was just so easy'.

Security is an important aspect of your business and you must have a written policy to ensure your people remain honest, a policy that all staff members agree to.

A typical policy would include:

Staff must be personally responsible for personal property.

Team members must not remove property from the business premises.

Management Memo

Australian statistics relating to employee shoplifting reveal that:

- Anywhere between 5 per cent to 75 per cent of employees steal (3 per cent of employees are responsible for 80 per cent of internal theft).
- 10-30 per cent of employees consistently steal (3 per cent will steal daily or weekly).
- Between 10-80 per cent of shrinkage is due to employee theft. [97]

Stealing will result in instant dismissal.

Nobody may personally accept free samples from suppliers.

All employees are to be liable to bag checks.

Employees are not permitted to record their own purchases.

Team members must not consume food from shelves without the item being first purchased.

No employee may operate a cash register unless authorised to do so.

Of course, you will need to consider other procedures that will be specific to your business.

7 Be committed to theft reduction.

Managers must be committed to strategies aimed at the reduction of shoplifting within the business. This means procedures must be put in place that reduce the opportunities for theft, and employees made aware of this commitment. Such procedures might include:

Pre-employment screening

Employee induction programs

Written company policies and procedures

Team malpractice awareness training

Investigation procedures for malpractice

Malpractice action plan.

How to apprehend a shoplifter

Shoplifting is a major challenge for retailers today but apprehending someone who has stolen from your store has many potential pitfalls for the unwary. Within the law, you must have your own procedures and all your team must be aware of these and be prepared to act accordingly.

1 Be able to identify a shoplifter.

Professional shoplifters use ingenious methods to hide products that they are planning to steal. Common things to look for include:

- Small articles placed in newspapers or inside gloves or coats
- Umbrellas, prams or briefcases used to hide products
- Slit pockets in outer coats
- Swapping price tags
- People wearing loose coats or baggy trousers.

2 Approach the person as a potential purchaser.

Remember, it's best to prevent shoplifting, not to catch people stealing. At the hint of suspicion, always approach from the front of the customer and greet them with a service approach, which could be:

'Good morning. Is that a gift you're purchasing?'

'Hello, I have an ideal cross merchandise product that will go wonderfully with the (product) you've just selected…'

3 Be certain.

You have the right to apprehend a person but this is always a difficult situation because, if you are in the wrong, you could face legal action yourself. *You* will have committed an offence, not the person you apprehended.

In most situations you are making a so-called citizen's arrest and you do not have the same powers as a police officer. For these reasons you need to consider:

- Did you actually see the person remove the item and hide it on their person?
- Are you confident they have not dumped the product in the store?
- Are you sure they have not paid for the product already?
- Have they actually left your store without paying?

If you have any doubt, it is safer to let the person leave without apprehending them.

4 Apprehend the person.

On the other hand, if you are confident that the person has stolen a

WINNING YOUR CUS

MANAGING YOUR STOR

PROMOTI YOUR PRO

MANAGING YOUR BUSINESS

DEX

231

Vol. 1: See 372

product, then approach the suspect outside your store and have a colleague as a witness.

When approaching, use words such as: 'We believe you have a product in your possession which is from our store and has not been paid for. Will you please accompany us back to our store so that we can discuss the matter?'

Take the person to a private office in your store and ask another colleague to contact your local police station. It's best to have the police ask the questions as they have the skills and authority to do so. If the police are not available, however, you must have a third party present who records in writing what happens at the interview. If you have apprehended a woman and a man is interviewing, then make sure the third party is a woman.

5 Conduct an interview.

If police are unavailable, the importance of conducting the interview correctly becomes critical.

Firstly, ask the person to place the suspected stolen product on a table in front of them. If they refuse you cannot search the person. You will have to wait for a police officer to arrive before a search can take place. After the products are placed on the table you then ask for a sales receipt. If this is not produced, you can hold a formal interview. The sole aim of the interview is to obtain the facts,

Management Memo

Cardboard cut-outs of police in stores were first used in Scandinavia and proved to be highly successful. It was then adopted by British retailers who found it reduced stealing. The replicas are now used in Australia, New Zealand, and many other countries.

The most effective use of cardboard cut-outs is when they are used seasonally, e.g. Christmas, to address high shop stealing times of the year. If you use them all the year round you will find their effectiveness is reduced. [98]

not to get a confession. All physical evidence must be saved for the police.

Keep the interview brief, objective and courteous. Remember to obtain the name, address and other identification of the person you are talking to. When the interview is taking place, never leave the person unsupervised.

6 Follow up.

The police will decide what action should take place next. You will need to advise the team of what has happened, but do not pass any specific details on to your staff.

Review your procedures, your aim being to prevent a similar incident from taking place. For example, a more secure display may be in order, or a repositioning of the product could reduce the risk.

How to reduce credit card and cheque fraud

With the passing years, consumers are using 'real' money less and less. The arrival of the cashless society means that credit cards will be used more often and this could lead to more fraud. Retailers are primary targets in this regard and you will need to ensure your staff are aware of procedures for reducing and preventing credit card fraud...

1 Authorise selected staff to handle transactions.

Do not allow any of your team to handle credit card transactions until they have been trained and authorised to do so. Make sure you have an audit control system so that you can trace each transaction to the team member who dealt with the customer. Ideally, always process cards in front of the shopper as this will reduce the potential for fraud.

2 Train the team to recognise fake cards.

All credit cards have certain common features and your team members need to know what valid cards look like. They must also be reminded that a VISA or Mastercard may look different when used by a traveller and they need to recognise international cards as well as national cards.

Pre-printed 4-digits appear just above or below the embossed account number. This number on the left of the card should match the first four embossed digits of the account number. This pre-printed number

cannot be removed by scratching the card.

There is no substitute for training and familiarisation of staff in these and other matters relating to the physical appearance of credit cards.

3 Follow set procedures.

Authorised team members should be trained to follow standard procedures in handling customers' credit cards. These might include:

- Always check the expiry date. The sale must be made within the dates on the card.
- Always check that the signature on the back of the card corresponds with that on the receipt which is signed in front of the team member.
- Ensure that the information on your store terminal matches the information on the card.
- If the card is not signed, ask for valid identification—such as a photo driver's licence or passport. If this is produced, ask the customer to sign the receipt and the card in your presence to validate the sale.
- If in doubt, you have a duty to contact the relevent bank and report your doubts.

WINNING
YOUR CUS

MANAGING
YOUR STOR

PROMOT
YOUR PRO

**MANAGING
YOUR BUSINESS**

DEX

233

 **Look for anything
suspicious.**

Treat every customer as being
honest, but be on the lookout for
irregularities. When dealing with
financial issues, it pays to be
suspicious, and to…

- be cautious about people who make
  strange, large or irregular purchases
  that seem to be out of step with their
  apparent lifestyle.

- treat as suspicious people who make a
  large purchase and keep returning to
  your store to make a series of irregular
  purchases using a credit card.

- watch customers who ask to split
  transactions into a number of small
  ones, particularly those asking the
  amount of floor limit or making
  multiple small transactions perhaps to
  avoid authorisation being contacted.

- be wary of customers who buy large
  products on a credit card, are adamant
  they take them straight away and
  resist any form of delivery service.

- observe where the customer keeps the
  card. Most people keep their card in a
  wallet or purse, although a person
  who keeps the card in a pocket may
  do so to hide the contents of their
  purse or wallet. Although not a good
  indicator by itself, it is a signal that
  other checks might be in order.

- check the way the customer signs the
  voucher. If they check the signature
  while signing, or are particularly slow
  when signing, this may indicate they
  have practised the signature and are
  trying to get it right.

- watch for shoppers with bandaged
  hands who say they cannot sign
  properly. Always check other
  identification like a driver's licence.

- be cautious if, when asked for other
  identification, the customer cannot
  produce any, particularly if the card
  was in the shopper's pocket.

- look for suspicious behaviour from
  members of the public in or around
  your store. This includes irregularities

Management Memo

Customers will still use cash, so have a
simple cash handling procedure.

- Total the sale and tell the customer the amount.
- Call the amount of money tendered by the
  customer.
- Place the amount on the cash drawer (do not
  put it in the register at this stage).
- Make up the change.
- Count the change back to the customer.
- Place the amount tendered into the appropriate
  compartment/s of the drawer
- Close the cash drawer.[99]

---

such as a customer giving you a card
of the opposite sex.

- be wary of companies coming to check
  your terminals without prior
  notification. Check that they are an
  authorised maintenance company that
  has bank approval.

**Be alert for
cheque fraud.**

Due to fraud, many retailers today
refuse to accept payment by cheque
and cheques are becoming less
common in retailing. To minimise
fraud, some retailers use cheque
guarantee companies to reduce the
risk by phoning the company to gain
authorisation of the cheque.

When receiving a cheque,
consider the following:

- Ensure the cheque is signed in front of
  a salesperson.

- Seek identification, via driver's
  licence, passport or credit card, to
  ensure the signature matches that
  provided on the cheque.

- Check that the amount written in
  words matches the amount written in
  figures.

- Make sure that the date on the cheque
  is correct.

- Ensure your company name is correct.

- In the case of an overseas cheque, call
  a supervisor for verification.

How to handle a hold-up

We are living in an increasingly violent society and the retail trade is becoming more and more vulnerable. Not so long ago, most retailers believed robbery was something that happened to other retailers, never to them. But times have changed, and it is best to be prepared for the day when your store also falls victim to an armed hold-up...

1 Be warned: it is likely to happen to you.

Research in the United Kingdom in 1998 revealed some frightening facts:

- Robbery increased 42 per cent between 1996 and 1997.
- The risk rose from 4 per cent to 6 per cent.
- There were 13,000 cases of violence to staff and 54 per cent of those physical attacks in stores were associated with a robbery.
- Retailers were the victims of 4.2 million criminal incidents. Looked at another way, on average, in 1997, each store in the United Kingdom could expect 14 criminal incidents.

2 Make safety your first priority.

Armed robbery is on the increase and your safety, and that of your staff and customers, must be your most important consideration. Your responsibility is to protect people's lives in a situation where the armed robber is usually nervous and unpredictable. The best advice is that you should take CARE:

C alm and controlled
A ct on instructions
R emember details
E vidence.

3 Remain calm.

It's not easy to remain calm in these circumstances, but if you can take deep breaths, insist that you keep control of yourself, and stay calm, you'll be better able to keep your wits in this difficult situation.

4 Do what the robber tells you to do.

The first few seconds of the encounter is when the robber is most emotional and most likely to be violent. It is imperative that at this time you do what the robber tells you to do. Keep quiet and speak only when spoken to. Do nothing to aggravate the situation. Don't try to be a hero. There's a difference between bravery and bravado. The latter can be life-threatening.

If possible, create a physical barrier between you and the robber. Avoid sudden movement. Raise your hands, the sign of submission. If a robber can see your hands they will, most likely, be less nervous. Stand side-on to the robber if you can, as this reduces your profile and is less threatening to the intruder.

5 Remember details for later.

The accompanying bandit description form is designed to assist in the apprehension of the criminal. Fill in the form immediately after the encounter. Talk to no one until you have completed it because you do not want other people's perspectives colouring yours.

6 Protect the evidence.

Do not disturb the area of the crime until police have arrived. They will want to know what the robbers said, what they touched, where they walked, their escape route, and how they got away.

7 Keep your wits after the encounter.

Check to ensure that nobody has been injured and, if they have, administer first aid. Contact the police and cordon off the area of the crime. Take names and addresses of witnesses and ask them to stay until police have arrived. Your adrenalin will be exceptionally high at this point. It is advisable to rest up. A cup of tea might be a good idea.

BANDIT DESCRIPTION FORM

Separate form required for each person. To be compiled immediately after incident by each staff member, customer(s) or other witnesses. If answer is unknown, write U/K against heading. Do not consult others during compilation. Senior staff members to collect forms and hand to police.

Name/Nickname used: ....

Gender: ☐ Male ☐ Female

Age approx.: ....

Complexion:
☐ Fair ☐ Dark ☐ Pale ☐ Fresh
☐ Pimply ☐ Ruddy ☐ Suntanned

Accent: ....

Stature: ☐ Erect ☐ Stooped ☐ Slouchy

Walk: ☐ Quick ☐ Limp ☐ Slow
☐ Springy ☐ Pigeon-toed

Hair: Colour: ....
☐ Wavy ☐ Long ☐ Thick ☐ Straight
☐ Crewcut ☐ Curly ☐ Bald

Eyes: Colour:............... Size: ....
☐ Squint ☐ Starey

Ears: Size: ....
Shape: ....

Nose: Size: ....
Shape: ....

Mouth: Size: ....
Shape: ....

Teeth: ☐ Good ☐ Bad ☐ Protruding
☐ Uneven ☐ Spaced ☐ Missing

Height: ....

Nationality: ....

Build: ☐ Thin ☐ Stout ☐ Medium ☐ Nuggety

Voice: ☐ Clear ☐ Loud ☐ Thick ☐ Slangy

Eyeglasses: ☐ Colour ☐ Tinted ☐ Thick
Shape:...

Disguise: Beard—Colour/Type...
Moustache—Colour/Type ....

Hands: Size: ....
☐ Soft ☐ Hairy ☐ Calloused
Missing/deformed fingers:.......................

Nails: ....

Gloves: Colour/Type ....

Jewellery (describe): ....
....

Scars/Marks: (describe) Tattoos, scars, location, discolourations ....
....

Weapon: Type ....
In which hand: ....

Clothing (describe): hat, tie, coat, trousers, dress, skirt, jeans, sweater etc. ....
....

Method and Direction of Escape: ....
Registration No. ....
Colour of car: ....
Make: ....

Method of operation: What did bandit do, say, touch?...
....
....

How to deal with emergencies

Fire, bomb scare, wall collapse, chemical spill—We all hope emergencies will not occur, but a sad fact of life is that they do. For this reason, we need to have in place procedures on how to handle crisis situations well before the event if we are to minimise the drama...

1 Install smoke alarms and fire extinguishers.

Some of the most common emergencies are fire-related. We can be prepared by taking some simple precautions.

Contact your local fire service and ask them to visit your store and provide advice on the strategic placement of fire extinguishers, smoke alarms, and other necessary precautions. In most stores several smoke alarms and fire extinguishers will be required. The key is to install and maintain. Have a procedure that ensures you test your equipment once a week. Clean the equipment annually and have regular alerts to check the efficiency of equipment and procedures.

2 Introduce procedures for bomb threats.

The bombing of retail stores has increased in recent years and can no longer be seen as an occurrence common only to politically sensitive areas of the world. Take bomb threats seriously and ensure your team is trained in the correct procedures. Specialists in this field can help you with your training, but general guidelines would include:

- Train the team in procedures for tracing telephone calls.
- Ensure your team know how to attract the attention of another team member without tipping off a telephone caller.
- Record the time and date of threatening phone calls.
- When a caller phones, try and obtain information on where the bomb is, what it looks like, when it is set to explode, what will detonate it, why it was set, and who the bomber is.
- Ensure people do not use radios, walkie-talkies, or cellular phones in the area of the bomb.
- Contact the police immediately.

3 Know what to do after a break-in.

Professional thieves may break into your store after you have closed for the day. If you arrive at the store next morning and find it has been broken into, take the following steps:

- Do not enter the store.
- Use the nearest telephone to call the police.
- If you do go into the store, do not touch anything.
- Wait for the arrival of the police

Vol. 1: See 356, 372, 404

before cleaning up or allowing access to customers and staff.

4 Compile a crisis phone directory.

It's the directory you'll never want to use, but it is an essential list that should be located near designated phone points. It should contain the phone numbers of:

- local police station
- fire station
- ambulance services
- Poison Control Centre (if relevant)
- water, gas and electricity utility services
- your local doctor.

5 Train your team in emergency phone use.

In Australia the emergency phone line is 000, in the United Kingdom 999, and in the United States it's 911. Such lines should only be used in an emergency. It is important that the caller stays calm, states the problem accurately, gives the location of the emergency, and answers all questions asked by the tele-communicator. Let the emergency operator guide the conversation and do not hang up until help has been organised.

6 Keep an emergency first aid kit ready.

Every store should have a well stocked first aid kit available to staff. It is important that a list of essential supplies is also with the kit, or supplies will be used and may not be replaced. A basic kit should include:

- towels and wash cloths

> ### Management Memo
>
> We all react differently in emergency situations. Some people take it all in their stride...
>
> 'There cannot be a crisis next week, my schedule is already full.'—*Henry Kissinger*
>
> 'The only thing we have to fear is fear itself.' —*Franklin D. Roosvelt*
>
> 'The crisis of yesterday is the joke of tomorrow.'—*H.G. Wells*

- cold packs
- assorted bandages
- adhesive tape
- antiseptic
- sterile gauze pads
- disposable rubber gloves
- allergy kit.

7 Know how to deal with the media in a crisis.

Emergencies are 'news' and it will not be long before the media arrive. You need to deal with the media in a professional manner that will not damage consumer confidence in your business. The following tips may be of value:

- Your goal is to inform the public with accurate information.
- Only talk to the press when it is appropriate.
- Be patient with the press and avoid using 'no comment' answers.
- Minimise media distraction.
- Do not embellish your answers.
- Never lie to the media.
- Tell the bad news and get it over with.
- Avoid retail jargon.
- Do not assume anything is 'off the record'.
- Decide who should talk to the media from your business.

How to develop and manage your store safety standards

Although the retail environment may be thought of as a relatively safe workplace, it has had its share of injury, even death, among employees, contractors, and customers of all age groups. Retailers have a legal and moral obligation to provide a safe working and shopping environment. The following points may assist you in developing appropriate standards towards that end...

1 Gather information on health and safety issues.

Consult your local authority on matters relating to health and safety in the workplace. Obtain a copy of the relevant legislation. If you are a member of an employer group ask how they can help. Investigate the services on offer from your workers' compensation insurer. Try the internet. Gather as much information on the topic as possible and understand the issues involved.

2 Develop a health and safety program.

Now that your have familiarised yourself with relevant background information, you should develop a policy and program which enables your managers and employees to establish and maintain a healthy and safe workplace.

Components of such a program could include procedures for training and recruitment; employee consultation; routine inspection; hazard identification, assessment and control; incident reporting; emergency situations; safe use of equipment/machinery; purchase of new equipment/machinery; customer safety; contractor and visitor safety; first aid; rehabilitation; promotion of health and safety; and security.

3 Gain the commitment of your managers.

Make your managers and supervisors accountable for safety in the workplace. Acquaint them fully with relevant health and safety legislation and your store policy and procedures. Bonuses should include health and safety targets being met.

Your departmental managers should know how much is spent on workers' compensation, the main hazards and injuries; and supervise employees and others to ensure they work in a safe manner. They should be responsible also for the regular training of new and existing employees in equipment/machinery.

4 Commit yourself publicly.

Health and safety policies should state your goals and your responsibility for employee health and safety at work. Good policies are concise and clearly express your intentions in providing a safe, healthy working environment. The policy should encourage employee involvement and foster their commitment from the beginning. It should also embrace procedures to guarantee the safety of customers, contractors, and visitors.

Display your policy on a staff noticeboard and/or in the trading area to endorse your commitment.

5 Make safety an integral part of your business.

Demonstrate your commitment to health and safety. The overall responsibility for health and safety in the workplace rests with the employer. All individuals, however, have a responsibility for their own health and safety and that of other people. Your commitment as a manager is demonstrated by the development of the health and safety program for your organisation, beginning with a policy and related procedures, and demonstrated daily by example.

Include in your regular meetings discussions on the health and safety concerns of employees and others. Health and safety should have the same importance as wages and sales, after all this is one area where loss *can* be prevented. Allocate resources to developing, implementing, and maintaining your program.

6 Keep your standards under review.

Identify and deal promptly with hazards—anything that can harm or injure— in the workplace. SAM will help in this regard:

S *Spotting Hazards.* This involves regular routine inspections; examining your accident history; knowledge of accidents in similar retail sectors; and regular reporting of hazards and incidents by employees and others.

A *Assessing Risks.* What is the risk of exposure to an identified hazard?— what type of injury/damage could be sustained? how often? how many? for how long? and so on.

M *Making Changes.* What control measures have been recommended by authorities, employees, or managers. Appoint someone in your store to be responsible for implementing these measures promptly.

SAM is also a useful device to help you develop the health and safety program itself.

7 Keep accurate records.

Detailed records should be kept to validate your commitment to the continuing health and safety of your staff and customers. Such records may be called upon by the authorities in the event of an injury or serious incident in the workplace. Your records should relate to accidents, procedures, training, instruction and supervision, meetings which include discussions on health and safety, inspections and subsequent actions. Records also assist you to highlight patterns of behaviour which result in injury or incident.

This topic was written by Kym Kaptein, Foodland Associated Limited, Perth, WA.

How to monitor safety in your store

How you choose to monitor staff and customer safety in your store will depend on the size and complexity of your premises. There are a variety of approaches which can be used either individually or in combination to monitor occupational health and safety (OHS) issues in your workplace...

1 Know what information to gather.

The first requirement in monitoring store safety is to know what it is that you need to monitor. You should be collecting information on safety issues—on hazards, accidents or potential accidents involving employees, equipment/machinery, contractors, demonstrators, suppliers, customers and other visitors.

To do this, consult first aid records, workers' compensation, injury or property damage reports. Consider the type of equipment/machinery and chemicals used, work processes, and who performs the work and how often. All such information will assist you in identifying your areas of risk, leading to corrective action.

2 Conduct daily safety inspections.

Workplace inspections should be a part of the normal routine of a retail manager's day. Such inspections identify changes occurring in the store and its close environment, which impact upon OHS and may

require corrective action to be taken before an accident occurs. Inspections also assist in the identification of gradual onset injuries. Conduct inspections on at least a daily basis and have a member of your staff accompany you. A checklist will make this task easier.

3 Develop a checklist.

An OHS checklist is used as a comprehensive tool to ensure that you cover the full range of conditions and safety situations within your particular store. If you design your own workplace checklist, make sure you take into account the requirements of relevant legislation as well as your store's individual circumstances. Some checklists are devised as simple questionnaires requiring 'yes/no' responses. Others use key words or phrases as cues: e.g. 'stairwell lighting adequate'.

You local OHS authority, OHS literature, OHS consultants, and the internet will provide you with copies of checklists used in various industries and workplaces. You will be able to adapt one of these to suit your own needs.

Do a safety audit.

As a management tool, a health and safety audit is in many respects similar to a financial budget audit. Audits are more sophisticated than checklists in that they convert 'what to look for' into a measurable standard which is then rated for each item as a grade or percentage.

Audits may be performed by internal or external personnel. They are used to measure the effectiveness of an organisation's OHS program and enable you to plan the future allocation of resources for the management of OHS.

5 Establish a safety committee.

Having a special committee, or setting aside time in your regular meetings, to discuss OHS issues is useful for several reasons—you can access, and assess, the accumulated store of knowledge and experience possessed by your employees in performing their work, and the employees gain the confidence and security of being involved in decisions relating to their own health

and safety at work. Committees can assist in developing, for example, recording systems for accidents and hazards, and in recommending practical control strategies.

6 Ensure hazards and accidents are reported.

Establish a store-wide procedure which demands prompt and consistent reporting of hazards and accidents in your store. A notebook may be all you need for staff and visitors to record such information. The reports assist you in identifying deficiencies so that you can take corrective action to prevent future injuries or property damage.

This topic was written by Kym Kaptein, Foodland Associated Limited, Perth, WA.

> **Management Memo**
>
> Effective monitoring can reduce the risk of costly workplace accidents and/or property damages. Audits, inspections, checklists, safety committees, and reporting procedures are valuable tools for identifying hazards and ensuring you are maintaining a safe working environment. The documentation generated as a result of your monitoring store safety may be used to support the fact that you are a safety conscious manager.[101]

Glossary

Terms that every retail manager should know…

Add Value. Provide extra product or service at a low cost to you, but at a high value to the receiver.

Advertising Subsidy. The amount of money paid to a retailer to be spent on specific advertising and promotion for a commercial brand.

Aisle. Customer access to products. Usually off the main customer racetrack.

APN. Australian Product Number. This is a unique number located under the bar code for this specific product.

Audit Roll. A duplicated copy of the customer's receipt produced by your cash register and used as your record of the transaction.

Average Sale. The amount of dollars spent by a typical customer in your store.

Baby Boomer. A person born between 1945 and 1955.

Barcode. A product code containing information about the product and its price. This information is stored in the form of bars of varying thickness, designed to be read by an optical scanner.

Benchmark. A point of measurement which can be used as a reference to measure business performance.

Benefits. An advantage of the product as seen in the consumer's eyes.

Body Language. How we use the body to communicate.

BOM. Beginning of Month.

Brand. The name used when identifying a specific group of products provided by one retailer or supplier. The brand differentiates the product from its competitors.

Browse Product. A product located where the consumer can have plenty of space when making a buying decision.

CBD. Central Business District. The area of a town or city which is a major location for shops, hotels and restaurants.

COGS. Cost Of Goods Sold. The actual total cost of stock sold by your business, normally worked out at the time of stocktake.

Category Killer. A retailer who specialises in one product group and sells in bulk within that product group.

Close. The point in a sales transaction where you decide the consumer is ready to buy.

Cold Selling. Selling to a customer without gathering information on the consumer's wants and needs.

Cold Spot. The area in your store where you get poor customer traffic or have difficulty in selling product.

Credit Card. A card which identifies the holder as entitled to obtain, without payment of cash, goods or services which are then charged to the holder's account.

Cross Merchandising Products. Products that naturally go together in the consumer's mind.

Customer Specific Marketing. Retailing aimed at specific, known consumers.

Demonstration. The physical activity of showing a consumer how to use or a tasting of the product on display.

Direct Mailer. A leaflet which is distributed to the potential consumer's home.

Discounting. Deducting money from the original selling price.

Display. A means of making specific products visible to a consumer.

Dodger. A circular on your store which is handed out on the streets or mass mail dropped in your catchment area.

Dump Bin. A display unit located in an aisle that is used to promote product. The products are displayed haphazardly to give the impression that it is a priced-motivated promotion.

EBIT. Expected net profit before interest and tax is paid by the business.

e-Business. The process of doing business using the internet.

e-Commerce. The process of doing business using the internet.

EHO. Environmental Health Officer

EOM. End of Month.

Everyday Low Pricing. Where you have a policy of having low prices every day in the store.

Features. Attributes of the product.

FIFO. First In, First Out. A term used for effective stock rotation. The first item you purchase as a retailer should be the first item the consumer buys.

FIS. Free Into Store. No freight charge is included in getting the product to your store.

Facing. The amount of the same product positioned at the front of the shelf.

Fad Product. A short-life product that is very fashionable for a few weeks.

Flagship Store. The leading store in a chain of stores which is used as the benchmark store.

FMCG's. Fast moving consumer goods.

Generation X. A person born between 1965 and 1980.

Gondola. A freestanding display for showing products on the shop floor.

GP. Gross Profit. The key yardstick to measure how your business is performing. Sales less the cost of sales equals gross profit.

GST. Goods and Service Tax.

HACCP. Hazard Analysis Critical Control Point. The term used for the system approach for managing food safety risk.

Hot Spot. A prime selling position in your store where you can maximise sales.

How-to Leaflet. An explanatory handout provided for consumers on how to use specific products.

Image. The form, appearance and impression of your business and team that you strive to create in the eye of the consumer.

Impulse Product. A product purchased, yet it was not a planned purchase when the consumer walked in your door.

Indenting. The taking away of a product to give the impression the product range has already been shopped.

ISP. Internet Service Provider. A company that sells access to e-commerce and the web.

Known Value Product. A product that is purchased by consumers based on price. The majority of your consumers believe they know the exact price of KV products.

KPI. Key Performance Indicators. A measurement guide normally based on the financial performance of the product, e.g. sales target, stockturn, etc.

Lay-by. A system that allows the

consumer to pay in small amounts over time until the payment has been made in full.

Line. A group of products, all of which do the same job for the consumer.

Link Products. Products that are naturally sold together in the consumer's mind.

Margin. The difference between the buying and selling price.

Margin of Safety. The amount of security your business has before it goes into a negative trading pattern.

Markdown. The amount of money you reduce a product from its original selling price in order to sell it.

Mystery Shopper. A person, not known to the salesperson, employed to make an assessment on your retail performance.

Non Known Value Product. A product whose exact price the majority of consumers do not know.

Non Price Sensitive Product. A product that achieves a high gross profit as consumers do not know the exact price of the product.

OHS. Occupational Health and Safety.

One on Eight Case Deal. Buy eight and we'll add one free.

Open Pricing. Pricing using a non computerised system.

OTB. Open To Buy. The amount of dollars you can spend in a given time frame to purchase stock to maximise sales.

Pallet. A moveable platform on which products are placed for storage, transportation, and display. They are designed to be used with a forklift system.

Planogram. A diagram showing the position of products on the shelf.

PLU. Product Look Up. A code number attached to the product which allows the retailer to 'look up' that product on a computer.

POS. Point of Sale. The position and location where money changes hand.

Power Product. A product that is a symbol of your industry and can be sold rapidly, due to its consumer demand.

Price Banding. The band between the minimum and maximum price that a consumer is willing to pay for a specific product.

Price Point. The ideal price for a specific product to maximise sales.

Product Promotion. A campaign held by the retailer or supplier to increase the sales of a specific product.

Product Range. The amount of different products within a retail category.

Purpose Product. A product the customer planned to purchase when the consumer walked in your door.

Quality Circle. A group of people who analyse the business with the aim of introducing improvement.

Race Track. The main customer flow path, which goes around the store.

Raincheck. A comment or note to a customer when an advertised or promotional line is out of stock. This acknowledgment allows the customer to purchase the product at the advertised price at a later date.

Rate of Sale. Total sales for, e.g. a month, divided by the number of weeks, giving you your average rate of sales a week.

Relays. A layout of products along a shop fitting.

Retail Price Maintenance. The restrictive trade practice of a supplier fixing the minimum price of a commodity for all subsequent levels of its distribution.

Retailer. The seller of products to the ultimate consumer.

Runway. The main customer flow path which goes down the centre of the store.

Sales Target. The planned financial objective of the business. This is achieved by selling specific products to consumers.

Scanner. The equipment at the payment point using laser technology that reads the barcode on products sold.

Sector Cluster. An area of a significant number of businesses of one type of business or services.

Shelftalker. A sign situated on the shop fitting to promote the product.

Shop Assistant. One who sells goods in a retail shop.

Shop Awning. A roof-like structure over the pavement at the front of the shop to protect customers from the elements.

Shoplifter. A person who steals from a shop while appearing to be a legitimate shopper.

Shrinkage. The difference between what you originally purchased and what you actually sold.

SKU. Stock Keeping Unit. The lowest level of identification of products for management purposes, i.e. one item of stock.

Smart Card. A new generation credit card which is often called the 'Electronic Wallet'. It can be used as a credit card, but also contains valuable information on your customer as a person, which can be used by the retailer.

SME. Small/Medium Sized Enterprise. Often used when talking to computer specialists.

SOH. Stock On Hand. The amount of product available for immediate sale.

Sponsor. A person or firm that finances an external promotion in return for advertisement of a commercial product or service.

Stockturn. The number of times that products are bought and sold over a given period of time.

Supplier. A person or company that provides product for sale. In retailing this is often the company that supplies the retailer.

SWOT Analysis. An analysis where one identifies the SWOT—Strengths, Weaknesses, Opportunities and Threats—of the business.

Team. A group of people working in association to achieve the same goal.

Trade Show. An exhibition of similar products that is only open to trade members.

Trolley. A low truck running on castors for carrying products.

Use By Date. The date on the product or shelf which indicates the life expectancy of the product on the shelf. After this date the product is unsaleable.

USP. Unique Selling Proposition. A point of difference concerning your business.

VAT. Value Added Tax. A Goods and Services Tax used in the United Kingdom.

VDP. Variable Day Pricing. Price variation that occurs on specific days of the week.

Vendor. A supplier who brings product into your store.

Vertical Merchandising. A layout where products are displayed in product categories based on a vertical layout.

Wall of Value. A wall of mixed promotional lines normally situated at the rear of the store.

Website. A setting on the internet where you can promote your business to the world. It is provided via your internet service provider.

Write-off. Reducing the value of the product to zero on your books.

YTD. Year To Date. Term used when referring to sales for a given period in the year.

John Stanley
Delivering Retail Customers

Are your team creating loyal customers, or just serving people**?**
Do your customers go away and rave to their friends about your amazing service**?**
Is your business turnover exploding through word of mouth**?**
Are your sales team excited and enthusiastic about coming to work each day**?**
Do your clientele love to visit your store and interact with your team**?**
Are your power displays increasing your sales by 540%**?**

John Stanley is an enthusiastic and charismatic international speaker and consultant specialising in the retail industry.

John has been motivating teams to push enterprises to greater heights through enthusiasm, self-empowerment and increased awareness of customer needs. Whatever your retail objectives, John Stanley can help fast track your business to reach amazing new heights. His valuable, practical and instantly effective ideas are based on over 25 years of international retail experience and ongoing international research.

With John's mentoring, training and on-site consultancy, small retail stores have grown into professional multi-million dollar business operations, while large international companies use John's skills to improve their professionalism and develop consistency throughout their stores.

John Stanley is one of few consultants in the world today who have the credibility, international knowledge and such a clear understanding of what today's customers are demanding and what retailers need to know to become more profitable.

John's skills include identifying your primary needs, working with you to fulfil those needs, building on your strengths, eliminating your weaknesses, understanding your customers and growing your profits.

Whether your goals be:

• Attracting more customers

• Improving your teams customer service

• Increasing sales

• Re-designing your store

• Improving customer flow

• Creating customers for life

• Increasing your stockturns

• Improving your merchandising strategy

• Designing more effective promotions

• Developing a retail business strategy

• Recruiting more effective sales people

John can help you achieve all this, and more…

Rave reviews from John Stanley's recent clients

John Stanley re-designed our farm shop to improve customer flow, merchandising and general image. As a result of the re-design we have achieved a 44% increase in turnover, and 18% increase in customer numbers, and a 22% increase in average spend over the same period last year. All this in spite of the current difficult trading time due to the Foot and Mouth outbreak here in the UK. We are also finding that running the shop is much easier and less stressful on many levels – especially stock control. Long may it continue. Thanks again for all your help – you inspire!!

Stuart Beare, Tulleys Farm, United Kingdom

I employed John Stanley as a consultant to work with my team on developing the overall appearance of the store. As a result of John's input and advice, within six months we achieved a growth that far exceeded our expectations. On a busy day we are achieving a turnover which is equivalent to one weeks turnover prior to us taking over the store.

Pierre Sequeira, 'Store of the Year 2001', Supa Valu Como, Western Australia

John has also created, written and sourced a range of products to help retailers to grow to new heights. For more information on John's services, products, or to subscribe to John's e-newsletter for retailers please visit John's website **www.johnstanley.cc**

For more information on John Stanley Associates services contact:

John Stanley Associates
142 Hummerston Road,
Kalamunda, WA 6076, Australia
Tel: +61 8 9293 4533
Fax: +61 8 9293 4561
Email: info@johnstanley.cc

Where other consultants discuss the problems, John offers practical, cost effective solutions.

www.johnstanley.cc

References

a. Spencer Johnson and Larry Wilson, *The One Minute Sales Person*, Willow Books, 1985, p. 80. **1.** Jarvis Finger and Neil Flanagan, *The Manager's 100*, Plum, Brisbane, 1998, p. 35. **2.** Ogden Nash. **3.** Helen Townsend, *Baby Boomers*, Simon & Schuster, Brookvale, 1988, p. 206. **4.** Betsy Sanders & Warren Bennis, *Fabled Service, Ordinary Acts, Extraordinary Outcomes*, Executive Briefing Series, Pfeiffer, 1995. **5.** *Image 7 Newsletter*, January 1999, Image 7, Western Australia. **6.** Victor Schwab, *How to Write a Good Advertisement*. **7.** Roy L. Smith in *The New Speaker's Sourcebook*, Eleanor Doan, Zonderan, Grand Rapids, Michigan, 1968. **8.** Jan Carlzon, *Moments of Truth*, Ballinger Publishing, 1989. **9.** Bobbie Gee, *Image Power*, audio presentation package, Bobbie Gee Enterprises, 1986. **10.** Betsy Sanders & Warren Bennis, *Fabled Service, Ordinary Acts, Extraordinary Outcomes*, Executive Briefing Series, Pfeiffer, 1995, p. 116. **11.** *DIY Retailing*, March 1998. **12.** Bob Vereen, '7 Things Never to Say', *Australian Hardware*, January 1998. **13.** Pat Weymes, *How to Perfect Your Selling Skills*, Kogan Page, UK, 1990, p. 112. **14.** Colin Pearce, *Make More Money from Every Sale*, A Westfield Retail Education Book, World Wide Success Media, 1997, p. 122. **15.** Scott Gross, *Positively Outrageous Service*. **16.** Ukrops Supermarkets USA. **17.** Robert Spector and Patrick McCarthy, *The Nordstrom Way: The Inside Story of America's No. 1 Customer Service Company*, John Wiley, NY, 1995, p. 202. **18.** Kenneth Stone, *Competing with the Retail Giants*, John Wiley & Sons, 1995, p. 194. **19.** Feargal Quinn, *Crowning the Customer: How to Become Customer Driven*, The O'Brien Press, 1990, p. 64. **20.** Murray Raphel & Neil Raphel, *Up the Loyalty Ladder*, Harper Business, 1995, p. 247. **21.** Janelle Barlow and Claus Moller, in *A Complaint is a Gift*, Koehler, 1996. **22.** Temasek Poly-Technic, January 1998, in *The Retailer*, TMPC Publishers, Queensland, April 1999, p. 14. **23.** Noreen Emery, Speech Dynamics, Perth Western Australia. **24.** Michael Le Boeuf, *How to Win and Keep Customers and Keep Them for Life*, Berkley Books, NY, 1987, p. 120. **25.** John Stanley, *John Stanley Says*, Vol. 1, Reference Publishing, NZ. **26.** Mark Wrice, *First Steps in a Retail Career*, National Retail & Wholesale Industry Training Council, Macmillan Educational Australia, 1995, p. 112. **27.** John Stanley, *John Stanley Says*, Vol. 2, Reference Publishing, NZ. **28.** Roy Morgan Research. **29.** Australian Marketing Association Report on Marketing Expenditure. **30.** Geoff Sirmai, *The Confident Consumer*, Allen & Unwin, 1999, p. 63. **31.** Chris Newton, *The Do-It-Yourself Advertising Guide*, Information Australia, 1984, p. 77. **32.** *John Stanley Says*, Volume 1. **33.** Chris Newton, *The Do-It-Yourself Advertising Guide*, Information Australia, 1984, p. 48. **34.** Pat Weymes, *How to perfect Your Selling Skills*, Kogan Page, UK, 1990, p. 75. **35.** John Stanley, *John Stanley Says*, Vol. 2, Reference Publishing, NZ. **36.** Alfred Alles, *Exhibitions: A Key to Effective Marketing*, Cassell, London, 1988, p. 116. **37.** Sonja Larsen, *Signs that Sell*, Insignia Systems, USA, 1991, p. 23. **38.** Kenneth Mills & Judith Paul, *Applied Visual Merchandising*, Prentice Hall, USA, 1974, p. 116. **39.** US Product Acceptance and Research Inc. **40.** John Stanley, *John Stanley Says*, Vol. 2, Reference Publishing, NZ. **41.** *Newsletter*, Insignia Systems, Inc. **42.** *Merchandising to Maximise Sales Productivity*, conducted on behalf of The Russell R. Mueller Retail Hardware Research Foundation, November 1989, p. 19. **43.** *Merchandising to Maximise Sales Productivity*, conducted on behalf of The Russell R. Mueller Retail Hardware Research Foundation, November 1989, p. 13. **44.** Kenneth Mills & Judith Paul, *Applied Visual Merchandising*, Prentice Hall, p. 118. **45.** John Stanley, *Merchandising Manual*, John Stanley Associates, February 1999. **46.** Edgar Falk, *1001 Ideas to Create Retail Excitement*, Prentice Hall, 1994, p. 49. **47.** Edgar Falk, *1001 Ideas to Create Retail Excitement*, Prentice Hall, 1994, p. 54. **48.** *Business Trader*, Brisbane, December 1998, p. 28. **49.** Source unknown. **50.** Chris Newton, Results Corporation, Queensland, *Newsletter*. **51.** *Flower Business International*, November 1998. **52.** US Product Acceptance and Research Inc, 1998. **53.** Lorraine Thornton, *Retailing: How to Lift Sales and Profits*, Stirling Press, 1996, p. 39. **54.** Bobbie Gee, *Creating a Million Dollar Image for Your Business*, Pagemill Press, USA, 1995, p. 37. **55.** Bobbie Gee, *Creating a Million Dollar Image for Your Business*, Pagemill Press, USA, 1995, prologue. **56.** Arthur Andersen, *Small Store Survival: Success Strategies for Retailers*, John Wiley, USA, 1997, p. 137. **57.** Lorraine Thornton, *Retailing: How to Lift Sales and Profits*, Stirling Press, 1996, p. 34. **58.** Mark Wrice, *First Steps in a Retail Career*, National Retail and Wholesale Industry Training Council, Australia, 1995, p.

140. **59.** *IGA Newsletter*. **60.** *Asian Retailer* August 1996. **61.** John Stanley, *John Stanley Says*, Vol. 1, Reference Publishing, NZ. **62.** John Stanley, *John Stanley Says*, Vol. 2, Reference Publishing, NZ. **63.** John Stanley. **64.** Lorraine Thornton, *Retailing: How to Lift Sales and Profits*, Stirling Press, 1996, p. 42. **65.** John Stanley, *John Stanley Says*, Vol. 1, Reference Publishing, NZ. **66.** Arthur Andersen, *Small Store Survival: Success Strategies for Retailers*, John Wiley, USA, 1997, p. 101. **67.** John Stanley. **68.** John Stanley. **69.** *The New Speakers Sourcebook* Eleanor Doan, Zondervan, Grand Rapids, Michigan, 1968. **70.** *The New Speakers Sourcebook* Eleanor Doan, Zondervan, Grand Rapids, Michigan, 1968. **71.** Jurek Leon, Terrific Trading. **72.** *John Stanley Says*, Vol. 1. **73.** E.P. Danger, *Using Colour to Sell*, Gower, London, 1968. **74.** E.P.Danger, *Using Colour to Sell*, Gower, London, 1968. **75.** Effective Marketing to the Retail Environment Workshop UK. **76.** John Stanley. **77.** John Stanley, *John Stanley Says*, Vol. 1, Reference Publishing, NZ. **78.** Mark Wrice, *First Steps in a Retail Career*, Macmillan Education Australia, 1995, p. 161. **79.** Ron Marciel, Western Nurseries, California, 1980. **80.** Arthur Andersen, *Small Store Survival: Success Strategies for Retailers*, John Wiley, USA, 1997, p. 91. **81.** Peter Latchford, *The Principles of Successful Retailing*, The Business Library, 1990, p. 195. **82.** Visual Merchandising VM & SD Magazine, St Publications, 1997, p. 5. **83.** Mark Wrice, *First Steps in a Retail Career*, National Retail & Wholesale Industry Training Council, Australia, 1995, p. 164. **84.** Arthur Andersen, *Small Store Survival: Success Strategies for Retailers*, John Wiley, USA, 1997, p. 100. **85.** Mark Wrice, *First Steps in a Retail Career*, National Retail & Wholesale Industry Training Council, Australia, 1995, p. 112. **86.** Mark Wrice, *Retail Management*, Macmillan Education Australia, 1998. **87.** Arthur Andersen, *Small Store Survival: Success Strategies for Retailers*, John Wiley, USA, 1997, p. 106. **88.** *Selection Interviewing*, Management Skills Guide SMS D5, UK Agricultural Training Board, p. 5. **89.** Celia Roberts, *The Interview Game and How It's Played*, BBC Books, 1985, p. 46. **90.** Jonathon Winchester, Shoppers Anonymous, Perth, Western Australia. **91.** Sam Deep and Lyle Sussman, *The Manager's Book of Lists*, SDD Publishers, Glenshaw, Pa., 1988, p.82. **92.** *Retail Challenge Newsletter*. **93.** Candy Tymson and Bill Sherman, *The Australian Public Relations Manual*, Millennium, Sydney, 1990, p. 122. **94.** Jarvis Finger, *Managing Your School*, Vol. 1, Fernfawn, Brisbane, 1993, p. 78. **95.** *Marketing Magazine*, July 1982. **96.** Michael Sacher of the Reject Shops **97.** Denny van Maanenberg, *Effective Retail Security*, Butterworth-Heinemann, 1995, p. 44. **98.** Denny van Maanenberg, *Effective Retail Security*, Butterworth-Heinemann, 1995, p. 44. **99.** Mark Wrice, *First Steps in a Retail Career*, National Retail & Wholesale Industry Training Council, Macmillan Educational Australia, 1995, p. 173. **100.** *Managing Occupational Health and Safety 1996*, eds. Wyatt A. and Oxenburgh M. **101.** Kym Kaptein, Foodland Associated Limited, WA.

Index

A

Actors, 101
Advertising
    budget, 186
    copy, 68
    floorgraphics, 88
    media, 60
    planning, 66
    promotion, 70
    recruitment, 209
Aisle, 123
Aroma, 162, 97
Australia Trade Show
    Bureau, 77
Average sale per customer,
    174
Awards, 47

B

Baby boomers, 8
Bag check policy, 229
Balloons, 113
Banded offers, 188
Bandit description form, 235
Benchmarking, 174, 206
Benefits, 36, 193
Best sellers, 140, 131
Body language, 20, 24, 44,
    116
Bomb threats, 236
Bounce merchandising, 117
Boutique layouts, 116
Branding, 3
Browse areas, 97
Bulk discounts, 197
Business cards, 33
Buying effectively, 196
Buying habits, 185
Buying policy, 202

C

Cash cows, 203
Categories, 135
Checklists
    customer friendliness, 25
    customer surveys, 38
    staff appraisal, 35
    through customer eyes,
    18
Checkouts
    body language, 21
    counter displays, 144
    customer flow, 116
    house keeping, 121
    last impressions, 120
    management policy, 121
    queue lengths, 34
    security, 226
Chemosensory research, 163
Cheques, 232
Children
    clubs, 5
    retailing for them, 4
    services, 12
Christmas, 102, 104
Closing a sale, 50
Cold spots, 96
Colour
    attracting the customer, 2
    concepts, 106
    cold spots, 97
    colour wheel, 165
    exterior use, 166
    interior use, 168
    merchandising, 164
    shop windows, 111
    signage, 152
    texture, 127
Competitions, 49
Consistency standards, 16
Corporate company
    blocking, 135
Cost price, 180
Coupons, 62
Credit cards, 232
Crisping, 148
Cross merchandising, 129,
    177

Cross selling, 89
Customer
    communications, 46
    complaints, 44
    expectations, 14, 28
    feedback, 23
    flow, 116
      aisle management, 125
      bounce management,
      128
    forums, 40
    loyalty, 36
    objections, 31
    overseas, 13, 21
    surveys 38, 40
Customer service
    baby boomers, 9
    closing the sales, 56
    customer doubt, 30, 28
    farewells, 30
    methods of
      improvement, 34
    overkill, 46
    policy, 50
    staff roles, 34
Cut case displays, 80

D

Database, 36
Demonstrations, 74, 109
Direct mailing, 62
Discounting, 179
Disneyland cleanliness, 122
Displays
    catch customer eye, 84
    movement, 112
    pallet displays, 86
    power, 90
    promotional, 72
Dogs, 142, 203
Dress codes, 16, 149
Dummy-up, 82
Dump bins, 81

WINNING
YOUR CUS
MANAGING
YOUR STOR
PROMOT
YOUR PRO
MAN
YOUR
INDEX
251

E

Emergencies, 236
Empathy, 45
End caps, 92
Entrance signs, 78
Everyday low price, 190

F

Facing, 71, 136, 99
Fashion trends,   ;
    generation X, 6
    baby boomers, 9
Features, 28
Female products, 129
First aid kits, 237
First impressions, 118
Floor hygiene, 88
Floor walking, 124
Food hygiene, 74, 142, 148
Fraud, 232

G

Generation X
    customers, 6
    employees, 212
Gift wrapping, 52
Gondolas, 132
Greeting customers, 24, 26
Greying tigers, 10
Grid layouts, 116
Gross profit, 180, 191, 199

H

Headlines, 69
Hiring, 208
Hold-ups, 234
Horizontal merchandising,
    132
Hot spots, 92, 104
Housekeeping counters,
    145
How-to leaflets, 64

Hygiene
    checkout, 120
    sanitation worksheet,
        123
    shelves, 98
    walls and floors, 122

I

Image
    creating image, 16
    freshness, 149
    image wheel, 118
Impulse products, 129
Increase average sale
    systems, 204
Indenting, 137
Induction, 211
In house signage, 79
Interviews
    job - salespeople, 210

J

Job descriptions, 208

K

Known value products
    product classification,
        128
    setting prices, 156
    signage, 182
    use, 158

L

Laser promotions, 89
Last impressions, 120

Less abled, 10, 12
Lifetime value of customers,
    32
Lighting, 127
    freshness image, 149
    colour interior, 167

    colour external, 167
Like by like relays, 134
Link products, 129
Low investment strategies,
    107
Loyalty ladder, 42

M

Magazines, 139, 221
Male products, 129
Mark up, 180
Markdowns, 175
Marketing
    communications
        checklist, 187
Marks and Spencer, 22
McDonalds, 3, 4, 122, 167
Meetings
    team, 101, 206
Music, 160
Mystery shoppers, 214

N

Name badges, 17
New products, 108, 139
Newsletters, 62, 41, 222,
Newspaper advertising, 187
Non known value products
    price sensitivity, 192
    products, 128
    setting prices, 182
    signage, 157
    use, 158
Nordstrom, 33, 37
Nostalgia retailing, 10

O

Open learning, 219
Open price policy, 194
Open questions, 205

Outdoor signage, 78

P

PA systems, 48
Pallet displays, 86
Percentages, 178
    departmental, 200
Perishable products, 148
Planograms, 137
Power displays, 82, 91
Press, 220
Price
    banding, 190
    barriers, 182
    increases, 183, 184
    points, 182
    points strategy, 204
Printed word, 406, 62, 41,
    222
Product
    placement, 128
    positioning price, 184
    range management,
    138
Product life cycle, 73
    signage, 73
    slow movers, 143
Profit pointers, 186
Promotions, 72
    fame, 95
    pricing, 190
    techniques, 188
Purpose products, 128
Pyramids, 84
    impact, 90
    hot spots, 93
    shop windows, 110

R

Recruitment, 208
Relays, 134
Request book, 139

Retail business strategy, 172
Retrenchment
    customers, 33
Ripple machines, 112
Rotating displays, 85

S

Safety
    audit, 241
    checklists, 240
    committees, 241
    displays, 126
    floors, 88
    heavy products, 131
    hold ups, 234
    margins, 206
    monitoring, 240
    pallets, 86
    power displays, 91
    programs, 238
    record keeping, 239
    store, 238
    shelf fillings, 98
    trolleys, 150
Sales per square metre, 174
Sampling, 188
Security
    workplace, 226,
Selling up, 204
Sell price, 180
Serif type, 65
Service
    quality service, 14
    research, 22
    special customers, 12
    special services, 13
Shelf filling, 98
Shelving, 131, 132
Shopfittings, 177
Shopping bags, 54
Shopping lists, 65
Shopping trolleys, 150, 205
Shop stealing, 228, 230
Shop windows, 110
Shrinkage, 226, 148, 174
Sight lines, 117
Signage
    management, 154
    ratios, 177
    security signs, 227
    stockturn, 199
    strategy, 155
    writing, 152
Silver tops, 10

Slow movers, 142, 197
Smoke alarms, 236
Sponsorships, 224
Staff appraisal, 35, 160
Staff monitoring, 19, 156
Staff theft, 229
Standards checklist, 177
Stockturn, 175, 198, 199
Suggestive selling, 204
Suppliers, 196, 146
SWOT, 172

T

Team meetings,
    follow up, 33
Texture, 12
Theatre, 100
Ticketing, 70
    categories, 135
    in house, 79
    management, 154
    on pallets, 87
    placement, 73
    signs that sell, 78
    slow movers, 143
    systems, 71
    strategy, 155
    words that sell, 79
    writing, 152
Tie-in selling, 205
Toilets, 122
Trade magazines, 107
Trade shows, 76
Training
    against shoplifting, 228
    best sellers, 140
    Christmas, 103
    counter displays, 144
    customer friendliness,
    46
    demonstrations, 74
    emergencies, 237
    features and benefits, 29
    methods, 218
    new products, 108
    selling up, 204
    sign writing, 152

smiling, 22
trolley assistants, 150

V

Variable day pricing, 190
Vertical merchandising, 130
Vouchers, 188

W

Wall of value, 94
Walk the floor, 176
Waste disposal records, 148
Words that sell, 153

X

X Generation, 6